For Lettice & G
Happy rea

From Norfolk
to Trafalgar

Tom Fremantle

A story of ships, battles, colonies and convicts

August 2020

Overy

From Norfolk to Trafalgar

A story of ships, battles, colonies and convicts

By T D Fremantle

First Printing: 2020
ISBN 978-0-244-24410-1

Published by T D Fremantle
tfremantle@talk21.com

Ordering Information:
Special discounts are available on quantity purchases by corporations, associations, educators, and others. For details, contact the publisher at the above listed address.

For my grandchildren,
and with warmest thanks to Alice,
Mark, Christopher and Emily.

Contents

Introduction

I became aware of my great great great grandfather Admiral Sir Thomas Fremantle when I was about five years old and it was that awareness and the news of my godfather Sir Edward 'Ted' Parry's promotion to Admiral which determined my choice of career. From that time my ambition was to emulate their prowess by becoming an Admiral myself. After about seven years' service my father died and I began to recognise a rather different set of priorities, and after completing ten years' service I became a civilian, married and had a family which became the focus of my life.

I was vaguely aware of Australian cousins when my mother received food parcels after the war in the late forties. I knew that she had enjoyed hugely a visit to Australia when she was nineteen – she very nearly stayed there. But we heard little about the Australian cousins and nothing about Governor King, also my great great great grandfather, beyond the print which was hung in a dark corner, showing the descendants of Governor King who had fought in the Great War.

After I retired from full time employment I began to read more about the Royal Navy in the late 18th and early 19th Centuries and to realise that the navy's achievement was not only in winning command of the English Channel and the wider sea routes to create a foundation for their Empire. At the same time, the navy had established a colony on the other side of the world. Two of my forbears had been intimately involved in that achievement. Fremantle, part of Nelson's band of brothers, secured a reasonable fortune, some fame and high rank; King, despite rescuing New South Wales when it was close to failure through drunkenness and disorder, and establishing a stable regime on which Governor Macquarrie could build, received no recognition, no thanks from a grateful Government, and only after his death was his widow granted a small pension. There seemed to be a story here, which I should try to tell my grandchildren.

This was the genesis of the book. The section about Nelson seemed to fit well because so much of the naval history of the time is dominated by him, and he was an exact contemporary of King who passed the Lieutenants' board the week before Nelson. But rather than focus on his triumphs at the Cape St Vincent, the Nile and Copenhagen, I wanted to direct some attention to his early career, which did not go at all well. He was fallible and made several serious errors of judgement which are often overlooked in favour of the populist perspective of the greatest admiral, who could be relied on to win important battles.

The story starts in Norfolk, largely because the salt marshes on the north coast at Overy Staithe have become a second home to me over many years' of holidays there. My children, and now my grandchildren, seem to have developed a similar love for the place, and I thought they would feel at once comfortable with an opening in that little harbour, where Nelson started to learn about boats and the sea.

Ben Luckett, his parents, wife and children are entirely fictional, as is the Master of Ben's first ship. Everyone else who features in the book is a character from documented history, although in one or two cases I have been unable to find a name for an officer, and have invented it. The events I have attempted to describe all happened, and the chronology is as accurate as I can make it.

Ben is somewhat unreal. It is unlikely that any sailor of his background would have been able to cover so much ground in his working life, and he is a bit too 'good' for reality. Unlike every other human he is always sure-footed and does not make mistakes which might knock his life off course. But I hope that does not damage my attempt to portray Nelson, Fremantle and King as they really were. They all remain worthy role models and I hope my own grandchildren as well as many others may feel inclined to recognise them as such.

Tom Fremantle
December 2019

Acknowledgements

Many people have helped bring this project to fruition. A continual source of inspiration has been the many words of encouragement from people polite enough to ask how I was occupying my time in retirement, only to find themselves overwhelmed by the torrent of information about my forbears. To all of them I apologise if I became a bore. Amongst them is my long-suffering wife, Alice, without whose patience and love the whole process would have been far more difficult.

I have been very well served by librarians and archivists at the National Archives at Kew, the National Maritime Museum Caird Library, and the Buckinghamshire archive in Aylesbury, all of whom have been very patient with me. In Australia I was given great help at the Mitchell Library in Sydney, and particularly by the small team on Norfolk Island, Leah Honeywood, Sallie Davie and Eric Hutchinson, who were all very enthusiastic and helpful. Both Fremantle and King relations have also helped and encouraged me along the way. And I must mention Carol Richardson-Bunbury from the Launceston Museum. Her enthusiasm for King and his Cornish origins has been both inspiring and helpful.

If it had not been for various people who kindly read the first draft of the book it would have turned out rather differently. Colin McGarrigle, Léonie Thorogood, Will Heaslop and Ash Faire-Ring have all made very helpful suggestions for which I am most grateful.

It was my cousin Dr Jonathan King, celebrated Australian author and historian, and co-author with his father of the only biography of Philip Gidley King, who issued a direct challenge to 'Get the novel finished and out of the way, and then write a new biography of our shared King forbear'.

'But you are the professional', I replied, 'It is your life's work to write this sort of book'.

'No, no', he said, 'I've forgotten most of what I knew about him and anyway you probably know more about him than anyone else now.

You owe it to the family to write down all that you know in a proper biography'.

So, this book may not be my last.

The key historical figures

Captain Horatio Nelson by Rigaud
(Royal Museums Greenwich)

Governor Philip Gidley King
(Mitchell Library, Sydney, NSW)

Admiral Sir Thomas Fremantle
(Fremantle Family Collection)

Maps

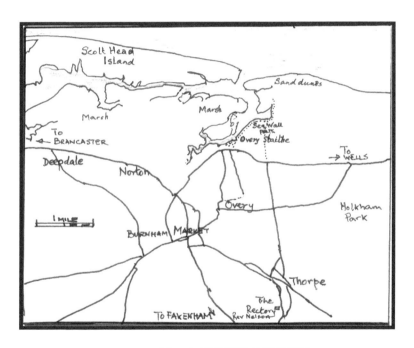

Map 1 OVERY STAITHE

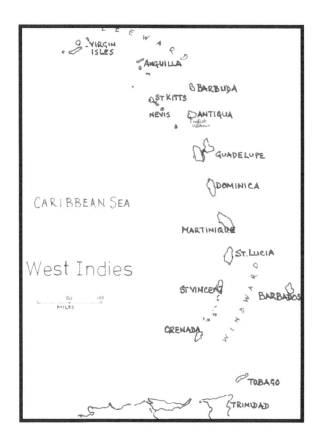

Map 2 THE WEST INDIES

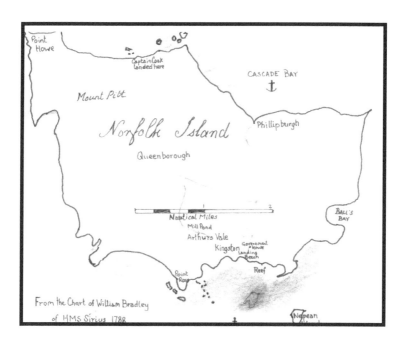

Map 3 NORFOLK ISLAND

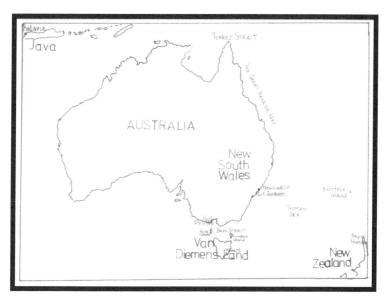

Map 4 AUSTRALIA

Map 5   WESTERN MEDITERRANEAN

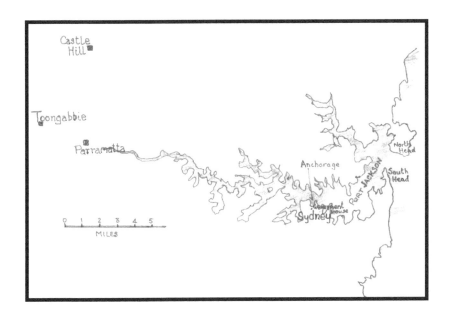

Map 6   PORT JACKSON, NEW SOUTH WALES

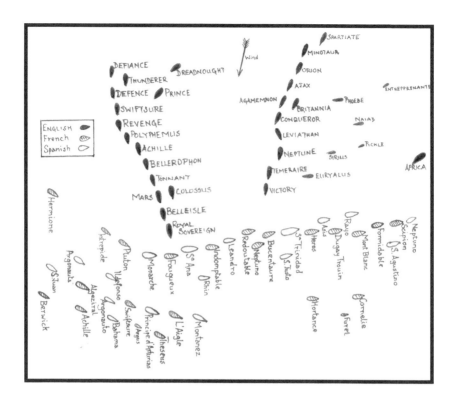

MAP 7 THE BATTLE OF TRAFALGAR

'At the commencement of the battle; Cape Trafalgar bearing ESE 4 Leagues'.

Position of the English Fleet and the Combined forces of France and Spain, from a design by Edward Orme dated 9th January 1806 and said to have been 'Certified as to its correctness by the Flag Officers of the Euryalus & Admiral Villeneuve'.

Part One - Overy Staithe and the Boreas

Chapter 1

It was on a day just like today when the wind whistled from the north west and the sun shone brightly on the surf as it piled up and roared into the beach in long silvery mountains of foam. Although the sun shone invitingly from time to time, Thomas and Lucy had not ventured out as they were caring for the new baby, their first-born son, to be known as Ben after his grandfather, who had arrived that very morning. Like all new parents the arrival suddenly brought home to them how different life would be in the future with another mouth to feed and a baby to defend from all the challenges of life in the 18th Century.

Thomas and Lucy Luckett lived in one of the cottages close by the water's edge at Burnham Overy Staithe, facing northwards across the marsh to the sand dunes which separated the harbour from the North Sea, where the wind whistles sharp and cold in summer as well as winter. But it is also where you can pause for a moment to watch pairs of oyster catchers screeching overhead practising their formation flying. There too you can listen to the haunting call of the curlew wheeling busily across the marsh. Thomas had been born on the marsh edge and had always lived there. He knew every inlet and tuft, and where to find the nests. He had learnt to be a fisherman like his father before him, and he understood the winds and the tides as well as any man. He also knew well the tell-tale signs which warned the fisher folk it would be unwise to venture out into the surf, and he was determined that his baby son would learn these same skills as he grew up.

Years passed and young Ben grew healthy and strong as younger brothers and sisters were added to the family year by year. Much of the time after he could walk by himself he would spend watching the boats as they came in and out of the little harbour, delivering coal and taking off grain from the local farms. He was well known to the villagers who worked on the boats, or fished, or worked the land. Life was hard in the late 1700s and every family faced the challenges of finding enough to eat as they struggled to keep warm and dry in the winter. In the summer many of the menfolk were forced to work as journeymen labourers, offering themselves for hire on the local farms, often finding they had to travel far and wide to find enough work to keep their family through the next winter.

As he grew, Ben became conscious of the exciting world around him. He would explore the marsh at low tide, encouraging the other boys in the village, and often causing his parents anxiety when he stayed too long and found himself wading or swimming back across the creek. He noticed how quickly the water rushed into the marsh as the tide rose and how, as it turned, the force might knock him off his feet. He felt the softness of the mud between his toes and the scratches of sea holly, the fierce sharp prick of the marram grass, and the knife-sharp edges of razor shells. He discovered where to find the best samphire which he would take home in bundles for his mother to cook for the family. He watched the seasons change and the marsh in front of the house turn from its winter brown into the spread of purple sea lavender of summer. He felt the bitter winds of a frosty February day when the water in the creek was cold enough to numb his toes in minutes, and the warmth of the sand on a hot summer day when he could gaze up to a bright sky of clear blue which stretched from one horizon to the other. He knew the north east wind cutting fiercely off the sea, blowing the sand in a haze across the beach, and the mild south-westerly bringing the smells of the countryside. He learnt about sea spinach and sweet alexander, wild barley, and blackberries so delicious and sweet that it was difficult to eat enough, and he would often return home with his friends, scratched and stained purple. He saw countless rabbits playing outside their burrows in the dunes, and occasionally he watched intently as a stoat or a weasel held the rabbit terrified in its beady glare. He wondered at the amazing skill of the little terns diving into a shallow pool in the sand to pick up a shrimp or a minnow, and was fascinated by the countless wading birds which would feed in the mud at low tide.

Within this coastal community many of the men went off to sea in the trading boats and barges which plied up and down the North Sea coast, or into the ships of the Royal Navy to seek a fortune from the prize money which they felt confident of earning. Many disappeared for years on end, and their wives and families never knew whether they were dead or alive. Occasionally they would receive a letter from somewhere far away, and they would visit the Vicar and ask him to read it for them.

While Ben saw and learnt more about of the lands beyond his sight he began to dream of travelling and seeing them for himself. They listened to stories from the sailors on the boats which loaded and unloaded at the Staithe, fascinated by them, and he always wanted to hear more. Where had they been? What was it like? 'Please Mr Bosun tell me about it. Tell me more about those hot places where you can barely touch the sand because the sun has made it so hot. Tell me about the icebergs at the end of the world where you dare not leave the safety of the ship for fear of freezing to death. Tell me about Captain Cook, for he was one of you before he went round the world. They talk of how he visited a new land called Van Diemen's land. Can I go there?' They came too with tales of great sea battles where ships with hundreds of guns fired broadsides at each other until one side surrendered, and the winner came home with prize money enough to keep a whole family for years. And they talked of Admiral Byng, so loved by his sailors, who was executed on his own flagship to save the consciences of the politicians. 'Can I be famous? Can I be rich?' the young boys would ask.

One evening when Ben was about twelve, as the sun reddened and sank into the western marsh beyond Burnham Norton, Thomas and Lucy sat down on the waterside with him. Life at Overy was not very easy and the family had grown so that there were now many more mouths to feed. It was time for Ben to begin to earn his keep and to learn a trade. Would he be wanting to go off to the fields to help grow the crops, or tend the sheep and cattle? Did he want to become a gamekeeper, which might be arranged through Lucy's cousin who worked on the great Holkham estate only a couple of miles away? Or would he like to go with his father and become a fisherman and experience all the risks and excitement of being at sea in a small boat? Ben listened respectfully to his father as he set out the possibilities. 'No, Father', he said, 'what I want to do is go to sea and find out about the whole wide world; I want to find new places and new people so that I can make a fortune and return here with enough money to look after the whole family. Can you please help me?'

Chapter 2

A few weeks later Ben was placed as an apprentice under the charge of the skipper, Mr Seago, of the Lisa Jane, and he began to learn the trade of a seaman. The little ship had a single mast with a gaff-arigged mainsail, a topsail and various foresails, and Ben's first job was to learn all the names and how each sail could be controlled in every possible state of wind. He stood uncertainly by the bowrope as the tide reached its height, waiting for the skipper's cry. 'Let go for'ard; aft the jib.' And so the wind caught the bow of the ship and eased it away from the hard. A south-westerly breeze was ideal for getting off, and the swift tide would set them easily down to the harbour mouth. Ben had explored the creek at low tide many times and knew all the hazards and sandbanks, but this view of the marsh from the deck of a boat moving downstream was less familiar. He looked ahead at the sand dunes and the gap to which they were heading, and then beyond into the Wash and the North Sea. He glanced back at the harbour as it receded into the distance, to a white line of buildings and the two windmills, gradually getting smaller. Over on the starboard side he could see the tower of the church at Holkham, home of the powerful Coke family, Earls of Leicester, who owned a vast amount of the local countryside. Stretching into the far distance on the port side were the marshes with which he was very familiar, beyond Burnham Deepdale to Brancaster Staithe, protected from the north by the row of sand dunes known as Scolt Head Island. Cattle grazed on the meadows, protected by the sea wall which had been built some two hundred years before, accompanied by flocks of grazing geese which from time to time would take off and wheel in their perfect flight formation around the sky above. Ben recalled how he had spent many hours during the summer lying in the sun amongst the sand dunes watching the birds singly, in pairs and in flocks, turning and wheeling against the backdrop of a bright blue sky. He had marvelled at the little terns hovering above a pool a mere six inches deep, before diving fearlessly into the water to emerge with a shrimp or minnow in their beaks. He had heard the click, click as the turnstones moved pebbles around the water's edge at low tide looking for a tasty morsel. He would always want to come back here, he thought, for this was the centre of his world. Wherever his new-found career would take him, he would always want to revisit this place, this harbour, this world in which he had spent his childhood. Of course it had been tough at times; father had left home to look for work because there was none at Overy Staithe. Food was not always plentiful, mother complaining how difficult it was to provide enough bread and potatoes for the whole family. And the wind could be evil when it blew from the north east, biting and cutting, freezing fingers and toes, so strong that it felt as though it would rip the clothes from your back as it soaked you with rain and chilled you with snow. And yet all that could be forgotten in the warm caress of the summer sun.

His musings were brought to an abrupt end by a shout from the captain, 'Harden up, aft the sheets. Look lively,' as he steered the Lisa Jane past the mussel beds, and then north westerly along the inside of the dunes. One more turn to starboard and they would be swept into the channel, through the dunes and out into the Wash. The south westerly wind was ideal for their passage.

On this voyage they were taking a cargo of barley to Whitby, where they were expecting to load coal for London, before returning with general goods for Overy to be sold in Burnham Market and the towns and villages inland. It was a good time for Ben to learn about life onboard. For the next two and a half years Ben continued to learn the ways of the sea under the care of Mr Seago, experiencing all sorts of weather and becoming familiar with the eastern coastline of England and little ports like Cromer, Blakeney, Wells, Hunstanton and King's Lynn which served the north coast line of Norfolk. He knew the Thames estuary, the hazards of the sand banks and the way up to the bustling port of London where they would deliver mostly wheat, barley or coal in exchange for the more exciting cargoes which arrived from other parts of England, from Europe, and from far across the oceans. Ben loved to watch the proud East Indiamen sailing confidently up to the Pool of London, and His Majesty's ships, frigates and line of battle ships, around Sheerness, Chatham and Deptford. Whenever he had the opportunity he would talk with the seamen from those ships and build a dream of what they might bring him.

In April 1784 the Lisa Jane was struggling through some foul weather at the mouth of the Thames. A strong north westerly had been blowing for several days and the little ship had taken a pounding in a choppy sea down the east coast. During the afternoon of 11th April they sighted the Nore light vessel, and began to pick out the ships anchored nearby. Mr Seago decided to anchor close to the light vessel to wait for a more favourable wind to enter the river, so it was with some relief that Ben let go the anchor and listened as the cable ran out and the ship gradually came to a complete stop. At six o'clock that same evening Ben watched as a frigate came to anchor not far from them. He could not make out the name, of course, but he could see that she was flying a white ensign, and he was able to count fourteen gun ports along the side of the ship. An hour or so later the peace of the Lisa Jane was broken as a naval boat pulled alongside and a Lieutenant with some marines came aboard and asked to see the Captain. Mr Seago knew exactly what this was about – the officer was under orders to find additional crew members for his ship, and Lisa Jane as one of the small vessels which regularly visited the Thames was bound to have some experienced seamen aboard.

'Good evening, Captain' Ben heard the lieutenant say, 'Lieutenant Dent of His Majesty's frigate Boreas, Captain Nelson. I have a warrant to take one of your seamen into His Majesty's service, and I would far prefer it if one of them were to volunteer.'

'Well, I'm short-handed as it is Mr Dent, and you know the weather has been less than kind to us in recent days, so I shall have a difficult job working up-river in any case,' replied Mr Seago. 'But did you say your ship is under Captain Nelson? Would that be him from Burnham Thorpe? We know him and I well remember him as a young lad on the creek at Overy. His father is the parson.'

'That must be the same Nelson,' replied Lieutenant Dent. 'He's recently taken command of the Boreas and we're ordered to the Caribbean. We sailed this morning from Woolwich. Despite many of the Captain's former shipmates volunteering to sail with him again we're still a number short. He would, I'm confident, be most grateful to be joined by another experienced man from his home county.'

Ben heard this and made a decision. It was probably the most important decision he would make in his fourteen and a half years, and it would set the course of the rest of his life. When he thought about it afterwards he wondered what it was that had made him be so bold, and he could only come to the conclusion that something, or someone had got into his head, taken hold of his brain and his tongue and forced the words out of him.

'Mr Seago, please forgive me for interrupting. I know things have been a bit difficult and it'd leave you short handed for the rest of this voyage but, sir, I'd like to volunteer. You must know I've always longed to see more of the world and travel to far away places and this is just the right chance. I've heard at home of Captain Nelson; my father once sailed with him in the Hinchinbroke.' Ben stopped, thinking that he may already have said far too much, and Mr Seago would be docking something off his pay for insolence.

'Well now, Mr Dent, that sounds to me like a pretty handsome offer from young Luckett here. I can tell you that he's a good lad and has served well during two years of his apprenticeship. Can you be assuring me that he'll receive the King's shilling for a volunteer?'

'Aye, that I can assure you both,' replied Dent.

'And, Mr Seago, when you get back to Overy, please tell my father, and I'm sure my brother Jess will gladly take my position and see that you're not short-handed for long.'

'Right then, look sharp, lad. Get below and bring up your kit, and don't keep the lieutenant waiting.'

In less than five minutes Ben had bade farewell to his shipmates, shaken Mr Seago by the hand, and thanked him for giving him the chance to get onto the next step of fulfilling his dream.

'I will always be very grateful, Mr Seago, for what I have learnt from you, and I hope that I shall see you again and be able to thank you after I return from whatever fate Boreas and Captain Nelson might have in store for me.'

As they climbed down into the whaler, the bowman let go with his boathook and took up his oar.

'Give way together,' ordered the coxswain, heading off towards the Boreas, a shadow against the darkening western sky. Ben was suddenly apprehensive. In a matter of minutes he had abandoned the relatively comfortable and well-known surroundings of the Lisa Jane with her unambitious master and crew, and stepped into a completely unfamiliar world. Then it was only ropes and sails, canvas and pitch, and steering a compass course. Now it would be all that plus guns and enemies, a much larger crew and stronger discipline. He had never encountered the bullies and the cheats he was sure to discover now; he had never seen a man flogged, or anyone wounded by splinters and cannon balls. He had climbed a mast, but only in the Lisa Jane, never up to the crows' nest or onto a yardarm. He knew about sailing a fore and aft rig but had never sailed a square rigger. He had known gales at sea, but had always been able to run for the safety of a harbour or the shelter of a bay. What would it be like on the open sea, especially when you have not seen land for days or even weeks and you know there is no bottom within hundreds of fathoms. Mr Seago had made him work hard and never accepted actions taken slowly or listlessly, but punishment was more likely to come from the thick end of his tongue rather than anything else, and the few lazy deckhands who had been aboard in the last two or three years never lasted more than a single voyage and were sometimes turned off a long way from home.

Ben could feel his heart pumping, worried he might accidentally step out of line or get on the wrong side of people who mattered most. Mr Dent seemed to be a reasonable sort, not much older than Ben himself. The sailors pulling at the oars looked a fairly rough bunch, hard and strong. It was difficult to know what stories and mysteries lay behind those hardened rugged features. I am at least as good as any of them thought Ben; this is an opportunity to learn new things and new skills. I may not be a gentleman but I will learn or die in the attempt. And he remembered the words of the Rector at Burnham Thorpe from last summer. 'There is nothing you can fail to achieve with the help of Almighty God; a life spent in His service and that of mankind will be well spent.' That was a good word, service, for surely it meant that you could help make things happen, for your mates, for your watch, for your ship, for your country, for your King, and ultimately for God.

He was brought suddenly back to the present as the boat bumped gently alongside the frigate, and Mr Dent climbed up the ladder to the deck, followed by the two marines. Ben looked questioningly at the coxswain who nodded. With his small kitbag containing his worldly belongings slung over his shoulder, he reached for the ladder and climbed up to the deck of HMS Boreas.

Standing on deck Ben saw an officer whom he later discovered was the First Lieutenant, James Wallis.

'Who do we have here, Mr Dent? It looks as though your visit was very worthwhile,' said the officer.

'We have an excellent extra hand here, by all accounts. He was apprenticed to the master of the Lisa Jane yonder, and has been at sea for three years, so knows well the difference betwixt larboard and starboard. According to the Master he can handle sails and ropes and is as quick with a bowline as any. What's more the vessel sails out of Overy Staithe in Norfolk and young Luckett here is acquainted with the Captain's father it seems. He took the bounty.'

'Today is your lucky day, Luckett; you've just joined the finest frigate in the finest navy of the finest country in the world. We could do with another hand on the mizzen top. Have you ever climbed a mast?'

'Only in the Lisa Jane, sir, which has not such a mast as these,' said Ben as he looked up at the peak of the mizzen mast. 'But I am strong and agile and quick with rope and canvas, so I would like the chance to learn.'

'Right Luckett, you are rated ordinary seaman, topman of the mizzen. Bosun's mate, take Luckett below and get him provided with some kit, and allocated to a gun crew and a watch.'

This brief and business-like conversation had been overheard by a neat and very smart officer who had been watching the proceedings with great attention. He slipped quickly down the ladder from the quarterdeck and walked briskly across to where Ben was standing.

'Tell me, Luckett, how was Norfolk when you left?'

'As good as ever, sir, and I am sure you would still recognise the Staithe which is little changed from year to year. I was fortunate enough to hear Reverend Nelson when I was last at home who seems to keep well.

9

And sir, if my father Tom Luckett were here he would want to pay you his respects; he often told me about the Hinchinbroke when you were commanding.' Ben was wondering whether he could also mention that he had seen the Captain when he was in Norfolk some three years previously, and that had been one of the reasons he had been so keen to go to sea shortly afterwards. But he had said enough and now waited for the Captain to reply.

'I am pleased to hear that, Luckett. And I do indeed recall your father, a fine man who came with me out of the Hinchinbroke and served me until we reached home. Prove yourself on the mizzen, Luckett, and let's see if you are as quick as your father.'

'Thank you, sir.' Ben had been dismissed and turned away to follow the Bosun's mate, patiently waiting for him. He was a little concerned that this conversation with the Captain might have him singled out and accused by his messmates of being a 'spy' for the officers. He would have to work hard to gain their confidence.

Ben was taken to the Purser and issued with kit from the Purser's slops. He had mess utensils, an earthenware bowl, a knife and spoon and a platter. He was also issued with cloth from which the ship's tailor might make him a jacket, and he would have to make his own trousers. The Purser provided a short coat for warmth and a tarred canvas apron, two hammock canvases, with the necessary length of rope, and a hammock lasher. Then he was taken onto the gundeck to the after gun on the starboard side, which would provide his 'family' for the purposes of messing. As a topman he would not fight with the crew of the gun, as his position in battle would be on the deck or up the mast providing the ship with continuing manoeuvrability, but he would still need to know how the gun's crew worked so that he could fit in with the team if someone was injured.

It was already past 8 o'clock in the evening, the start of the first watch, and the larboard watch was below, so Ben had some time to find his way around. As hammocks had now been slung, movement along the gundeck was difficult. So he returned to the upper deck and made his way for'ard, looking carefully at the ropes which were neatly secured around the foot of the masts and along the bulwarks, trying to fathom out what purpose each one served. Compared with the little Lisa Jane, there seemed to be an enormous quantity of them. Having visited the furthest point of the fo'c'sle he returned aft until he reached the ladders up to the quarterdeck where he knew he would not be welcome unless he had some specific task to accomplish. He returned to his hammock station to complete the business of slinging his hammock. This would be the last night he would have before joining the routine of watch keeping when he would never have more than four hours of sleep at a stretch.

The following morning at six am – four bells of the morning watch – he was woken from his dreams by the piercing cry of the bosun's call shrilly waking all hands. 'All hands. Lash up and stow. Weigh anchor at six bells.' Ben jumped out of his hammock and pulled on his clothes. He must watch the sailors alongside him carefully as they lashed up their hammocks each in exactly the same way so that it would pass through the ring before being stowed in the nettings on the upper deck. The daily process of holystoning and swabbing the deck had been completed and the decks were drying out as the sun rose. It looked grey and threatening to the south and there might be a blow coming on. Within minutes Ben had joined other mizzen topmen preparing to hoist their sail whilst others went up to the topsail yard.

All was busy on the quarterdeck while the Captain and several other officers watched the preparations for sea. He could see the master, much older than the Captain, limping around the deck, looking dissatisfied with almost everything. The First Lieutenant was concerned with the weighing of the anchor and ensuring that the two midshipmen who had been given the task of supervising the capstan were ready, and as the ship's bell was struck six times the order to weigh anchor was given. The sailors leant against the capstan poles, and the cable began to come in. At the same moment the mizzen was hoisted to help the ship turn into the wind. All was ready as the anchor cleared the sand and the bow paid off in an easterly direction. The sails were adjusted and the course set.

So Ben's routine began and he quickly became familiar with the detailed workings of the mizzen mast and sails so that he could react in an instant if the Captain or Master ordered a change to the set of the sails. As everything was new to him those first few days were full of frantic activity as he needed to become quickly familiar both with the routine and how the ship would be fought. Very quickly he became familiar with many different situations, pulling in boats, sailing in boats, watching the guns' crews practising their skills, learning his way around the mizzen and keeping all ropes in good condition and properly secured. He climbed the mainmast and learnt to drop back to the deck, sliding hand over hand for speed. Although his primary station was at the mizzen, at any moment he might be required to scale one of the other masts, and he needed to know the purpose of each rope and how and where it should be secured.

He also began to get to know some of his fellow crew members, not all of whom proved likeable. One he feared was Thomas Johnston who spoke rough and was clearly a bully, feared also by many of the other sailors. He had brushed with the Captain when his wife had been ordered ashore – hardly surprising since sailors were generally not permitted to take wives to sea, although some of the warrant officers were allowed to do so. Johnston started putting it about that if his wife were not allowed onboard then there should be no women aboard, even as passengers. Even after Johnston had been called to the quarterdeck and reprimanded by the Captain, he continued to brag to anyone who would listen what mischief he would be doing during the Boreas's commission.

Within a few days the Boreas reached Portsmouth and a few more passengers were embarked there, one of whom was Lady Hughes with her daughter Rose Mary. They were to travel out to the Leeward Islands where her husband Sir Richard was Governor. An hour or two after their arrival Ben was sent for by the First Lieutenant.

'Luckett, the Captain has particularly asked for you to be assigned the additional duty of keeping an eye out for the needs of Lady Hughes and Miss Hughes. They will need assistance now to ensure proper securing of their baggage, and during the voyage you will see that they are provided with as much comfort as possible. Is that clear?'

'Thank you, Sir. I shall be happy to do all I can to make them comfortable.' Ben was pleased to have a reason to be present in the visitors' quarters which would bring him closer to the other officers, especially the Captain.

'Let us go and find the ladies so that I may introduce you to them.' And so they proceeded aft.

Chapter 3

The Boreas sailed from Spithead with a full complement of crew, all in high spirits. Despite the country being at peace without the promise of finding enemy ships to capture, there remained a good opportunity to generate additional earnings from American vessels which were trading illegally with the British colonies. The ship's company strongly believed that their young Captain was very likely to find ways of winning prizes and bringing riches to everyone onboard.

As the ship turned and caught the breeze Ben saw the panorama of Portsdown Hill marking the landward side of Portsmouth, and as he looked out to the East from the mizzen top he could pick out the entrance to Chichester harbour. To starboard he saw Ryde and Bembridge on the Isle of Wight, while astern of the ship, the Solent stretched down to Southampton Water. He might not see any of these places again; it was very unlikely the ship would be back in less than three years, and the risks were great that he might never return. But he felt no fear, only excitement at the prospect of seeing new places and enjoying exciting new experiences. His heart pounded at the thought of returning home to Overy Staithe with a purse full of prize money and a wealth of stories of bravery and hardship to tell to his family back home. This was a life worth living, with the sun shining warmly on your back and the breeze ruffling your hair.

A few days out, crossing the Bay of Biscay Boreas was making good progress southwards with a quarter wind. Ben had been sent up the main mast to check the top-gallant and had taken great delight in sliding down the rope set up for descent from the masthead, landing lightly on the deck more or less at the feet of the Captain. Nelson was, at that moment, engaging with one of his 'young gentlemen', a nervous-looking boy of about twelve whose name was Maurice.

'Well, young sir,' said Nelson, 'I am going to race with you to the masthead and beg I may meet with you there.' So saying, the Captain set off for the larboard shrouds, whilst Maurice headed rather nervously for the starboard side. One of the Bosun's mates standing close by and hearing the conversation turned to Ben and said quietly.

'Follow him up Luckett. We don't want the Captain's enthusiasm to turn into a mishap.'

Maurice made reasonable progress finding foot and hand holds with more care than a practised topman, and he finally reached the masthead where the Captain had already arrived and was surveying the horizon as if he was accustomed to doing this every day.

'Well, it's a fine view we have from up here isn't it?' he said to Maurice as he clung tightly to the topmast. 'It always seems strange to me how so many people see this as a difficult and dangerous place to get to, or an uncomfortable place to end up in. Don't you think it's worth the climb just to see the view and feel the power of the wind in your face?'

Maurice was becoming more confident, but even so he could only utter 'Yes Sir,' in acknowledgement. A few minutes later they were on their way down, reaching the deck without mishap. Before going off to his other duties Maurice turned to Ben. 'Thanks for staying around when I climbed up. I won't need you next time. After all, having been shown such an example by one's Captain it would be difficult not to agree with him that there is really no hardship or difficulty in climbing to the masthead. If he challenges me to another race to the masthead I'll get there first.' With which he turned and headed for the gunroom, head held high, looking very pleased with himself.

Ben reflected that what Captain Nelson had just done demonstrated that he was quite prepared to do anything that he expected his officers and men to do. He clearly demanded of himself at least the same if not better standards of behaviour and performance than he did from those for whom he was responsible. 'That's the sort of Captain I want to serve with,' thought Ben. 'He gives you the confidence that he knows the implication of what he orders you to do. And he's probably done it himself, or something very similar.' Ben recalled his father's account of serving with Nelson in the Hinchinbrooke; how Nelson, though suffering from a severe fever himself, had been meticulous in visiting each of the guns laying siege to Fort San Juan to make sure that the guns' crews were at least as well as he was. Nelson had been fortunate then to be recalled to Jamaica before the fever could kill him, and Tom Luckett had been lucky to escape with Nelson at the same time.

Shortly before Boreas arrived in Madeira, Ben witnessed his first flogging. A marine, John Nairns, was frequently drunk and when in that state he became aggressive and truculent, striking out with his fists at anyone who appeared to stand in his way, whether a fellow-marine, a sailor or an officer. Generally, everyone knew what he was like and made a point of keeping out of the way, but occasionally a blow was landed, as one had on this occasion upon the nose of the Sergeant of Marines. Nairns was duly taken before the Captain who ordered twelve lashes. Nairns was stripped to the waist and tied face down to one of the gratings, his arms outstretched. The Bosun's mates prepared their cat-o-nine-tails and the torture began as the first one raised his arm high and brought the cat slashing down upon Nairns' back. Eleven further blows followed, by which time the skin was beginning to tear and blood was drawn. He had heard stories of sailors receiving 100 lashes and more, and of being flogged around the fleet where every ship was required to administer a certain number of lashes and the survival of the culprit was unlikely. Ben wondered whether fear, though understandable as a deterrent, really could be a good way of winning loyal followers.

When Boreas reached Funchal in Madeira, Ben was one of the oarsmen pulling ashore with the Captain and Lady Hughes and most of the 'young gentlemen' who were being given experience of some of the diplomatic niceties of the Royal Navy.

'I wonder Captain Nelson,' Lady Hughes was saying, 'that you consider making an official visit upon the Governor accompanied by your entire group of young gentlemen.'

'Well, it is simply that they do not get much opportunity to see how things work since they are confined for most of their lives to the restricted scope of the ship. I make it a rule to introduce them to all the good company I can as they have few to look up to beside myself during their time at sea. It's important that they should begin to get some idea of the way diplomacy works and how international relationships are developed,' replied the Captain.

As they drew alongside the landing stage the oars were lifted vertically and the bowman stood smartly with a boathook and painter ready to jump ashore. The coxswain judged the speed of the boat and the angle to perfection and the boat drew gently alongside with the smallest of bumps. The Captain stepped onto the landing stage and helped Lady Hughes to follow, whilst the young gentlemen all waited patiently before jumping vigorously ashore and re-starting their cackle of excited conversation. A messenger from the Governor was waiting to lead them to Government House and they set off at a brisk pace, while the boat's crew shipped their oars and settled down to await their return.

The next few days were occupied with the loading of stores, in particular several casks of wine which the Captain wanted as a gift for the Governor of Dominica whom he would be visiting on behalf of his old friend Captain Locker. There was fresh food to be brought on board, and a continual succession of tradesmen's boats plied to and from the town bringing supplies for the purser and for the sailors. Ben found himself a good deal in the Captain's gig pulling to and fro as the Captain came and went to the various parties and dinners held ashore in his honour. Dignitaries, including the Portuguese Governor himself, came aboard and were entertained in the Captain's cabin, and the ship's band was called upon daily to help entertain the guests. The Boreas was six days in Funchal before setting sail again towards the Windward Islands.

Nearly three weeks later as the cry of 'Land ahoy' went up from the masthead, preparations were made for arrival in Carlisle Bay, Barbados. Ben was much involved with arrangements for the disembarkation of Lady Hughes and her daughter. In some ways it would be sad to see them go for Lady Hughes had been gracious and kind to Ben, and appreciative of his attention to her needs. He realised that what had made his job all the more agreeable was that she spoke to him as if he was almost her equal. When she greeted him of a morning, her words were always accompanied with eye contact and a smile, however uncomfortable her night might have been. And even young Rosie had not behaved in a pompous or over-bearing manner, remembering unfailingly to say 'Thank you', so that Ben felt that he was valued and respected for his knowledge and for what he could do for them.

When the anchor ran out in Carlisle Bay, the anchorage for Bridgetown, on 28th July, they did not have long to wait before Admiral Sir Richard Hughes came aboard amidst much firing of salutes and the shrill call of bosun's calls signalling the still. Ben had heard about the Captain's previous meeting with Sir Richard which had not been a very happy one, but this time everything seemed to be very cheerful, and Sir Richard, with a patch over his sightless eye, was jolly and welcoming and for all one could tell, very pleased to see his wife and daughter again. As they greeted one another Ben overheard Lady Hughes.

'We've had a wonderful voyage. Captain Nelson and his staff have been most attentive to our needs. If every voyage was as pleasant as this, one might well enjoy a lifetime at sea.'

During the three weeks anchored in Carlisle Bay activities centred around the usual business of fresh supplies of food and water while constant repairs were carried out on the rigging and sails. Ben discovered a little about the naval practice of Courts Martial. Captain Nelson, being next in seniority to the Admiral, would be President of any court convened. There were four other ships in the anchorage at the time, enough for a court to be convened, and the captain's cabin was turned into a court. The other captains came aboard with much pomp and ceremony and accused men were marched under marine guards, and usually in chains, to stand before the court and be judged.

Towards the end of July as the temperature soared into the eighties an air of lethargy seemed to permeate the crew. They set sail into a fresh breeze, bound for Antigua where they were expected to lay up for the season of hurricanes. But when they anchored in English Harbour, an even greater sense of lethargy descended upon the crew and Ben found himself struggling to keep busy. It was there that he learnt to juggle using, at first, three small balls made of gash pieces of rope. He watched the young gentlemen performing a variety of plays which gave them something of a purpose.

But most firmly etched in Ben's mind was the experience of a Court Martial which was convened aboard HMS Unicorn, for which Captain Nelson had been called as a witness. Both the sailors concerned had been in trouble earlier in the voyage. Able Seaman John Johnston was obviously rough and tough, knew his way around and was fearless when it came to running aloft. He had taught Ben many of the ways of living in a ship, but he was rather too fond of the daily ration of grog and regularly persuaded his mates to give him 'sippers' until he was definitely 'groggy'. During the voyage he had said to Ben: 'Look here,' he said, 'you need to know that I'm reckoned to be one of the worst men aboard; I'll show you the ropes, but you mind you don't get the same reputation as me.'

So it was hardly surprising to Ben when, after they arrived in English Harbour, Able Seaman Johnston, and the marine who had already been in trouble, Nairns, had their grog ration stopped by the Second Lieutenant as a result of their surly bad behaviour. Johnston's reaction to having his grog stopped was simple. 'Well then', he had said to the Lieutenant, 'No grog, no work.' Whereupon he had been confined below, amidst a torrent of abuse, saying amongst other things 'I'll be damned if I can't open the Captain's eyes to what's going on below decks.'

Ben had seen Johnston and Nairns being returned to the Boreas after the court martial, still wearing leg irons, although their heads were held high. Their marine escort had overheard what was said at the court and talked to Ben about it.

'After all the evidence had been given the Captain was called as a character witness. And he stuck up for Johnston, particularly; he said he had never had any complaint about him except for sometimes using the wrong sort of language, and if he had not received complaints from others, he would have believed him one of the finest sailors he had ever served with. Well, you can't get a better comment from the Captain than that. But in the end it was very clear that the authority of the Second Lieutenant had to be upheld and Johnston was found guilty. We're going to see him get 200 round the fleet.' For the first time Ben saw the horrible effects of such cruel punishment; but even at the end of it Johnston remained defiant and after his raw back had healed he was again his normal self, taking a bit too much grog and still managing to say the wrong thing at just the wrong moment.

Tropical heat, relentless sun and the airless stench of bodies cramped together on the gundeck began to give Ben a feeling of hopeless boredom. At sea he could enjoy the wind and watch the rippling waves, exalt in the antics of porpoises running alongside and the abandon of the flying fish. There was always plenty to do, repairs to be made, adjustments to the set of the sails and a course to be steered. In English Harbour the main enemy was boredom. Some of his messmates seemed to be happy with nothing to do. Others sought their amusement by drinking more than was good for them, but that did not seem to Ben to be enough. He started by talking to the Captain's brother William who was onboard as the Chaplain.

'I can understand entirely what you mean, Luckett, and sympathise with your predicament. In fact I so much agree that I have asked my brother to give me a passage home on the first available ship to return to England and I am off in the Fury. But you cannot do that, I know. You might think about reading and studying, though.' Reverend William Nelson was not entirely without ideas.

'That's all very well, Sir, but my reading is not very good; I only had a couple of years at school before I went to sea. I'd very much like to read and try to improve myself but I need a teacher.'

'Let's have a word with one of the young gentlemen for a start,' suggested the Reverend William. 'Why don't we see if young Maurice Suckling would help you?'

Ben felt quite positive about that, especially as he knew Midshipman Suckling to be one of the kinder and more intelligent characters in the gunroom.

'It would be very kind of you, Sir, to have a word with him, and I'll do my best to be a good student.'

'Leave it to me. I'll also mention to my brother that you are interested in improving yourself. He's always keen to help young people to learn and do better and I feel sure he'll support the idea.'

Ben did not have long to wait and was soon to be found frequently in the company of young Maurice. They discovered more in common since Maurice was a Norfolk boy and also knew the coastline around Overy Staithe where he had visited his Nelson cousins. Besides which he was a patient teacher, and over the following weeks Ben's ability to read and write began to develop with Maurice's support and guidance.

Meanwhile the months of early autumn 1784 passed by and the sailors in all the ships sheltering in English Harbour got through their boredom in any way possible. Ben was frequently one of the boat's crew ferrying officers ashore and from ship to ship, and because he had been recognised as trustworthy he was a member of the crew of the Captain's gig. On one occasion Captain Nelson said to his regular coxswain, Able Seaman Frank Lepee, who had been with him in previous ships; 'Lepee, I think it is time we let young Luckett show us what he can do. Would you be good enough to give him the helm.'

Ben's heart leapt into his mouth. Would he be able to control the boat? Would he bump it into the jetty so that the Captain would fall over? But he stepped up into the stern sheets and took hold of the tiller.

'Let go for'ard; let go aft. Give way together,' he ordered and he turned the gig towards the jetty. That was the start of something, as from then onwards Ben and Frank would complement each other, and Ben's boat-handling skills improved with every trip.

The Captain was much ashore, visiting the resident naval officer Captain John Moutray and his very attractive wife, Mary. Ben would sometimes help to entertain and instruct the Moutray twins, James and Kate, a lively pair who were keen to learn all they could about boats and the sea. The boats would ply to and fro, not only between the ship and the shore but between ships. One ship which was frequently visited was the Mediator, commanded by Captain Cuthbert Collingwood. He and Captain Nelson, Ben noticed, seemed to be very good friends, and whenever they were together Captain Nelson's spirits seemed to be raised. They spoke often about Mrs Moutray and it was clear that both found her very attractive. When she came on board the Boreas to dine, Ben could well understand why. Mary Moutray was elegant and refined, had a beautiful smile and a bright spark in her eye. When she stepped aboard the gig Ben was always greeted with a direct look, eye to eye contact and a cheery 'Good day Luckett.' And when she stepped onboard and was handed up the gangway, there would always be that same direct look and cheerful 'Thank you.' As had been the case with Lady Hughes, Ben felt that he was being treated as a human being, not equal of course, but at least as a person of value, and that made him all the more keen to be helpful to her.

The Captain frequently enquired of Ben how his reading and writing were progressing and Ben was very happy to talk about the books he

21

was tackling.   He always remembered to tell the Captain how helpful
Midshipman Suckling had been, and the Captain would encourage him
further and say he hoped in due course it would be possible for Ben to
learn some navigation.   He felt good about that, and such an objective
would help him put up with all the discomforts of life on board.

In October, after a great dinner and ball given for all the officers, the
Commander-in-Chief finally led his squadron out to sea amidst sighs of
relief that the boredom of the torrid harbour days were over, at least for
a spell.

Chapter 4

At sea again after months in English Harbour, Admiral Hughes' squadron exercised at manoeuvres which often involved sailing in line ahead or abreast and making turns together or in sequence. Skill in sailing and in controlling speed and direction was vitally important, and the topmen were kept hard at work adjusting the sails to the point of wind and the required speed to remain in station. The guns were exercised every afternoon so that within a few days their crews became expert in the routine of clearing, sponging, loading, ramming, hauling out and firing. There was always competition between individual crews as to who could be ready to fire first after a broadside. It took Ben some time to get used to the smoke which filled the gundeck the moment the first broadside was fired. It was often so thick you could barely see your hand in front of your face. Every man had to listen for the voice of the gun captain, and of the Lieutenant who was transmitting the orders to fire from the Captain. The Midshipmen would be running with messages between the Lieutenants and the Captain on the quarterdeck where he could see the signals from the Admiral's ship, while another midshipman at his side would spot the signal flags, interpret their meaning from the signal book, and hoist an answering pennant or the full signal to signify the message had been received.

Captain Nelson was always appreciative of the efforts of the gun crews and the topmen, but he did not like Boreas to be out-performed by another of the ships. 'I can't have Collingwood beating me,' he would often say. 'He may be a good friend, but I want him to know that the men of Boreas are the best.'

After ten days at sea, the squadron anchored in Carlisle Bay, Barbados, where they had last been three months previously. During the days that followed Ben became vaguely aware of a tension between his Captain and the Admiral. He overheard remarks which passed between Nelson and Collingwood seeming to suggest that the Admiral had given them orders which they could not possibly agree with or follow. It was surprising, thought Ben, how much one can pick up, going about one's normal business on the quarterdeck, keeping one's head down, but listening carefully to all that was said. Ben's relationship with Maurice Suckling was another source of information and learning.

'The Captain is in a difficult position,' said Maurice one day to Ben as they relaxed beside each other during the middle watch under a clear and starry sky. 'It's all about the Navigation Acts which were passed by Parliament in London, and which are therefore the law as far as all of us are concerned. But in this case many of the local people in these islands don't like the law and think it shouldn't apply to them. The Navigation Acts say that all trade between British territories, both England itself and all its colonies, must be in British vessels; the logic behind this is that it helps to make sure that Britain has a strong body of seamen and plenty of ships. Otherwise it would be too easy for other countries to build up their merchant fleets and sailors.

'Everything was fine until the American colonies fought for and won their independence in 84. Until then a ship from America could trade with the Leeward Islands quite legally and good business in sugar developed, important to the American colonies. After independence the American ships no longer qualified as British, and the Navigation Acts therefore meant that any American merchant vessel arriving in Carlisle Bay should be sent away and prevented from landing or loading anything It's hardly surprising that the local people don't much like being deprived of a part of their traditional market. Our Captain and Collingwood say that it is none of their business to make judgements as to whether the British Parliament was right or wrong; their duty, our duty, is to uphold the law.

'I can tell you, Ben, there was an awful row when Nelson and Collingwood went to see the Admiral to complain that their orders from him made no reference to enforcing the Navigation Acts. Admiral Hughes told them "I have no orders relating to these matters and I don't have a copy of the Navigation Acts to hand."

' "Excuse me Sir," said Nelson, "but this is most odd. My understanding is that every Captain is issued with copies of the Admiralty statutes as a matter of course. I have my copy here, as it happens; Collingwood has one too, as I know for certain. And, please allow me a moment to read some of the detail for you." And Nelson went on to read out various clauses in the Acts, while the Admiral was going redder and redder in the face, and he looked as though he was about to explode.

'The following day Captain Nelson went back with Collingwood to see the Admiral and the discussion continued, but it seems as though the Admiral must have admitted defeat for the two Captains had broad smiles on their faces when they returned to their ships.

'But I'll tell you what, Ben, I have a sort of feeling that we are going to have some difficulties with that act, and although our Captain may have won a battle with the Admiral, I suspect the war may not be over.'

Admiral Hughes sailed from Barbados the following day leaving Captain Nelson in charge there. Two American traders came in and tried to anchor, and Ben was in one of two boats sent out to them immediately with orders for them to move on. The Masters of the merchant vessels were completely taken by surprise, but left quietly.

A few days later Boreas set sail and headed for English Harbour, calling briefly so that the Captain could visit Mrs Moutray, on the way to the Virgin Islands. Once they had anchored there, the boats' crews were actively involved in Coral Bay, St John Island, making a survey of the harbour in order to assess whether the anchorage could be a safe shelter from hurricanes. Ben spent many hours in a boat pulling gently along a straight course towards a fixed mark onshore, measuring the depth of the water at regular intervals as the results were plotted on a chart. It was arduous and particularly tricky because soundings might vary enormously from one point to the next as they passed over the coral formations, but it would be a valuable service to future mariners seeking a safe anchorage.

Boreas was in English Harbour for Christmas 1784 and the Captain spent the day ashore with the Moutray family. The ship's company enjoyed an extra tot and sang a concert of songs, most of which had very little to do with the birth of Christ and were more about the sailor's perpetual longing to find a pretty girl and settle down somewhere away from the sea. But there was a rather greater sense of goodwill than was often the case, and for one day the Bosun's mates were rather less active with their starters than on a normal day.

Before going off on patrol again Boreas moved north to St John's Antigua's capital, where the Captain consulted with Captains Cuthbert (HMS Mediator) and Wilfred Collingwood (HMS Rattler), whose ships were both anchored there. The stern look on Nelson's face as Ben pulled him back to the Boreas suggested that the meeting had not been straightforward. It turned out later that they had discussed the enforcement of the Navigation Acts. Both the Collingwoods had discovered that the civil authorities in the islands had little intention of observing the Acts and, indeed, were encouraging American vessels and their captains to continue trading. It had become clear that if Nelson and the Collingwoods were to enforce the law, they would find some very strong and determined opposition.

One night, when they both had the middle watch, Ben and Maurice Suckling discussed all this, sitting against the mizzen mast under a perfectly clear tropical sky, lit by the millions of stars, and cooled by a gentle and steady breeze.

'I heard that the Captain wrote to Admiral Hughes and more or less declared that he would disobey the Admiral's orders. That's a pretty serious thing for him to do. After all if you or I were to disobey an order from our superior we would be for the cat in your case or at least a court martial in mine. But our Captain is so passionate about the importance of upholding the law which parliament has made that he can't avoid clashing with an order even from his Admiral which requires him to do something he believes is wrong and illegal.'

The conversation between Ben and Maurice which followed was tortuous and explored situations demanding moral courage and how any thinking person should behave when faced with an order which appeared to be illegal or immoral. Beyond hoping that they would be spared such dilemma they could think of no better action than to respect their Captain's position and resolve to obey his orders to the letter.

Their discussion was suddenly interrupted with a sharp; 'Aft the main sheet,' as the mainsail showed signs of spilling the wind, and Ben knew he must look sharp and check the mizzen.

By the end of February Captain Nelson had got into even deeper water, creating a situation which further heightened tensions between him and his Admiral. The Admiral had written an order confirming that Mr Moutray had a special commission as Commissioner of English Harbour which entitled him to fly the broad pennant of a Commodore, and for all captains on the station to obey any of 'Commodore' Moutray's orders. Nelson clearly believed that a retired officer without a command, as Moutray was, even when acting as Commissioner could not be a Commodore, and that he, Nelson, as the senior captain on the station should be in charge in the absence of the Commander-in-Chief himself. Collingwood wrote to Hughes objecting to the order but proposing a tactful solution; Nelson, by contrast, wrote defiantly 'I will never obey any order of his [Moutray's]'.

When Boreas entered English Harbour in February 1785 Moutray's broad pennant was flying from the Latona (Captain Sandys). Nelson refused to salute the pennant and wrote to Sandys with a reprimand for not saluting him, as senior captain on the station.

Luckett and Suckling both happened to be in the great cabin when Captain Sandys came aboard to call on Captain Nelson.

'Have you any order from Sir Richard Hughes to wear a broad pennant?' asked Nelson.

'No,' replied Sandys.

'For what reason do you then wear it in the presence of a senior officer?' continued Nelson.

'I hoisted it by order of Commissioner Moutray.'

'Have you seen by what authority Commissioner Moutray was empowered to give you orders?'

'No.'

'Sir,' said Nelson, 'you have acted wrong to obey any man who you do not know is authorised to command you.'

Sandys was desperate to offer some justification, feeling that he had been caught between a rock and a hard place.

'I feel I have acted wrong, but being a junior captain did not think it proper to interfere in this matter, as there were you and other senior captains upon this station.' The poor man had been placed in an impossible position and Nelson was offering him no escape, and when Luckett and Suckling had a chance to talk about it later they both felt very sorry for him. But equally they noted that Captain Nelson had made it quite clear that he expected anyone who served with him, or alongside, to observe the letter of the law and the customs of the service.

Nelson was wrestling with the issue of seniority and orders while not wishing to lose the friendship of the Moutrays, least of all of Mary. He had allowed himself to become overwhelmed by a detail which would sour relations with his superior officer, rather than recognising a problem and finding a tactful way around it. Collingwood's reaction was far more mature, stating his objection but proposing a solution which might allow everyone to agree and feel justified. Nelson had taken a position which might be strictly correct, but took no account of broader issues, nor of the potential upset and hard-feeling which would surely follow. Perhaps the boredom of peacetime in the West Indies gave him too much time to ponder such details which were unimportant in a wider context. Hard feeling evidently turned into resentment and, in the fullness of time, contributed to Nelson's long period ashore without a command. He had displayed moral courage for sure, but it would not lead to better achievement of the enterprise. Everyone involved was upset. Moutray was slighted and confused, Hughes was vulnerable and undermined, Nelson and Collingwood were upset that their seniority was being overlooked, and Captain Sandys of Latona was being used like a ball batted to and fro between the other parties. Although Moutray had received perfectly clear orders from the Admiralty ordering him to act as commander-in-chief at English Harbour in the absence of the Admiral, he must have felt that if he had shown the order to Nelson a difficult situation would have been further inflamed.

Towards the end of February Nelson received a letter from Mary Moutray telling him that her husband had been recalled, and it was clear that the dockyard at English Harbour would be down-graded. So much misery and upset had been caused to so many people by one somewhat thoughtless officer attempting to batter his way through an imaginary wall, instead of being clever and diplomatic enough to find a less painful solution.

'Well,' said Maurice to Ben, 'at least that solves one problem, and we won't have any more nonsense about who flies the Commodore's pennant in English Harbour.'

Chapter 5

During the early months of 1785 the tensions over implementing the Navigation Acts became ever greater. Ben and Maurice noticed how the Captain was seldom seen with a smile on his face. At first they put his misery down to the departure of Mrs Moutray to whom he had been greatly attracted. But as weeks turned into months it was clear that there was more to it. They talked over the chatter in the gunroom, where it was said that the captain had been upheld by no lesser person than the Home Secretary, Lord Sydney, who had written to the Governor and the Commander-in-Chief urging them both to enforce the Navigation Acts, just as Nelson had insisted should be done.

'Part of the trouble,' declared Maurice at one point, 'is that the government is so far away. It takes weeks for letters from here to get to London and for a reply to be received back. And it seems that the captain has been writing to Lord Sydney without sending his Admiral or the Governor a copy of what he's written. And then in London Lord Sydney assumes that the Commander-in-Chief is commanding his Captains and knows what's going on when in fact he doesn't. It'd be far easier if they could all get together and talk about the problem; then each one could simply ask the others to explain their position, and everyone would know at the end what the government decision was and why, and they could get on and implement it.'

On 19th March the Boreas intercepted an American brig heading for an anchorage in Basseterre Roads off St Kitts. Ben was on deck as Captain Nelson ordered one of the gun's crews to close up and prepare to fire some warning shots. A signal was hoisted ordering the brig to anchor and not to communicate with the shore. Ben was one of Lieutenant Wallis' boarding party to visit the American, and they were disgusted by the state of the ship which was poorly maintained and taking on water. The Boreas's carpenter and sailors did as much as they could to man the pumps and stop the leaks and, on the following day, the ship was allowed to enter the harbour and anchor while repairs were made.

But far from being complimented on having helped and repaired a leaking ship, Captain Nelson and his crew were accused of cruelty in ordering a ship in distress back to sea. Local merchants in St Kitts were determined to paint Captain Nelson in the worst possible light. Then out of the gunroom came the news that the possibility of some prize money was approaching. The Captain had evidently issued a declaration around all the islands that American trading vessels which were found to be trading in contravention of the navigation acts would be taken as legitimate prizes and sold independently.

On 2nd May Ben was in the gig which had been called away to pick up the master and mate of the Eclipse, flying English colours and apparently entering St Kitts, which had attempted to flee as soon as the Boreas drew near. It turned out that the schooner was actually the American vessel Amity, from Philadelphia, and from the master downwards all were pretending to be British. A second register found onboard made it clear that they were all American. So the ship was sent in custody to the local vice-admiralty court for trial, something which had not happened since the end of the American war.

About ten days later Nelson heard that four American brigs had anchored off Nevis to trade there. Ben was in one of the boats which was sent, with a government lawyer from St Kitts, to investigate and arrest the brigs. When they had covered the few miles to Nevis they saw that the Americans were showing white flags with a red cross – St George's flags – which were said locally to be 'island colours.' They left some marines onboard to secure the ships and see that they did not escape and Ben thought how happy he was not to be one of those marines isolated in a strange ship where the crew was hostile.

On 23rd May Ben was Coxswain of the Captain's gig as he rowed ashore in St Kitts.

'It's an important day today, Luckett,' Nelson had said. 'We are to hear the court declare whether the Eclipse is condemned as a prize or not. All the local traders are desperate in their determination to free her, whilst the law of our land makes it wholly clear that she was attempting to trade illegally.'

At the end of the day, returning onboard, Nelson had something of a smile on his face.

'We won that round,' he said as the men pulled back towards Boreas, 'but only after I intervened to stiffen the lawyer's resolve. The court ruled in our favour and even Sir Richard seemed to be impressed by the outcome. But we have four more to go, at Nevis, and that will be much harder I suspect.'

For the next five weeks Ben and his shipmates often found themselves escorting officials to see the captain. However the First Lieutenant had given orders that no-one, under any circumstances, was to be taken to the Captain without him or Lieutenant Dent meeting them first. Some of these visitors were evidently attempting to arrest Nelson or serve him with writs issued by the local traders and it was clear to the whole ship's company that a battle was being fought with words rather than with guns.

Ben took his captain ashore at Nevis for the first time on 8th June, once again dressed in his best uniform, to attend the court. On the landing stage there was a small crowd waiting for him with officials of the judge advocate to protect the Captain. Various local people had asked the marshall to arrest Nelson as soon as he stepped ashore, and the judge advocate was determined to stop that happening. The court case took two days this time, but again Nelson's case prevailed and the four American ships were condemned.

In the gig on the second evening Ben saw the captain smiling and smiled back.

'Forgive me for being impertinent, Sir, but it's good to see a smile on your face again,' said Ben.

'Well Luckett, I'm bound to say it has been difficult. But it's good news indeed to know that Sir Richard is now evidently entirely convinced of the rightness of my approach to the scandal of the local officials' and traders' doings. Hopefully attitudes have changed enough to ensure that at least the government officials will now support our efforts.'

When the Boreas sailed at last from Nevis in the middle of June it was not long before Maurice and Ben once again had the chance of sitting together enjoying the stars during the night watches.

'At least we shall have a chance of a slightly happier Captain now all that courtroom stuff is over,' declared Maurice.

''Doubly so, I suspect,' replied Ben. 'The Captain asked me to take a message up to Mrs Nisbet a few days ago and I was able to visit the house of her uncle Mr Herbert.   He seems to be a very important person, President or something of the island, and very wealthy.'

'What did you manage to see when you were there?'

'Well, you know, it's fairly difficult visiting a place like that to get to see much as one cannot just walk up to the front door and ring the bell. But I got inside and was able to talk to some of the servants.   One of them told me that Mr Herbert obviously very much likes the Captain, and how on one occasion when he visited, Mr Herbert had found him under a table playing games with Josiah, Mrs Nisbet's three-year-old. It's quite difficult to imagine him like that when all we've seen over recent months has been someone who was worried and angry.'

'I heard from a Midshipman from one of the other ships who had been up to the big house for an entertainment at which our Captain was present, that he and Mrs Nisbet looked very attached to one another.   I often dream of finding a nice girl somewhere here and enjoying some time with her.'

'Such a chance would be a fine thing,' answered Ben. 'There's not much hope I reckon.   All us fellows can do is dream and hope that we live long enough to enjoy it.'

Boreas had been given the task of intercepting a French frigate, L'Iris, which had been spotted off the island.   Nelson took the Boreas off to the Dutch Island of St Eustatius where he found the Frenchman at anchor. The Dutch Governor invited the French and English Captains to dinner which, Nelson told Ben, had been a very congenial affair, and he had offered to escort L'Iris around the British colonies.   But the Frenchman had no time, he said, and was bound for the French colony at Martinique.

Once again from the middle of August they spent the hurricane season anchored in English Harbour, but this year time passed quite easily as

33

Ben always seemed to have something to do, repairing torn sails, cracked blocks and frayed ropes. There were boats to be pulled between the ships as their captains sent messages to and fro, and joined each other for dinner or recreation. And there was always the battle of trying to stay cool and catch every last breath of the slightest breeze. Throughout the months Ben also continued his studies and could often be found reading a book borrowed from the officers' library, despite disparaging and unwelcome remarks from most of his shipmates.

In October the Captain announced that they would be returning to Nevis shortly, once again on the lookout for illegal traders. Nelson was up and down the hillside at Nevis, visiting Montpelier, Mr Herbert's residence, so frequently that some of the ship's company began to wonder whether their captain was still fighting a legal battle, rather than cruising around looking for more Americans. The difference Ben noted was that earlier in the year the Captain had been more or less unable to go ashore, but now there was no restriction at all. Then, he always looked glum; now, he came back aboard with a smile; stepping into the barge with a 'Hello Luckett, have you had a good day?' and making it abundantly clear that he had. The rumour onboard was that he was courting Mrs Nisbet and that there might be a wedding in the offing before too long.

But just when everything seemed to be pleasantly relaxed the unexpected interfered. Mrs Parry, wife of the Governor of Barbados, had been embarked at Nevis so that she could be taken home to Barbados, and the ship weighed anchor without anyone thinking that this would be other than a routine cruise. With the prevailing wind from the East a south-easterly course was set to pass between Guadaloupe and Antigua before easing onto a broad reach to the south for Barbados. But during the first night at sea it became clear that they were in for a very strong blow. Ben and his fellow topmen were called out to shorten sail several times during the night. The sea continued to rise and the ship was beginning to suffer as she rose and fell to the waves and the breakers increasingly plunged the main deck into feet of water. In the early hours of the morning there was a series of sharp cracks and the sections of the mainmast opened up. They fought to take all sail off the main and relieve the pressure on the mast. The Captain and the Master decided that they must take the ship into Antigua to assess the damage and carry out some repairs. With the mainmast in a dangerous state it took several more days to beat up against the wind into English Harbour.

Once safely anchored the dockyard officers visited and examined the mast.   Evidently their advice was that a new mast should be fitted, which would take some weeks to achieve.   Meanwhile, the passenger Mrs Parry would be stranded and unable to return home.   Ben saw the Captain arguing with the dockyard officers.

'In a perfect world,' said Nelson, 'you are quite right.   But I have to weigh up the risks and I am fearful that some in Barbados might well say I never intended to go there in the first place and will impugn my honour and my reputation.   I am determined to go on but beg you to be good enough to secure an additional iron collar to the mast where the cracks have appeared.   We will adjust the stays to pull it back into the right position and then we will be gone.'

Two days later they were on their way again, the wind having moderated to a steady 10 knots from the east allowing them to set on a broad reach directly for their destination.   In Carlisle Bay they rapidly disembarked Mrs Parry and set off back to Nevis, which they made in quick time, arriving on Christmas Eve.   Before any Christmas celebrations happened onboard the Captain landed and was last seen setting off up the hill for Montpelier.

During the early months of 86 Boreas continued to patrol, but spent an increasing amount of time at Nevis and Barbados.   Carlisle Bay, the anchorage for Barbados, was a busy place with frequent arrivals and departures.   Governor Parry had shown no inclination to press for the observance of the Navigation Acts, and trading vessels of all nationalities were frequent visitors, although in most cases they would fly a white flag with a red cross – St George's flag – or British colours whether they were entitled to do so or not.   Most Royal Navy ships were content to accept the outward signs as valid.   Besides it was well known that the legal authorities, notably Judge Weeks, and the Attorney General Mr Brandford, held sympathies more closely aligned with the local merchants and planters than with the government in London.

Now that her Captain had been vindicated by the recent judgements in the courts at Nevis and St Kitts, and the subsequent endorsement of his actions by the Commander in Chief and the Home Secretary, Lord Sydney, in London, Boreas had a very different welcome. Boarding parties were sent to every merchant vessel to check its register and confirm whether or not it was a British vessel. Ben and his shipmates were kept very busy and were often left onboard the merchantmen as prize crews whilst the master and his crew were taken ashore pending full enquiries.

It was clear to Ben and to most of Boreas' company that Barbados had become another place in which their Captain was going to make a stand. Early in March Ben had been with him as he boarded the Lovely Lass suspecting it of trading illegally. Later in the day they had been ashore to consult with Mr Brandford, the island's attorney general, on the case, and the master had admitted how grateful he was that Captain Nelson had drawn his attention to some irregularities in his register which he was happy to put right. He affirmed publicly that he had been treated very properly by the Captain and his men, and he was permitted to go on his way.

That evening they arrived back onboard to find considerable commotion. Lieutenant Dent, who had been left in charge during the First Lieutenant's sick leave ashore in Nevis, reported to the captain that the master of the Brilliant, a schooner under British colours, had been brought onboard shortly after dropping anchor and was not very happy about it. Ben followed the Captain as he strode off towards his quarters and not long afterwards he was in charge of the boat which took the master ashore whilst a prize crew was sent aboard the Brilliant, and her own crew sent ashore to accompany their master. Captain Nelson had decided that the ship was almost certainly foreign built and owned, and therefore not allowed to trade. The same had happened with the Jane and Elizabeth a couple of days earlier. There were clearly going to be some more fireworks and no doubt the Captain would be vilified and pressurised to withdraw the cases.

When first the case was brought before the notorious Judge Weeks he at once refused to try it on a technicality, which was fiercely rejected by the Attorney General Mr Brandford. In the meantime the customs were trying to get a cut of any deal by claiming that they had taken the prize despite arriving a few minutes after the Boreas' men.

The waterfront in Carlisle Bay where all the boats and cargo were landed was a busy place and Royal Navy sailors, especially those from Boreas, were not at all popular. Insults would fly and the occasional punch would be thrown. Ben and his fellow sailors were regularly briefed by Boreas' officers about the situation and warned to be extremely careful when ashore and not to respond to provocation. Officers normally carry pistols with them and would often be accompanied by sailors armed with cutlasses.

Local people were further inflamed by the landing of press gangs from the naval ships looking to add to their crew, and even Boreas had signed on a number of local men, by force.

On 14th April 1786 Mr Scotland, Boreas' Bosun, went ashore as ordered to administer some form of punishment to some sailors in the hospital. He had permission from Lieutenant Dent to remain on shore after completing the task until the evening gun at 8pm. During the course of the afternoon he walked down towards the waterfront and there found Midshipman Nowell and a party of armed sailors acting as a press gang and holding various other sailors at the point of a pistol in an attempt to recruit them. Scotland observed that the young midshipman seemed to be getting increasingly out of his depth in the face of ever greater threats, and instead of acting judiciously and withdrawing to allow tempers to cool, pressed on ever more fiercely. Scotland drew his pistols and intervened positively by ordering the Midshipman and his men to follow him, and he led off inland in the direction of St Michael's church away from the waterside and the crowd of sailors. As they approached the churchyard they found themselves followed threateningly by the mob, and a number of Boreas' sailors started to run, some of them to the left towards Spry street and others to the right onto St Michael Row. Scotland found himself deserted by his fellows as the mob ran up behind and split in all directions attempting to follow and catch the other sailors.

Meanwhile Captain Nelson was walking back from Government House escorted by Frank Lepee and Ben Luckett when they heard a shot from St Michael's churchyard.

'We'd better get over there and see what's up,' ordered Nelson. So the three men quickened their pace and headed to the source of the shot. Only minutes later they entered the churchyard and found the Bosun Mr

Scotland holding a young man in his arms, who had evidently been shot. Other passers-by seemed to be disinterested and took no notice as they went on their way.

'What has happened here, Mr Scotland?' asked the captain.

'I was being threatened and chased,' replied Mr Scotland, 'and in waving my pistol to warn people off it caught one of them and accidentally discharged. Unfortunately this young man stopped the ball and it seems to have caused a serious injury. He says he is James Elliott of the brig Fortitude from Grenada.'

'We need to get him to the hospital as quickly as we can. We could do with some help.' Saying which Nelson stopped a couple of men in the churchyard and asked if they would be kind enough to help take the injured man to the hospital. They bent over him to see how best to lift him without aggravating his pain or making the flow of blood any faster.

Mr Scotland stood up and spoke quietly to the Captain.

'It was my fault, Sir, but it was all so confusing with people running everywhere and awful threats being made against our men. It should not have happened; I should give myself up to the authorities and take whatever is coming.'

'No, no,' replied Nelson. 'That is the way to certain death as there is no possibility of a fair hearing and justice from this place. Go off and take the young man to hospital and get back on board as quickly as you can. Speak with no one, admit nothing, and ditch the pistols as soon as you spot a drain where they will be lost.'

And to the helpers who had now lifted the injured man gently. 'Thank you for doing that service; when he recovers Mr Elliott will be for ever grateful to you. Now go quickly.'

And Nelson turned to his bodyguard and said abruptly, 'Back onboard. Look sharp.'

Meanwhile Scotland went with Elliott and the two helpers as far as the hospital. As they entered carrying Elliott, he ran off as fast as possible cutting down to the river where he disposed of his pistols and, within minutes, getting back to the waterfront. There he spotted one of Boreas' boats and jumped aboard saying to the coxswain, 'Back to the ship as quick as you can.'

Lieutenant Dent was on deck when Mr Scotland came aboard and, having been warned by the Captain that he would be returning shortly, Dent and Scotland went aft together and reported to the Captain.

'Ah, Mr Scotland; you seem to have made good time. Before anything else you must make a deposition before Lieutenant Dent and myself,' and he called out, 'Luckett, please be kind enough to fetch my clerk with a pen and some paper.'

And then to Scotland he went on, 'While we are waiting for him, just tell us what happened.' And Scotland told it all just as he remembered it and finishing with the words 'It was sheer bad luck that young Mr Elliott stopped the ball.'

'Ah, scribes', said Nelson as the clerk arrived in his cabin. 'Thank you for attending so promptly. Mr Scotland has a deposition to make and I'd be obliged if you would kindly record his words.'

The clerk settled himself at Nelson's writing desk and began to write:

'I, John Scotland, Boatswain of HM Frigate Boreas under the command of Captain Horatio Nelson, do willingly make the following deposition and swear by Almighty God that all is true.

'On this day Friday 14th April.......'

Scotland's deposition followed very much the words he had spoken minutes earlier to the Captain and Lieutenant Dent.

The deposition continued;
'Having carried Mr Elliott to the hospital I surrendered my pistols and left to return onboard to my place of duty and to report to my Captain.'

The Captain allowed the clerk to finish writing and then asked, 'Will you please read the account you have recorded and I will then ask Mr Scotland to sign it.'

The document was duly read and Scotland signed, followed by the Captain and Lieutenant Dent as witnesses.

'Thank you, scribes, that will be all for now.' The clerk left the cabin before the Captain continued.

'Mr Dent, what are your thoughts on this case?'

'The account Scotland has given seems entirely reasonable and well accords to the character we know of him. There must be people who witnessed what happened who would affirm that the discharge was accidental. The likely problem is that there were plenty of men who were clearly unhappy with the actions of Mr Nowell and his men and they will probably wish to find a way of ensuring that there is a scapegoat. Sad to say it's Mr Scotland who will be that.'

'I'm quite clear that there's little chance of getting proper justice in this place. We've already witnessed how Judge Weeks treats the law when it comes to upholding the Navigation Acts and I see it as highly likely that he will use this case as a means of getting back at me personally. If we were at Nevis matters would be much fairer.' He paused, thinking.

'Mr Scotland, you must disappear early tomorrow morning and make your way back to England as best you can. Eventually we may be able to meet and ensure your name is cleared and that you can recover all your pay. Delay is out of the question; if Elliott dies there will be an inquest and it's very likely that will find that he was murdered and a warrant will be sent out for you. I cannot be seen to obstruct the law by preventing your arrest and that will, in my opinion, be fatal to you, regardless of the facts. I think the Cyrus will be sailing back to England in a day or so with Captain Sandys onboard. Lieutenant Dent please find some surplus items which should be returned to England and carry them to the Cyrus tomorrow. Scotland will accompany them and not get back into the boat. Make sure that the boat's crew is briefed that they have not seen Mr Scotland in the boat. Goodbye Mr Scotland, I have been very satisfied with the way in which you have performed your duties as Bosun and I will gladly testify as much before any reasonable court. Good luck, and I hope we may meet again.'

'Thank you, Sir. I'm grateful for your advice in this matter and I'll do the best I can to get back to England and plead for a proper trial if such is deemed necessary. It's been a privilege to serve under you, Sir, and I wish you the best of good fortune too.'

So saying Scotland and Dent left the cabin.

The following afternoon a boat left the Boreas with some staves and made for the Cyrus. No one ashore would have noticed that there was one less person in the boat as it pulled back to the Boreas. A few minutes later the Cyrus weighed anchor and set sail for Antigua before heading for England.

On the following evening word came from the hospital that James Elliott had failed to recover from the surgery to remove a bullet from his stomach, and had died. Furthermore an inquest had been arranged for the following day.

The next day, Sunday 16th, Captain Nelson was once again flanked by Lepee and Luckett as he made his way to the Court House for the inquest. The coroner called the Captain and asked him to describe how he came to be in the churchyard and what he had seen. He told how he had heard a shot and gone quickly to the churchyard to find his Bosun, Scotland, cradling the deceased in his arms, suffering from a gunshot wound. He told how Scotland had taken the injured man himself with two others to the hospital and handed him over to the steward before leaving. The Hospital Steward, when called, confirmed the arrival of the injured man but could not say who it was who handed him over; he knew Mr Scotland since he had been in the hospital earlier in the day on ship's business.

The coroner asked for other witnesses, and two men came forward. James McCormick was a thick set man who looked and sounded rough, the sort of bully you might expect to find as a bouncer outside a house of ill repute. He swore to tell the truth and gave his name, describing himself as a seaman from His Majesty's ship Latona, taking leave ashore. He described the activities of the press gang as very violent with the officer holding a loaded pistol at the head of each man apprehended until he should give the right answers. Some of the sailors being held by the press had made a run for it and the midshipman with his men and Mr Scotland had given chase. McCormick was with Elliott, the deceased, who had been a bit too slow and had been caught again just inside the churchyard. McCormick described what happened next.

'Mr Elliott said he had surrendered and would come quietly, but begged them not to drag him and manhandle him roughly. The press gang released him, taking his word, but a moment later he made a run for it guessing that he could get into the cover of the church before the press gang realised. But Mr Scotland shouted 'Stop or I'll drop you.' Elliott went on running but the shot felled him.'

'Are you in any doubt as to the identity of the person who fired the shot?'

'No Sir, I am not. Earlier in the day he had held a pistol at my head demanding to know which ship I was from and I asked him who was asking the question and on what authority. He told me and only dropped his pistol when I said I was from the Latona.'

The Coroner then called John Mitchell who in a weasly high pitched voice told the coroner that he was unemployed and currently residing in the same house as Mr Elliott the deceased. He had been with Elliott the whole day and had watched the violence of the press gang. 'I am of such a weak and unimpressive appearance,' he went on, 'that the press was not interested in me.'

He added that it was he and McCormick who had been at hand when Captain Nelson appeared, and they had carried Elliott to the hospital. 'This fellow who seems to be called Scotland came with us but we told him to push off as we needed no help from a murderer.'

The conclusion of the inquest was inevitably that the killing had been illegal and that John Scotland, Boatswain of His Majesty's ship Boreas, should be arrested and brought for trial. Governor Parry followed normal protocol and asked the Commander-in-Chief, Admiral Hughes, to arrange for Mr Scotland to be handed over to the civil authorities for trial. When he went aboard the Boreas on 20th April in connection with a court martial of three deserters from Rattler, he took the opportunity to ask the Captain to hand Scotland over.

'The truth is, Sir, that no such man, answering the description given by the coroner is onboard my ship' responded Captain Nelson. That was the message returned to the Governor. The following day the Admiral delivered an order to all his ships informing them that Scotland had been accused of murder and ordering them to inform him at once should they identify the person in question.

Six days after the inquest five Captains from His Majesty's ships anchored in the bay gathered onboard Boreas for a court martial which had been convened to review the sinking of the Cyrus. Hours after weighing anchor from Carlisle Bay, bound for Antigua she had been driven onto an uncharted rock off the north-west coast of Barbados and rapidly sank in seventy fathoms. During his evidence the Master told how the majority of the crew had managed to swim and scramble to safety although some poor souls had been lost. A number of survivors had presented themselves for further duty and were available to serve aboard other ships, but the Master could not be sure whether there were any others who had disappeared into the plantations and might or might not be seen again.

The next day McCormick and Mitchell were to be seen loafing around the waterside, as unemployed sailors are accustomed to do. A boat from Boreas came alongside with some water casks to be filled and while that was being done the remaining members of the boat's crew were engaged in conversation by McCormick and his friend.

'So what do you fellows know about that rogue Scotland?' asked McCormick.

'He keeps himself to himself,' answered the Boreas seaman, knowing that he was warned to give nothing away.

'So you are protecting him onboard, are you?' continued McCormick trying to draw him out.

'That's none of your business where Mr Scotland is,' responded the Boreas man.

'It's very much my business to see the law upheld and no murderer getting away through protection onboard the Boreas. I shall make sure the attorney knows where he is.' And with that McCormick, accompanied by his wheedling and wheezing friend Mitchell, set off from the waterfront up towards the law courts.

Later that day Judge Weeks ordered the marshall, Thomas Gretton, to send men to Boreas to arrest Scotland. Under-marshalls Arthur and Jones were rowed out to the ship and presented their warrant of arrest to Lieutenant Dent, saying that they had sound information that the man was hiding onboard. Dent asked them most politely to wait a few moments on the gangway whilst he went and consulted his Captain. When he reached the great cabin, Nelson was clearly in a bad way.

'What is it now Mr Dent? I am not in a mood for much, as all this nonsense about Mr Scotland has made my head hurt, and I have a dreadful migraine.'

'Two under-marshalls have just delivered a warrant for Mr Scotland's arrest, Sir. They say they have positive information that he is onboard.'

'Well we shall have to make a thorough inspection and find out where he is hiding out. I don't recall having seen him since the day of the incident, do you? You had better tell them that we will send the papers on to the Admiral to ensure that due process is followed.'

'Aye, aye, Sir,' replied Dent turning on his heel and heading back towards the gangway.

'The Captain asks me to thank you for the papers and says he will send them along to the Admiral for his attention. Thank you gentlemen.' With that the lieutenant gestured the visitors toward the gangway and they had no option but to withdraw back into their boat, having achieved nothing at all.

Later that day Governor Parry received a note from the Admiral confirming that Captain Nelson had informed him that the wanted man was not on board. The Governor then issued an order to all officials to cause 'all and any places and place throughout the island' to be scoured for the offender. A reward of £20 was offered for information leading to his arrest and merchant ships were cautioned against taking him on board.

Meanwhile the cases of the Brilliant and the Jane and Elizabeth had still not been heard and the prize crews were increasingly reporting concerns at the way in which the ships were deteriorating. The Captain had succeeded in having a hearing on 6th April but it had only lasted a few minutes because Judge Weeks had refused to hear it, on a technicality. Governor Parry proved powerless because the Judge maintained that the Governor had no authority over him, and, after the incident of Boatswain Scotland, Parry had decided that he had been cheated and was not going to do anything to help the process.

They languished in the harbour a further four weeks before Nelson received a note from Attorney Brandford saying that there was very little chance of the matter being resolved locally and that he would send the case to England for trial. Nelson knew that the two ships would have dropped to pieces before any judgement could be received back from London.

On the 21st May Ben escorted his Captain up to the court house where he requested the return of all the papers relating to the Jane and Elizabeth and the Brilliant. The King's Proctor who was responsible for their safe keeping was amazed, but had no reason to prevent their removal by the person who had lodged them in the first place. They hurried back on board.

'Mr Jameson,' Nelson ordered the master, 'to sea at once. Signal the two prizes to get under weigh and follow us to sea. North west until we are clear of Barbados and then the shortest course for Nevis.'

There was a flurry of activity onboard as the Bosun's mates chased the sailors about their duties and the sails began to unfurl for the first time in several weeks. The capstan was turning to haul up the anchor and the cable was being washed as free as possible of sand and weed as it came through the hawse to be laid out below. The easterly breeze caught the sails and as the cry of 'Anchor aweigh' was passed aft the ship began to creep forward ripples working outwards from the bow and a stream of bubbles formed the wake. The Captain on the quarterdeck looked over the starboard quarter to the two trading vessels and was content to see activity there. Focussing his telescope on the waterfront he was pleased to see that no one seemed to have taken any notice of the fact that Boreas and her two prizes were leaving.

That night Maurice and Ben were again able to have a chat under the stars.

'It's a relief to be away from there,' offered Ben.

'Everyone seems to have been against us all the time. It was awful to go ashore and find oneself being jeered at by a mob. Several of our people were attacked and so it is hardly surprising that the incident of our Bosun occurred.'

'He was a good man, and fair. I know he issued punishments to a number of fellows, but only when they were well deserved, and unlike some Bosuns he was no bully. I cannot believe he ever intended to kill that poor fellow.'

'And the Captain was quite right – if he had given himself up there would never have been a fair trial and he would have been convicted of murder and hanged. He admitted firing the pistol although he said it was unintentional and I believe that – there were so many people rushing about. Confusion, half darkness.'

'I wonder where he is now. I saw him slipping into the boat which took some staves across to the Cyrus and as far as I know he never came back with them. So he must have been onboard when the Cyrus went down. Perhaps he drowned. We shall probably never know.'

'The Captain took a huge risk, you know. He must have believed very profoundly in Mr. Scotland's innocence; he could, even now, be accused of perverting the course of justice, or of sheltering a wanted man. But actually that makes me feel pretty good – to be serving a Captain who will do so much for one of his men. If he will defend and support us in a tight spot then I guess we can do no more than support him as best we can. My father always used to tell me that moral courage was just as important as physical courage, but much more difficult as you cannot see it and feel it in the same way.'

'I hadn't thought of it like that,' replied Ben. 'I just feel that the Captain is someone who seems right and just; whether it is a matter of how he speaks to me or what, I am not sure.   But with him I feel as though I matter to him – I am not just being treated like cannon fodder, an expendable sailor.   You know that he himself could do everything he asks of you and that he will do his best to look after you.'

'I heard the Captain order course for Nevis, so I presume that he is aiming to take our two prizes to the Vice-Admiralty court there, which we know is more friendly.   Rumour has it that the president may become the Captain's father-in-law before the year's out, so the judges may be sympathetic to our claim.   Let's hope there may still be a pound or two of prize money in it for us all.'

The general morale in the ship was good as similar conversations took place amongst the sailors and the officers.   Everyone was happy to be on the move and to feel once again the motion of the deck underfoot and the breeze flowing through the rigging.   Wind vanes had been set to divert fresh air through the gun decks and clear some of the foetid and foul smells which hung heavily within the ship whilst at anchor. Gradually the whole ship, timbers creaking, ropes straining, sails taut in the wind, seemed to be heaving a sigh of relief as she responded to the coaxing of the crew tending the canvas.

A few days later Boreas arrived in the familiar anchorage off Nevis with the two merchant vessels close at hand.   The Captain went ashore and began the process for the condemnation of the two prizes and by stark contrast with Barbados the whole process was complete by the end of June.   Seldom a day passed without the Captain being taken ashore, either to pursue the progress of the case or to visit Montpelier and dine with Mr Herbert and his niece.   Wherever he had been he would always return with a smile on his face and much more of a spring in his step than had ever been the case in Barbados.

There were some other tasks to be fulfilled.   In July Boreas took another prize, the Eagle, which was escorted in to Nevis and rapidly condemned without any fuss.   On 13th July they called in at St Bartholomew, an island some 65 miles north west of Antigua owned by the Swedes.   Captain Nelson had first met the Governor, Baron Rayalin, six months earlier and was asked to visit again in order to reassure the Antiguans that they were not going to entice black slaves away from the British territories to sanctuary in St Bartholomew.

On 1st August the Commander-in-Chief Admiral Hughes sailed for England handing command to Captain Nelson. But that coincided with the retreat of the fleet to English Harbour to sit out the hurricane season once again, and for Boreas it would be for the last time.

Chapter 6

The island of Dominica is one of the most beautiful and unspoilt places in the West Indies, enjoying a climate of plentiful rainfall and a landscape which is largely rainforest, the home to many unique species of birds and animals. During the recent American War of Independence the French had finally decided to ally themselves with the Americans against the British, which gave them an excuse to re-take Dominica as a French colony. In 1778 a French force had overwhelmed the small British garrison whilst the Royal Navy's back was turned, waiting for orders from England in Barbados. The island was returned to British sovereignty in 1784 under the Treaty of Paris, although the majority of the inhabitants were either of French or African origin. In 1786 it was important that the British reinforced their sovereignty, and the best way of doing that was by a visit from the British West Indies Squadron now commanded by Captain Nelson.

Early in December 1786 Boreas was joined in Roseau Bay off the island's capital by Amphion, Solebay, and Rattler, accompanied by a 28 gun frigate which had not been seen in these waters before. Pegasus was commanded by the King's son Prince William Henry and Nelson had received orders to show him around the West Indies. The whole company of Boreas had been ordered to smarten themselves up for the arrival of Pegasus and the firing of the appropriate twenty one gun salute. There was much ceremonial as the Captain and officers all dressed in their best uniforms welcomed the royal Prince onboard.

The following day Ben accompanied his Captain paying a return visit to Pegasus and while the Captain was speaking with the Prince in his cabin Ben had a chance to talk with other members of the crew.

'It must be good to sail with a Prince as your captain,' suggested Ben to one of the seamen.

'Don't believe it,' came the rather surly reply. 'We never know where we are, and the First Lieutenant, Mr Schomberg, isn't happy at all. You can always tell if it's going to be a happy ship if the captain gets on well with his lieutenants. Here they always seem at odds. The Prince wants us to dress up even in this heat; Mr Schomberg defends us and says it's not reasonable and the Prince then loses his rag and demands obedience from Mr Schomberg. Jack is always at the back end of the argument.'

'That can't be much of a life,' admitted Ben. 'Boreas is quite different and the Captain is always on our side. I've been lucky enough to go with him to many different places and he's always grateful. He could so easily treat me as a mere sailor to be disposed of, but I really feel as if he values me as much as he would anyone. And when it came to our Bosun Mr Scotland who was likely to be unreasonably convicted of a murder the Captain made sure he could sneak away; he didn't believe Mr Scotland could possibly have killed a man in cold blood, and stood by him.'

'Sounds like he's the man to follow; any chance of a transfer?' asked the seaman knowing that it would be very unlikely.

Over subsequent weeks Ben had many opportunities to talk with the men of Pegasus and he learnt from them how the Prince was very keen on using the cat for the most minor offences. He once had a German artist to visit him and the poor man found himself not just falling out with the Prince but bent across a cannon with his backside being beaten. Apparently he was later repaid the costs of medical treatment, but it was not the sort of behaviour which endeared the Prince to anyone.

'He's a regular piss-pot, too,' one sailor told Ben. 'He seldom goes ashore for dinner without coming back completely drunk. It's said that many of the ladies fear being in his company because he is so likely to misbehave. And it's when he is most pissed that you need to watch out – he'll throw his weight about and order the cat for the least slip-up.'

Ben watched his Captain in the company of the Prince and it seemed as if the Prince was the senior officer, despite the fact that Nelson was very much his senior in rank, and older too, and much more experienced at the navy's business. But Nelson seemed to agree with the Prince and praise his firmness, whereas any other junior captain would never presume to advise his superior and would look to Nelson for encouragement and advice. And as for drunkenness he had never ever seen Nelson unsteady after he returned from dinner ashore, and he knew that when dining onboard he would never drink wine, however much he offered to his guests. The Prince's behaviour did nothing to endear him to either officers or sailors, let alone the government officials and civilians he met when ashore.

Boreas and Pegasus spent two months in English Harbour from December 1786 during which time the Prince was frequently entertained at balls and parties of one sort or another with Nelson frequently having to dance attendance upon him. Nelson would ride a horse from English Harbour to St Johns in order to attend these balls and he asked Ben whether he could ride well enough to accompany him.

'No Sir,' said Ben, 'I've never been on a horse, but if it will help you I'll be happy to learn, and escort you.' So after two or three lessons in horse-riding with the English Harbour livery Ben was confident enough to attend Nelson as he went to a ball. Whilst there he was able to observe all the other people attending, most of them dressed up in their finest clothes bought especially for the occasion and excited beyond belief to have the chance of attending a ball in the company of a real Prince. On the return journey Nelson had told Ben about some of the people at the ball.

'Governor Shirley was there, of course, and although he has just been appointed a baronet you couldn't believe how nervous he was. He'd been invited to propose His Royal Highness's health and was scarcely able to say a word. There seem to be plenty of people who are delighted with all this ceremony but I'm bound to say it doesn't suit me. Tell me Luckett, what have you observed aboard Pegasus?'

'Well, Sir,' Ben replied, 'The men don't seem to be very happy. I hear their captain will put every small thing down in an order book and that the First Lieutenant has been confined to his cabin after asking for a court martial.'

'His Royal Highness has been doing his best to maintain discipline and doesn't want to see his officers and men becoming slack and failing to attend to a proper level of detail. We depend for our success in battle on everyone doing exactly the right thing at the right moment so it's important for them to know what standard is expected.'

Ben thought that his Captain's remarks did not really match the way he behaved in Boreas. Trivial things did not get recorded in an order book – it was not necessary. But he also recognised that if he said too much, however much he respected his Captain, someone might find himself in trouble. 'Perhaps,' he thought to himself, 'this is nothing more than a function of the pressure the Captain has been under what with all the legal issues in Barbados. If we were to get an order to return home that might change things back to normal; or perhaps a wedding would help.'

There was talk of a Court martial for Lieutenant Schomberg but there were never enough ships in the harbour to be able to appoint five of them for a court. It would have been appallingly difficult if it had happened because either Lieutenant Schomberg would be found guilty of some crime or misdemeanour and would probably be broken, which would end his naval career, or he would be found 'not guilty', in which case the Prince would be made to look a fool, or incompetent, which would be very embarrassing for all concerned.

By the end of January Boreas was on the move again with a quick trip to collect the President, Mr Herbert, and bring him to Antigua. But before he got ashore he went down with a fever and, in company with Pegasus, they turned round and went back with him, calling on the way at Montserrat for the Prince to enjoy some more entertainment. By the middle of February they had reached Nevis and the Prince began a succession of entertainments and social events in St Kitts and Nevis, which included balls, cockfights, formal dinners and horseracing. Despite dancing attendance on the Prince, Nelson knew that if Mrs Nisbet was to become his wife he must arrange the wedding quickly because the Prince was due to go to Canada shortly and he himself was due to be relieved and return to England. Fanny Nisbet must be his wife before then.

The wedding was set for Sunday 11th March which dawned with a steady drizzle, which soon cleared. Frank Lepee and Ben Luckett busily engaged preparing the Captain for his wedding, making sure that his uniform was in perfect condition for such an important occasion. As he donned a clean and perfectly white shirt he declared, 'Undoubtedly the most important day of my life. I don't believe that any man can be truly fulfilled until he finds the right woman with whom to devote and dedicate the efforts of his life. What I've done and will do will surely still be for my King and country, but my inspiration will also come from the woman I love. And today I shall dedicate myself to her. So everything must be just right.'

'May we rejoice for you, Sir,' responded Ben.

'It is true,' continued the Captain, 'there are many who profess to see a wife as a diversion, and I suppose that they speak from their own experience and observation. It would be true if the woman attempts to dominate her husband and prevent him from achieving the greatest things to which he aspires. Mrs Nisbet, soon to be Mrs Nelson, knows well what drives me and that I seek glory in the eyes of my King and my country. She understands, I am sure, that this means that I must continue to strive my utmost to achieve sea commands and rise through my exertions to a position of standing in the country. And if glory means death, then so be it; it will be the will of God.'

Frank buckled his sword to his belt, Ben handed him his hat, and he strode out of the cabin into the sunshine of the upper deck. His gig was waiting for him and he boarded without delay. Once ashore he walked briskly up the hill to St John Figtree church.

All the grandest people of Nevis were attending the wedding and the reception which followed. Nelson's young cousin Maurice Suckling was the only member of his family to be present. Prince William Henry fulfilled his promise to give the bride away and signed the marriage register as a witness. The Rector, William Jones, performed the ceremony and declared that they 'be man and wife together, as long as ye both shall live,' following with the exhortation to the congregation 'Those whom God hath joined, let no man put asunder.'

Arrangements had been made for the newly married couple to stay in lodgings where Frank and Ben had taken some of the Captain's necessities, but work had to continue and added to the Captain's responsibilities the new Mrs Nelson still had commitments to her uncle at Montpelier. On 19th March the Boreas sailed to Tortola.

By 6th April they were at English Harbour again with a heavy programme of repairs to ensure that the Boreas was fit for her return across the Atlantic within the next few months. It was on this visit that

Ben met Mr Wilkinson and Mr Higgins, both merchants, who had visited the Captain in his role as acting Commander-in-Chief. He overheard them making their case to the Captain, that they had detailed information which would be able to expose the massive extent of fraud that had been going on for years in connection with the provision of government supplies, especially to the dockyard at English Harbour. The two gentlemen urged the Captain to engage the Prince with the issue, asking him to arrange a government investigation. In the event, despite Nelson's enthusiasm, the Prince was little interested in taking up the issue until Wilkinson and Higgins mentioned the fact that the company owned by a certain Mr Whitehead had 'stolen' a significant proportion of the prize money earned during the American war by British ships.

'I cannot let that pass without action,' Nelson had said to Ben after Wilkinson and Higgins had left. 'I have been successful in pursuing those who would act illegally by failing to impose the Navigation Acts, surely I must now persuade the government to act when the fraud so clearly affects the money received by our gallant sailors and their officers. It would be so easy to forget about it or delay it – to leave the matter to the next Commander in Chief; go home and enjoy life.

'But that would be dishonest,' he went on. 'I cannot bear the thought that I might let those sailors down, that I did not do something for them when I could.' During the coming weeks the Captain was often buried under piles of ledgers and papers from the dockyard and the hospital searching for evidence of the fraud to which the two informers had pointed. Letters were written to the Comptroller of the Navy, to the First Lord of the Admiralty, and to the Master General of the Ordnance Board but, as Nelson confided in Ben, 'We have to be very secretive to avoid too many people knowing what we are doing and preventing any further investigations.' This would be an investigation likely to run on for months and possibly years.

Many of the sailors aboard the Boreas, including the Captain, suffered from a fever during the month of April, and Nelson's pace of work was affected. Nonetheless a court martial was convened on 9th and 10th April. Most of the cases were routine and involved desertion or attempted desertion from Solebay and Rattler. The final case was that of William Clark of Rattler, who had been a persistent deserter. The prisoner was found guilty and due to his record no sentence less than execution could be delivered.

Ben and his shipmates were all required to be on the upper deck or in the rigging on 16th April at the appointed hour of 1030 as drums rolled and the yellow flag was hoisted aboard Rattler. Clark was taken onto the cathead, a black hood placed over his head and a noose around his neck whose rope led aloft to a block on the fore yardarm. A number of the Rattler's sailors manned the tail of the rope with space on deck for them to run together to hoist the noose aloft. Just as the order was about to be given, activity could be seen on the Rattler's deck and the Captain, Wilfrid Collingwood, urgently consulted a paper which had been handed to him. This turned out to be a letter from Prince William Henry asking for the sailor to be reprieved. Clark was freed and discharged from the navy.

'I shall be in trouble again, I daresay,' mentioned the Captain to Ben afterwards.

'He is a lucky man, Sir,' replied Ben.

'Sure enough, and he was properly convicted. The problem is that I am rather afraid that the reprieve, despite being from a Prince, is not really good enough. The Royal prerogative of mercy can only be dispensed by the sovereign, the King himself. So, by accepting the Prince's reprieve I have undermined the King, and there will be plenty of people in the Admiralty who will find that quite unacceptable.'

'Surely not, Sir,' replied Ben, 'it shows the men that their officers are capable of showing mercy from time to time.'

'Thank you, Luckett. We'll have to wait and see what comes of it. I just hope that Clark will accept the gesture of mercy and will go and make something useful of his life outside the navy. His record on that count is not very promising.'

Just a few days later a letter arrived for the Captain from the Prince who had accompanied Rattler to sea. The letter told of the death of her captain, Wilfrid Collingwood. He was the younger of the two Collingwood brothers and Nelson had clearly found in him a good friend and a solid honest supporter. He had suffered from the same fever as others in English Harbour and the doctor had advised him to put to sea to get some fresh air. But he had not recovered and died quietly on the evening of 21st April. The Boreas followed on 25th, glad to be away from the pestilence from which so many had suffered, and headed for St Vincent and Collingwood's funeral.

The following day Nelson sent for his First Lieutenant and informed him that he was to assume command of Rattler as an acting Commander. He would be replaced as First Lieutenant by Dent, who in his turn would be replaced by Lieutenant Hope, who had asked to be transferred out of Pegasus. Lieutenant Wallis was delighted that this would give him the chance of early confirmation as a post Captain. He received a warm send-off from Boreas and approached his new responsibilities with confidence.

So April turned into May and Boreas spent the time anchored off Nevis whilst the Captain assisted his wife and Mr Herbert to prepare for their journey to England. It was arranged for them to travel in a merchant vessel, the Roehampton. Meanwhile the Prince paid a brief visit to Nevis to take leave of the Nelsons, and on 20th May the saluting guns fired their final 21 gun salute as the Prince sailed off in Pegasus. He was to go by Jamaica and report there to Commodore Gardner in order to settle the business of the court martial of his First Lieutenant Schomberg, and Rattler was to sail in company as far as Jamaica, before returning to England.

Like the rest of the ship's company Ben was sensing the end of their duty in the Leeward Islands and they were all beginning to look forward to setting a course for home. It was no surprise when a brig dropped anchor at Nevis with orders from the new Commander in Chief, Commodore William Parker, to sail at once to St John's Antigua and meet him in Jupiter, and Sir Richard Bickerton in Sybil.

Boreas was already at anchor at St John's when Jupiter and Sybil arrived but Captain Nelson was very ill that day.

'Luckett, I feel atrocious, with a head from which fifty drummers must be trying to escape and a stomach which will hold nothing. I cannot possibly meet the new Commodore without being carried on a stretcher.

Please ask Lieutenant Dent to send to Commodore Parker to ask him if I might be excused calling upon him until tomorrow.'

The meeting with the Commodore took place on the following day and afterwards Nelson returned to Boreas looking tired and dejected.

'The only good thing that happened today, Luckett, is that I have in my hand orders to sail to England, and we are to go by way of Nevis and St Eustatius. Everything else seems to have rebounded against me. But I am clear that there is no point at all in fighting with this Commodore, nor of trying any further to justify myself. Please ask the Master and the First Lieutenant to come to the cabin so that I can discuss our movements with them.'

'Aye, aye, Sir,' said Ben as he left the cabin. He was thinking how sad it was that the Captain seemed so low just at the moment he should be looking forward to the return voyage and the prospect of some leave to set up a home with his wife.

They called briefly at Nevis where the Captain bade farewell to Mrs Nelson and Mr Herbert and wished them a comfortable and safe voyage. Both health and morale onboard improved as the ship set her course to the east and the Atlantic breezes began to freshen the ship below. Young Maurice Suckling once again found an opportunity to chat with Ben during the night watches.

'What will you do when we pay off?' asked Maurice.

'I will first deposit a large part of my wages with a bank,' replied Ben, 'and I would be grateful if you could advise me where I should go. I don't want to find that an unscrupulous banker removes my hard-earned wages through some fraud or other. I just want it kept safe from the highwaymen and robbers who frequent some of the inns at the waterside.'

'That seems like a good start, but what then? Will you look for another ship or go back home, or find a wife?'

'For sure I should like to see my home again and find out how my mother and father are getting on. We lead a pretty tough life out here

57

but it is not easy for the likes of them trying to scrape a living out of fishing and some occasional farm jobs. I should really like to take some money to them to help with my brothers and sisters. What about you?'

'Noble thoughts, my friend. Me? Well my family all think that they sent me away so that I would make a fortune. I don't think that will happen on this trip and my only hope is to find another berth as a Midshipman so that I can clock up enough years to qualify as Lieutenant. That will be hard in peacetime. And what do you think our Captain will do? He seems to be a bit more cheerful since we turned for home, but really he is worn out and dispirited – he is certainly not the young and enthusiastic captain we started out with two years ago; the one who challenged me to race to the masthead, do you remember?'

'I do indeed. I see a lot of him of course and I must be careful not to betray his confidence. As I see it, he has been fighting hard for what he believes is right, whether it is the implementation of the Navigation Acts where at first the senior officers all seemed to be disposed to ignore them, or the fraud he has worked on within the dockyard and the hospital at English Harbour. Then he seems to have got on the wrong side of everyone by standing up for Boatswain Scotland, because he believed that there was no chance of a fair trial if he surrendered. More recently it has been that drunken deserter from Rattler who was reprieved by the Prince. He has been driving himself mad as well over the reception he had from Commodore Parker; apparently he should not have sent Pegasus to Jamaica, nor appointed Lieutenant Wallis to command Rattler. It seems he fearlessly does what he believes is right without thinking of the consequences.'

'Isn't it strange how the idea of getting into a battle, firing broadsides, boarding enemy ships and so on, seems much simpler and more straightforward. That might result in an injury or death, which I suppose is unpleasant. But this business of standing by what you believe is right regardless of the consequences is much more complicated. You can't really see your adversary and you have to guess what's going on in his mind. You have to guess what the outcome might be and once you have started something you probably can't undo it or go back and start again. And if you were to change your mind you'd have to justify to yourself why your belief has changed, or why you now wish to pursue an easier path.'

'I still say,' concluded Ben, 'that Captain Nelson is a great person to serve. You know you'll get an honest and straightforward answer and that if you do your best for him, he'll do his best for you. I think one thing I've learnt over the past couple of years is that I'm a follower, not a leader, and the captain is someone I can follow. So I guess that, if I can, I'll stick with him and see how things go. At least if he goes to his home in Norfolk I'll be not more than a few minutes' walk from my own folk.'

On 4th July the anchor finally went down at Spithead and the whole ship's company were able to feast their eyes on the familiar view of Portsmouth and its harbour. Ben was amongst the first boat's crew to pull into the harbour with the Captain so that he could call on Admiral Hood, in Triumph, and the Captain of the Dockyard, and arrange for the Customs to visit the ship.

Within a day or so the ship's company was paid a proportion of the wages they were due and most were allowed ashore to stretch their legs on dry land. For some it was the first time they felt land under their feet for three years and their first steps ashore were uncertain as the ground appeared to sway under them and they staggered as if they were drunk. Many of the men soon found their way to the taverns around the waterfront, where the barmen and owners were notoriously clever at relieving Jack of his pay with great speed and efficiency. Some risked deserting, though most knew that they would not be paid the remainder of what was owed to them if they did.

Luckett and Lepee continued to serve the Captain as best they could, attending to his needs and accompanying him ashore on official business. And then in the middle of August orders came for the Boreas to join the impress service at the Nore which meant that they would be anchored in the Thames estuary sending boats ashore with armed parties to collect any seamen they could find, and into all the merchant ships returning home to gather their sailors before they were able to get ashore. This was a tedious and boring business which involved placing others into unhappy circumstances at a time when Boreas' men were looking forward to going home to their wives or sweethearts. They did what was necessary, but without enthusiasm.

Eventually the time for paying off arrived, and on 30th November 1787 the ship paid off at Sheerness. As Ben and Frank packed up their Captain's belongings, Nelson was at hand to give instructions.

'I'd like you both to accompany me if you will. I can't pay you much but I'll do my best to ensure you're well housed and fed and in return that you'll help me ensure my smart and proper appearance, and that you'll render such service as my wife and I may require as we go about our business.'

'Thank you, Sir,' responded Ben; and Frank nodded firmly in agreement.

Nelson went on 'Thank you both. I'm sure we'll continue to get along well. In the event we may only have a short time to wait before the government needs to increase the number of ships in commission and man a new fleet, but at this moment nothing is sure. For now, I'll take the coach to London and would be obliged if you'll bring my effects to 10 Great Marlborough Street where I've taken rooms.'

The lower decks were cleared and all the remaining men gathered by the gangway to take leave of the ship which had been their home for the past three years. Before he departed Captain Nelson addressed them briefly.

'Thank you all for your service during these past years. The Leeward Islands have not always been as welcoming as we might have hoped and English Harbour has tried our health and my patience. But we have come through it together and I hope that when their Lordships of the Admiralty are next willing to assign me to command a ship any of you who so desire may come and serve with me again. When that will be none can tell. In the meantime I wish you all well and may good fortune attend you and those you love.'

The Bosun raised his voice above the murmur of the sailors, 'Three cheers for Captain Nelson. Hip, hip, hip....' And three times came a rousing cry of 'Huzzah' as the sailors willingly saluted their Captain, before he stepped onto the quay and made his way to the posting house to pick up the coach for London.

Luckett and Lepee left not long after having commandeered a dockyard trolley upon which to transport the Captain's chests and furniture. Not only were they carrying his uniforms and clothing, but they had a writing desk and various other less important items, and all his papers, letters and writing material, and a full set of tableware. They went into the dockyard office to find out when a carrier was expected to leave next for London and were told that one was expected at dawn the following day from the Red Lion. They would stop for a night at Dartford before crossing Bexley Heath and continuing past Greenwich and on to the Old Kent Road.

Chapter 7

London in 1787 was not a very agreeable place. Everything about the place was dirty and crowded and stepping onto the street meant being beset by beggars and hawkers of every description doing their utmost to remove any pennies you might have. Ben longed to be back at sea, enjoying the fresh air and the smell of the ocean, the open space and the excitement of arriving somewhere new. London seemed, for Ben, to lack interest. But first he must make the journey to Norfolk to visit his home and see how his parents and siblings were faring.

Meanwhile Captain Nelson had welcomed his wife to London after her voyage from Nevis and, after a few days in her uncle's lodgings, she moved in with him as husband and wife for the first time in a house in Prince's Street. The Captain always seemed to be busy, meeting people and writing letters. One morning not long before Christmas he said to Ben; 'Do you recall a seaman in Boreas called James Carse?'

'Yes, Sir, I do indeed. He was a cooper I believe – not a young man but he knew his trade. Why do you ask?'

'I've a letter from a lawyer asking me to appear for Carse as a defence witness. He's been charged with murder. From my memory of him he's less likely to have murdered someone than you or me; it doesn't match the character I recall. What do you think?'

'It seems very unlikely unless he was severely provoked or totally drunk. But he never used to be such a great drinker – he drank his tot like the rest of us, and enjoyed it, but he was never looking for extra. But I do remember him having a curious turn one day off Antigua, not long before we sailed for home. He suddenly seemed to lose himself and spoke gibberish and couldn't control his limbs; and then he completely retired into himself, and couldn't work. I think you sent him off to the hospital.'

'That's right, it's coming back to me. The hospital told us he had recovered and we took him back aboard just before we sailed. He couldn't work properly though, could he? Melancholy is how I'd describe him. Well apparently he went ashore with a pocket full of money and found his way to the Ship in Distress, on the waterfront in Wapping where they say he met a lady who took him off to her house whilst he was very drunk, presumably offering him her favours. No sooner had he got into her bed than he noticed her room mate and went quite mad, believing she was about to rob him. He leapt out of bed, pushed her into a corner and cut her throat with a clasp knife. Meanwhile the girl in the bed ran for her life and fetched the watch. It's a cut and dried case – no doubt that he killed the girl. But it doesn't seem to be in character.'

'Is there anything we can do for him, do you think?'

'Well I'll certainly appear for him at the trial and hope to make some statement in mitigation, which just might keep him away from the gallows. But I wonder if there might be someone down there in Wapping who knows a little more about what actually happened. It'd be no good me going down there as they'd know me at once for an officer and tell me nothing. But you might be able to find out something which would help him. Why don't you take a walk down to Wapping and look around the waterfront at the Ship in Distress. Someone might be able to talk – but watch your back – and don't take more than a penny or two with you.'

'I'll do that for him, Sir. But I'd better look out my old sea-going kit – it'll not be much good if I turn up in that hole looking like Captain Nelson's servant, if you know what I mean.'

An hour later Ben was on his way. He had left his money safely behind in the Nelson's lodgings and had dressed in his rough clothes, looking more a sailor than a landsman. In wartime it would have been a dangerous thing to do for fear of being picked up by a press gang. But now, with the country at peace there would be no press gang and the greatest danger was that of being robbed or swindled out of any money he happened to have with him – a few pence would be quite enough.

As he walked he could see the vast dome of St Pauls dominating the skyline and felt that he must take a look inside that magnificent building which had been completed less than a hundred years before. He passed into the City of London along Fleet Street where all the newspapers were produced, down to the Fleet which was still a stinking drain running down to the river, carrying all manner of frightful rubbish, and on to the East up Ludgate Hill to St Paul's at the top. The west front of the cathedral was massive and he felt even smaller as he ascended the steps up to the doorway. And once inside he could do nothing more than stand in awe at the magnificence and grandeur of what he saw. The dimensions were vast, strong and powerful, obviously a message to him, and others, that the God who dwelt there was all-powerful. He felt over-awed as he began to walk towards the crossing, and there he looked up in amazement at the dome with all its magnificent decoration. A few minutes later he climbed up and up until he reached a new level where he could look out across the dome and down to the floor where people, like ants, seemed to be scurrying across the detailed and precise patchwork of the black and white marble floor. Ben had never really questioned the existence and power of God, for he had seen what that power could do through an Atlantic storm, and he had seen the devastation of a hurricane. But this building told a different story, about the resilience of mankind who, after the disaster of the fire of London had destroyed the old cathedral, built a new one much stronger and greater than the old one. Men would never go to such expense and effort without believing very sincerely and deeply in the presence, and goodness, of God. Well, he thought, if it is good enough for them, it must be good enough for me too.

He walked on to the Tower of London, wondering about all the people who had been locked up in that forbidding tower and a shiver ran down his spine to think of how many had ended up being executed. Beyond the Tower he could see the mass of shipping in St Katherine's dock whose masts seemed nothing less than a forest. There were so many people coming and going, quite apart from the carts hauling cargoes to and from the waterfront and he had to fight his way through the busy throng to get down to the water's side. An old man was sitting on a box smoking a pipe, watching everyone. He must see everything that went on hereabouts. Ben approached him and asked, 'Good day to you, Sir, it's a fine day to be out and watching, what's up hereabout?'

''tis and all,' replied the smoker, 'and what's brought you along here.'

'Well, you know how it is for a seaman, it's hard to stay away too long. I used to sail into here from Norfolk when I was a young'un, and having a day to spare I thought I'd come down and see what's up. Is the tavern under the Ship in Distress still as rough as it used to be?'

'Aye, that it is. The girls still know a good fishing ground when they see one, though one of'em got herself killed a few days back.'

'Hasn't changed much then,' said Ben. 'What was the story this time? I suppose Jack was drunk and didn't know himself, and I daresay he had already been robbed, and imagined the girl was going to lift the rest of his pay.'

'Well if you are really interested,' continues the old man, 'you might catch the friend of her that was done, in the tavern right now. I saw her pass by not five minutes ago and she hasn't picked her man yet.'

'Thank you for that; and who should I ask for?'

'They call her Mary, though I don't know as whether there's more than one of'em. Dark she is, and quite a good looker.' Armed with the information he needed Ben wished the smoker a good day and strolled on down the quay.

He pushed through the open doorway of the tavern under the sign of the Ship in Distress, into the stale air and stench of unwashed bodies mixed with rum, beer and tobacco smoke – not unlike the smell between decks of a frigate in the tropics. For a few minutes he allowed his eyes and ears to get used to the thick atmosphere, and he looked around to see if he could pick out someone who might be Mary. Over in the corner was a table with four girls at it, talking animatedly; that would be a good place to start.

'Good morning, ladies,' Ben started, 'And would any of you be taking a drink with me, or shall I get in four and make it a broadside.'

'Well, there's a generous gentleman, if ever I saw one,' says one of them, 'I think it's the more the merrier, don't you girls?'

Ben placed an order and turned back to them.

'I don't suppose one of you is Mary?' he asked.

'And why do you ask that?' replied a girl with dark long hair.

'Well they tell me that an old shipmate of mine has been here with her. James, they call him; James Carse.'

'Well we all know about him,' replied another. 'Good thing they caught him and locked him up. He'll be for the gallows in a day or too, I shouldn't wonder. He went quite mad and thought Sal was trying to rob him.'

'That can't be right, the James I knew was a gentle man and I never saw him drunk in four years we served together. He suffered dreadfully from the sun out in the Indies and would have stayed in hospital if we'd not been sailing for home. What happened? Do you know?'

'I was in here with Mary that day, and he was buying drinks all round. He'd had a few himself but still seemed in command of himself. Well, after a bit, he and Mary are getting close and she invites him to take her home, and off they go. All normal, routine you might say.'

'Mary said that as soon as they got to her place, Sal had met them – she and Mary shared the place – and he asked for some rum and a plate of beef. Then he took off all his clothes save his shirt and headed for the bed. Mary was getting down to her shift and Sal brought in the meat and drink before settling down out of the way to smoke her pipe. Then suddenly he jumps off the bed shouting "I must, I must." And his eyes are blazing. He pulls a knife from his pocket, charges over to Sal and pushes her up to the wall and sticks the knife into her. An eight inch cut they say. Mary rushes off in fear of her life dressed in nothing more than her shift and finds the constable.'

'And when he talked to us,' the third of them broke in, 'he said that by the time he got to the house Sal was dead and Carse made no attempt to get away. Calm and docile, like a lamb, he said.'

'It all seems very strange,' said Ben, 'and quite unlike the James I knew. I wonder if the mixture of drink had been just enough to send him mad for a minute, working on a head already suffering from the Indies sun. There are plenty of sailors I know who'd be much more likely to do something like that than him.   You've been very kind to tell me all that, ladies, and I shall take myself off, and think if there's anything I can do to help the poor soul.'

'What can you possibly do?' said one of the four, 'It's a cut and dried case.'

'Well, I'm not sure.   But the Captain did say that if any of us got into trouble we should let him know as he might be able to speak up for us. And I think I might be able to find him if I'm quick about it.'

'Well, he sounds an interesting one.   I thought all those naval Captains simply beat the living daylight out of the crew and then took all their prize money.'

'Not this one,' replied Ben, 'Everything he does is for the men; he works himself to the bone to make sure we're all content.   Most of us would follow him anywhere.   He has ordered the cat, but on those occasions everyone knows it's well-deserved.   If you ask me, this is a man to watch if we ever go to war again.   He'll do great things, you mark my words.'

'So now you'll have to tell us his name or else your words won't mean a thing to us.'

'Horatio Nelson,' replied Ben, 'and don't you forget it.   He'll beat hell out of the frenchies and the dons and end up in St Pauls over there, I shouldn't wonder,' nodding in the direction of the cathedral, little knowing how prophetic his words were.

It was time for Ben to withdraw and leave the girls thinking about the next war, if ever it would come, and how they might take some of the pickings when sailors came home after the battles.'

When he arrived back at Prince's Street the Captain was at his desk writing letters but he broke off when Ben knocked on the door of the study.
'Ah, Luckett, how did you get on?'

Ben recounted his visit and meeting the girls, and concluded, 'It just seems quite out of character.   The drink must have combined with the effects of the heat stroke he suffered in Antigua in some way we cannot understand.'

'Well it looks quite bad for poor Carse, but I'll agree to attend his trial and do my best to mitigate the sentence. We all experienced the effects of that sun and the heat out there and I know it got to me, giving me severe headaches and feeling out of my mind. Besides I never did think Carse had fully recovered when we took him back aboard for the voyage home.'

On 17th December the Captain went to court and pleaded in mitigation, as a result of which, although Carse was found guilty he was ordered to return to the sea service as soon as possible. No one could tell what had caused Carse's awful lapse of sanity, nor, more especially, whether he might do the same thing again after too many strong drinks.

The Nelsons spent Christmas together in London. In the New Year the Captain decided that young Josiah, his stepson, should go to school and that Frank Lepee should escort him to Norfolk and put him into school there. The Captain himself was preoccupied trying to get himself another command at sea, but Lord Howe always seemed too busy to see him. The Nelsons then decided that taking the waters at Bath would be helpful to Mrs Nelson in her acclimatisation to the English winter, and Ben accompanied them as they took to the road – whilst they rode inside the carriage, Ben was outside with the coachmen huddled up within one of their massively thick and heavy coats to keep out the worst of the cold as they drove westwards.

After a few weeks in Bath both the Nelsons felt refreshed and they took to the road again to visit the homes of a number of friends and then to travel on down to Plymouth and Exmouth where the Captain hoped to find the Prince in order to prevail upon him to use his influence to secure him another command.

One morning as Ben was helping the Captain to dress for the day ahead, he ventured, 'You're looking much fitter now, Sir.'

'Well I'm certainly beginning to feel a bit more human,' replied Nelson. 'I was becoming totally frustrated with what happened in Boreas towards the end of last year; I worry for all of you, especially given our experience with Carse, as well as for myself. And I'm bound to say that I'm frustrated again now that I don't seem able to break through their Lordships' defences to get another ship. But at least I'm being better fed and feeling stronger. We'll have to see what the next few weeks bring.'

'I know all the lads of the Boreas are keen for you to get another command, and we'll all follow you if we can. I know you have sent Master Josiah to school in Norfolk and I wonder whether you are thinking of a visit there with Mrs Nelson. I'm anxious to see how all my family is getting on – life must be quite tough for them, I fear.'

'Yes, Norfolk. My father's still there of course although he's quite old now and I'm not sure what he can do. We must go, and you shall come with us, though I doubt I can continue to keep you up there for long unless there is a real prospect of another ship.'

'I'd like to stay with you and Mrs Nelson, Sir. And when we get to Norfolk I will take leave of you whilst I visit my family. Depending on how things are, I may be able to pick up some work at Holkham. It seems that Mr Coke has some new methods for agriculture so perhaps he could use another able body.'

'Yes, indeed. Coke has got quite a reputation for changing the way agriculture works, just as those fellows Wilkinson and Higgins wanted to expose all the corruption in Antigua. It's been very difficult to get any of the Naval Boards to take any interest; but I suppose we should not be surprised about that, for if they did get interested it'd give them an enormous volume of extra work which could also bring trouble and controversy. People don't like change; that was one of the things I learnt out in the Indies – most people didn't want to bring about the changes which were a direct result of the War of Independence and its impact on the Navigation Acts.'

'Have Mr Wilkinson and Mr Higgins been vindicated yet, Sir?' asked Ben.

'They write to me, Luckett, as if I can wave some magic wand and have the Ordnance Board or the Victualling Board immediately drop everything and investigate all their accusations. I keep on pressing the case as much as I can, but it's hard to get anyone to take proper notice. If only I could get some real influence through one of the great people…. the Prince would be ideal, although I fear he may have lost some of his own influence as a result of his performance in Pegasus. I must keep trying for Wilkinson and Higgins, though; they are honest men amongst a hoard of vipers and if they are not successful in their claims they will surely be ruined.'

Spring was beginning to emerge as they returned to London in April of 1788 and some of the chill seemed to have come off the air, leaving the city perhaps just a little less smothered by the smoke of a million fires trying to keep the inhabitants warm. Just two months later the house in Prince's Street was packed up and some of the Nelson's things placed in storage and they set off for Norfolk.

As the coach took them past Fakenham Ben found himself getting more and more excited. There was something wonderfully familiar about returning home, and yet he peered around every corner to see what might have changed in his five years away. Finally they arrived at the Crown in Wells-next-the-Sea and climbed down for some refreshment in the inn, whilst they found someone to take them the last few miles. An hour later they were in a more modest vehicle plodding gently towards Burnham Thorpe. They passed along through Holkham village following the wall of the park. Where the road divided, Ben jumped down, took his leave of the Captain and Mrs Nelson, and set off towards Overy Staithe with his kit slung over his shoulder. His heart was light and his soul expectant. He had fifty pounds still in his pocket, the sort of money his parents had probably never known. Surely they would all be glad to see him.

The curious feeling as he walked along the hard at Overy Staithe was a mixture of surprise and relief. Surprise that whilst he had changed, and grown, and experienced life beyond England in the world of the Royal Navy, everything here seemed almost as if he had never been away. The boats in the creek seemed to be the same, the marshes were the same, the creek itself had not changed as far as he could see; the houses were unchanged too though some had received a more recent coat of whitewash. And relief, at the same time, that the world of his childhood was still there, his happy memories had not been washed away by change.

Since it was only a few minutes from the edge of the village to his family home there was little chance for anyone to prepare a great welcome for him so he walked up to the door almost unremarked upon by anyone. Thomas and Lucy were in the kitchen, she all of a fluster, whilst he remained solid and unmoved as if this were simply a normal part of another day. But if you looked carefully you would have noticed the corner of his mouth relax, his lips widen across his face and his eyes begin to light up. That was about as far as Thomas did emotion; in truth he was overjoyed for this, his first-born son on whom rested so many hopes, had returned home looking fit and well.

During the next few weeks Ben told stories to his siblings and to many of the other children in the Staithe. He regaled his parents with descriptions of some of the places he had visited – of Antigua and Barbados, St Kitts and Nevis – and the sort of life he had been leading. He told them how wonderfully well he had been treated by Captain Nelson and how, as soon as he had another ship, Ben would certainly volunteer to go with him. He gave them most of his money and suggested they might use some of it at least on his siblings' education; he told them how lucky he had been to serve in the Boreas where he had the advantage of being encouraged to read and study, and how he could now read a chart and take an altitude at midday.

Summer turned through autumn, and winter came with its brown and grey colours and the cold north-easterly winds when the hardest task was to stay warm in the frost, and still no news came from Captain Nelson that he had another ship. Gradually Ben found himself absorbed again into the life of the Staithe and his family. But he was always restless, whether taking work as a casual labourer at Holkham estate or going to sea with one of the local fishermen or traders. Their world was too small for him, their horizons far too narrow; he yearned to explore. He would have to wait.

Part Two - From Norfolk to Norfolk Island

Chapter 8

The year had nearly reached its end and the trees were all bare, the marsh had taken on its winter colour, predominantly brown. Christmas was not far away. But on that particular day the sun was shining and there still seemed to be a little warmth in it as Ben decided to take a walk out to the sea. A new year would be upon him soon and he must decide about his next move along the pathway of his life. The tide was rushing into the Staithe as Ben walked along the hard and onto the sea wall. It was time to go, he was thinking to himself. But go where, and to what purpose? He set off along the sea wall, zig-zagging towards the distant sand dunes, pondering whether there might be some merit in heading north to Whitby where Captain Cook had started his famous journeys to the Pacific; or should he go to Bristol or Liverpool and join the fleet of trading ships voyaging across the Atlantic and further afield. Or, perhaps he should aim to rejoin a fighting ship even though no war had been declared, and head for one of the naval ports at Chatham, Portsmouth or Plymouth.

A voice seemed to be calling him from the side of the wall, lower down amongst the thick grass. 'Good morning, Luckett,' it seemed to say. 'Is that you, Luckett?' He knew the voice, surely, but he could not see where it was coming from. And then a head popped up, and he knew instantly, that it was none other than his former Captain, Nelson.

'Good day, Sir,' said Luckett with a broad smile, delighted that he should happen across his former captain at such a moment. 'What brings you out here?'

'I often come here when I have the Gazette from London, especially when the weather is as fine as it is today. This is a wonderful place to sit and contemplate, to wonder what one should be doing, and to dream of great happenings in far-away places. And what about you?'

'I'm restless; I've definitely decided that agricultural work around here is not for me. It's very hard and offers very small rewards and absolutely no security or opportunity. The labourers are in a hole and nothing they can do can hoist them out of it. There's fishing, of course, but that too is a hard existence and doesn't bring in much; but it's always the same, and always here. I feel I want to go back to sea – not in one of these small trading vessels running up and down the coast but something larger like the Boreas, which will travel round the world.'

'It sounds as though your feelings are very like mine. But it seems there is no future at sea for me unless there is another war. No one seems to want me in a ship at the moment despite my continuous and urgent pleading to the Admiralty. But, Luckett, we may be in luck. The news from France is of revolution and that may stir governments into making war with each other. But I've also just been reading about the new colony in New Holland. Have you heard about that?'

'No, Sir; tell me what that is about?'

'Well, it was shortly before we arrived back in Boreas that a fleet set out under Captain Arthur Phillip with 750 convicts to set up a colony in New Holland at a place identified by Captain Cook, and called by him Botany Bay. It seems that this fleet arrived out there early in '88, but instead of settling in Botany Bay they chose another harbour which was named Port Jackson, and there they established themselves and began to create a town which they called Sydney. Earlier this year the new colony seems to have been suffering badly from dwindling stores and the fact that they had been unable to grow sufficient food to keep themselves. Starvation loomed. So Captain Phillip sent one of his Lieutenants, called King, back to London to plead for supplies and help so that they can establish themselves properly. Lieutenant King described his voyage home, via Batavia, where he arranged for some supplies to be sent down to Port Jackson, and the Cape. It seems that the entire crew and the master of the packet from Batavia succumbed to a deadly fever, picked up in that pestilential port. King managed to survive with a mere four crew members by building them a sort of tent on the upper deck and never going below at all while they crossed the Indian Ocean. They made harbour in Mauritius, where the master died. King himself survived, arranged a new master and crew, and organised the thorough cleaning of the vessel before setting off again for London. Now there is an officer after my own heart – what do you think?'

'If it had been you, Sir, you'd've done the same. I don't see how it is you seem always to know what to do. I need someone to point me in the right direction and tell me; then I can find the energy and courage to do it.'

'Well, Luckett, Lieutenant King may be someone you'd do well to watch, and you might even like to find him. I've read that the Gorgon is being fitted out in Portsmouth, under a Commander Parker, and that he's likely to be sent out to Port Jackson; my guess is that Lieutenant King will go with them. So if you want to set off for somewhere a little further afield you could do much worse than take yourself with all despatch down to Portsmouth and see if you can volunteer for the Gorgon. If you'd like to do that, let me know, and I'll write a letter of recommendation for you to Commander Parker. Perhaps you should mull it over and let me know in the next day or two.'

'Thank you, Sir. I appreciate that, but I am not sure that I need so much time to think about it. The only problem is that I was hoping to be able to serve under you again, and that will be very difficult if I'm on the other side of the world.'

'Well you know what the landsmen say – a bird in the hand is worth two in the bush. If you wait for me you might have a very long wait. And, in any case, if you were to attach yourself to this Lieutenant King you might find that you were even better off. Why not spend Christmas Day with your family and call on me the following day at the Rectory in Thorpe. I'll have a letter for you, and I may ask you to deliver some other letters for me in London on your way by. How will that serve?'

'Very well indeed, Sir. You've given me just exactly the push I needed. I'll go to Portsmouth and try to sign on to the Gorgon and see what comes of it. But I'll not lose sight of a hope of serving under you again at some time, God willing. I can't believe that you will not have a ship of the line, which will surely be the best in whatever fleet it is appointed to join.'

'Thank you Luckett, I'll see you on the appointed day. Meanwhile may I offer you and your family every good wish as you celebrate the arrival of God upon this earth. May He go with you and with all you love.'

And so saying Nelson turned and sat down again on the bank burying himself in the detail of the printed pages. Ben smiled to himself, and a sense of relief washed through him as he strode off towards the sand dunes and the sea. His mind was already made up beyond doubt. Another parting from his family would be a moment of sadness, but he knew in his heart that it must be right. He had contributed to the family's life especially by enabling his siblings to go to school, but there was no space in the cottage for him. Now he had a plan and a determination to set out again to seek a new fortune, perhaps on the other side of the world. As he walked up the dunes and caught sight of the North Sea waves crashing onto the beach ahead of him he knew how much he wanted to be at sea.

So, Christmas Day came and went, and Ben rose the following day, put a few things into his bag, embraced his siblings and his mother and father for the last time and set off towards Burnham Thorpe. At the Rectory he slipped in to the kitchen, and the maid was sent off to tell the Captain. Nelson came himself after a few minutes with a packet of letters, which he handed over with the minimum of fuss. With a cheerful 'Good luck Luckett,' Ben was quickly dismissed and set off on the road to Wells. He could not help himself from thinking that perhaps Captain Nelson was in some way jealous seeing him, a mere seaman, setting off for sea with purpose, whilst he was left kicking his heels at home, without any prospect of doing what he longed to do.

Ben arrived in Portsmouth in the middle of January and made his way down to the Dockyard to find the Gorgon. She was berthed alongside with much activity suggesting that she was being loaded for a long voyage and, to his sailor's eye, seemed a fine enough ship. It looked as though she had been built with guns on a lower deck as well as on the upper, but now he could only see 11 guns on each side of the upper deck, 12 if you counted the bow chasers on the forecastle. The lower deck must have been converted for carrying people or supplies.

He made his way up the gangway and asked the Bosun's mate whether he might deliver a letter to the Captain. Captain Parker looked a bold and welcoming man with a big smile and received the letter with a pleasant 'Thank you.' Ben waited as the Captain opened the letter carefully. He read, looked at Ben, and looked down again at the letter.

'You will be aware that Captain Nelson recommends you to me,' said Captain Parker. His voice was warm and kind, but crisp and clear. 'It's not often that men such as you volunteer for a project which carries so much that is unknown. We'll sail for Port Jackson, at first, and then, after carrying out whatever local tasks the Governor may wish, we'll return home across the Pacific and round Cape Horn.'

'I've spent the past year at my home in Norfolk,' responded Ben, 'and am anxious to go off and find somewhere new. They tell me that free settlers are being encouraged to travel to Port Jackson, and that they're not just taking convicts. So I'm also wondering whether it might be possible to spend a few years in this new colony and help explore around about.'

'Are you suggesting working your passage and leaving the ship at Port Jackson? That might be quite helpful since we shall have onboard some extra passengers who'll need to be looked after. I'll happily take you onto the books as an Able Seaman and arrange with the First Lieutenant for your duties to be centred on the care of the passengers. Would that be agreeable to you?'

'Thank you very much Sir.'

So Ben was listed as a volunteer, an able seaman aboard the Gorgon. He found out that the ship had been built as a frigate with 44 guns, but that the guns had been removed from the gun deck to convert her into a hospital or troopship. Now she was being loaded with stores for Port Jackson and with thirty soldiers of the New South Wales Regiment, which explained all the activity when Ben arrived. By the end of January all was safely stowed away and the ship moved to Spithead and anchored there to await final orders and the arrival of the passengers.

First of the passengers to arrive was Mrs Mary-Anne Parker, the Captain's wife, who arrived in a great fluster, for she had received very little notice of the possibility of accompanying her husband on his voyage. She had to make arrangements for their two children to be cared for by her mother, and clearly the separation from them had been very emotional. But it was not often that the opportunity arose for a lady to make a voyage around the world and to share all the perils and dangers with her husband, and she was brave and bold enough to do so. Orders then arrived for the New South Wales detachment to disembark and transfer to another vessel, in order to make way for thirty convicts, for whom the accommodation had to be made secure.

Finally on 12th March, Commander Philip Gidley King, Lieutenant Governor of Norfolk Island, and his wife Anna Josepha arrived, having been married only the day before, and on 15th March, the weather being fair and the wind favourable the Gorgon sailed.

Ben had helped the carpenter to erect a partition to create a small cabin for the Kings, but still they had very little space to give them any privacy. Mrs King seemed, like Mrs Parker, to be bold and brave and quite prepared to endure discomfort in following her husband's calling. Ben immediately enjoyed the west country burr in her voice, not unlike his own from Norfolk and almost within minutes the natural friendliness of both of them had them exchanging descriptions of the countryside in which they had grown up. Hers was the remote and hilly seaside of Cornwall where all was up and down and roads were deep and sheltered; his were marshes and dunes where the vastness of the sky gave a sense of the greatness of creation.

After two weeks of being buffeted in the channel the weather moderated and the Gorgon was able to make a good passage to Tenerife. Ben took the opportunity whilst looking after the needs of the Kings to ask the Commander about his earlier voyage to Botany Bay.

'We really were sailing into the unknown then and we had no idea what to expect. I think God smiled upon us as we sailed first to Tenerife and then to Rio de Janeiro before reaching Cape Town. This time I trust it will be easier – at least I know where we are going.'

'Well, Sir, I don't know whether Captain Parker mentioned it to you but when I came aboard I asked him if I might serve him for the outward voyage but then remain in the colony as a settler. I wonder if it might be possible to accompany you to Norfolk Island when you return there as Lieutenant Governor. I don't really know what to expect but it will, for sure, be a new experience and no more hazardous than continuing a life at sea. And by all accounts it is probably less disagreeable than working on the land near my home in Norfolk. I hope you don't mind me asking.'

'Not at all, not at all,' replied King. 'I'd be delighted to have you on the island and I could certainly ensure that you would have a place to live, though fairly basic, and a plot of land to call your own. Besides very few of the convicts have any experience of handling a boat so having you there would be extremely helpful. We tend to go fishing whenever the sea allows so there is often the need for a boat handler. Your agricultural experience in Norfolk will be useful too.'

The few days' break in Tenerife allowed the Kings and other passengers to spend some time ashore exploring the local area but as soon as water and fresh food had been replenished the Gorgon set sail for the Cape. The Captain had decided to put in at Simon's Bay rather than Capetown because at that time of year Simon's Bay provided the better anchorage and shelter from the hurricanes. Soon after anchoring, the Kings and the Parkers and some of the other passengers went ashore and headed for Capetown where they would pay their respects to the Governor and arrange for necessary supplies for their onward journey. Commander King had told Ben about his first visit there on the way to Botany Bay when they had filled the ships as much as possible with farm animals to help them start the colony. They would now repeat the process and take as much as they could. Making all the arrangements took several days and the Gorgon was moved to Capetown to load the dry stores, livestock, fruit trees and anything they could imagine might be useful in helping the colony. On 31st July, some six weeks after arriving, the passengers returned onboard and were ready to set sail on the final leg of the voyage.

Chapter 9

The Southern Ocean which the Gorgon now had to cross to reach its destination was, and is now, one of the fiercest and roughest places to be at sea. Commander King talked to Ben about his experience in 1787 when Captain Phillip's fleet had sailed from Capetown rather later in the year. Then he had experienced high winds and mountainous seas, when the helmsman had to be lashed to the wheel and, on one occasion, he had become so cold he had almost frozen to death. This passage proved to be a little easier although not without incident.

Ben took the opportunity to get to know one of the other passengers, William Chapman, for it was clear that they would often be working together to support Lieutenant Governor King. William came from a very different background, and having been well educated was quite happy to help continue the informal education which Ben had begun whilst aboard Boreas. They talked whenever the opportunity arose and Ben was able to regale him with tales of Captain Nelson and life aboard a frigate. William wrote copious letters to his mother and his sister Fanny, and he talked about them so much that Ben began to think he knew them very well.

On 7th September at the end of the first dog watch (6pm) the cry went up, 'Man overboard'. As quickly as possible the ship was hove to and a boat was lowered, despite the very considerable sea. Ben was one of the seamen at the oars on that day when they pulled as hard as they could back down the track of the ship in the hope of finding the carpenter who had slipped and fallen overboard. They searched as best they could for an hour but found no trace of the man; like so many other seamen he had probably been unable to swim and would have found that the cold shock of hitting the water had quickly numbed him, his heavy clothing had pulled him down, and he had sunk under the waves within a few minutes. The boat returned to the Gorgon, its crew wet and exhausted after pulling the boat for an hour. They had hooked the boat onto the falls and were readying themselves to be hoisted back onto the ship when a particularly large wave struck, the ship rolled heavily and the boat's crew were caught off balance. Thrown off his feet, Ben nonetheless reached out frantically to grasp one of his fellows, but with the force of the movement he could not get a grip and the man fell into the sea. At once another man shinned down the falls to make up the crew and the boat was released again to try to make a rescue. Again the crew pulled for all they were worth, but again there was no sign of the man; his brother had been lost only a couple of weeks before. Such are the dangers of a ship crossing the Southern Ocean.

Twelve days later, on 19th September, Gorgon rounded Van Diemen's land and was heading northwards with every expectation of making Port Jackson within a few days. The Point named 'Long Nose' by Captain Cook was in sight when thunderclouds began to build up from the East, and, as the sun set a heavy squall hit the ship, accompanied by the fiercest and most threatening thunder and lightning. After an hour and a half of storm a tremendous crack was heard as lightning struck the pole at the head of the mainmast. The main topgallant mast was split to pieces and the main topmast itself was severely damaged. The lightning then seemed to explode along the yards and through the sails into a terrifying sphere. Everyone on the quarterdeck was thrown off his feet and temporarily stunned, though fortunately not permanently hurt. The storm continued for another two hours when there was another deafening explosion and the whole ship shook as if she had struck a reef. Those on deck had experienced something which was described as a ball of fire landing very close by and the whole ship being enveloped in lightning. Miraculously no-one onboard was hurt, and an hour or two later the wind subsided as suddenly as it had risen, and backed to the west. By the morning the weather was fine.

That morning Ben asked Commander King if he had experienced anything similar at another time.

'Not exactly like that,' replied King, 'but when I was last on Norfolk Island we experienced a hurricane. That was frightening, but also frustrating because of the damage it did. We had been on the island nearly a year and our little community was beginning to take shape. We had several crops which, despite the rats and the caterpillars, seemed to be doing well when the hurricane hit. It came in from the South East and the force of the wind tore up everything which was growing. Massive trees were ripped up like weeds and it was only by the greatest good fortune that none fell upon our huts. Our new grain store was severely damaged and I had to call on everyone to turn out and shift the grain into another house to stop it being ruined. The worst part of that hurricane was losing the possibility of the island being able to feed itself, and having to continue to rely on supplies arriving from Port Jackson. But I've never seen lightning like we experienced last night.'

'I don't mind if I don't see it again, Sir,' replied Ben.

On 21st September the Gorgon entered the Heads at the mouth of Port Jackson and Ben saw for the first time the wonderful harbour on which the new settlement of Sydney stood. It was clear from the number of boats which pulled out to greet them that their arrival was enormously welcome and within minutes of dropping anchor officers from the colony came onboard to greet them. Very soon the Captain's gig was lowered and Ben accompanied Commander King to call on the Governor, Captain Arthur Phillip, and deliver the official despatches.

Later that day Ben went with Mrs King as she moved in to Government house as guest of the Governor. He was fascinated by all he saw, strange birds particularly. The people they passed looked rough and underfed, and Ben soon learnt that the colony had been expecting the Gorgon's arrival for more than nine months, and that the food stocks had declined so severely that rations had been cut for everyone. Indeed at the dinner given by the Governor that very evening they learnt that the normal practice was that guests were expected to bring their own bread. The main dish on that occasion was announced as 'Bow-wow pie' which was made with the meat of a local dog and was declared to be very tasty.

Over the next few days Ben saw more ships arriving in Port Jackson loaded with convicts from England, most of whom were in very poor condition having been kept below decks for the previous six months. Many had died on the voyage and those who were still alive were diseased and weak, certainly unable to contribute at once to the life of the colony. His heart was torn by what he saw, and he wondered how men could be so utterly cruel to their fellow men; surely those poor convicts had a right to some sort of life. But then he was reminded of the harshness of life in England and how most of them had been convicted of crimes which would normally carry the death sentence; they had been spared the gallows, only to suffer appalling conditions and often a slow death in the bowels of a hot and unhealthy ship. But some of them survived, and would hopefully recover their health; some would flourish, a tribute to human resilience.

Ben took leave of the Gorgon, and Captain and Mrs Parker, thanking the Captain especially for the opportunity to serve onboard on the outward voyage. He wished them well for their return journey. By this time Ben was unquestionably Lieutenant Governor King's man and was pleased to be able to accompany him every day as he went about the colony observing the developments since his last visit.

'What was it like when you first arrived here?' asked Ben.

'It seemed an almost perfect place to build a new colony,' replied King. 'We landed first at Botany Bay which Captain Cook said was ideal, but down there we found that there was nowhere suitable to establish ourselves with a good supply of water. Here was much better. You know, during the voyage out here, I spent many hours with Captain Phillip talking about our plans. We shared a vision of the new colony arising in a heathen land, based firmly on Christian principles in which everyone worked for the common good. It would gradually become self-sufficient and would, in due course, be able to repay the mother country by sending goods back to them. As you know I went almost immediately to Norfolk Island and set about achieving the same over there, and in about 18 months we very nearly became self-sufficient.'

'Some people might say that trying to start such a place with convicted criminals serving a punishment, would make it impossible. Have you found that punishment is the best way?' asked Ben.

'Every time I have sentenced someone to a number of lashes; I feel uncomfortable. And very often I have relented and changed the punishment to something less. I very much want people to recognise that there is a better way, and stealing from other people, or from the government store actually hurts everyone. People are so different from one another, which makes it hard to make rigid rules. One convict sentenced to hang in England may see himself as spared by transportation, and given another opportunity to live and do good for others no matter how hard life may be. Another may feel his conviction was unjust, and he must do everything he possibly can to escape, or make life more difficult for the authorities. The reality is that very few people have managed to escape and live – many have walked away from Port Jackson into the interior thinking that they only have a few miles to walk to freedom; in reality it's thousands of miles, and they will die of starvation or thirst.'

One of the stories circulating around the colony at the time was how Mary Bryant, daughter of a fisherman from Fowey in Cornwall, had led a party with her husband and two infant children away in a stolen boat. It was a few years later before the full story was told, of how she and her crew survived an epic voyage up the eastern coast of Australia, buffeted by strong winds, but just surviving to be able to land and find fresh water and food. Eventually they arrived in Batavia (the modern Jakarta) which was full of typhoid and other tropical diseases, from which William Bryant and their infant son soon died. To begin with Mary pretended they were the survivors of a shipwreck and they were welcomed by the Dutch; but for some reason they admitted later to being escaped convicts and the Dutch took them into custody, handing them over to Captain Edwards and his fellow survivors from the wrecked British frigate, the Pandora. They were shipped out of Batavia, and transferred at Capetown to the Gorgon, then on her return voyage from Port Jackson. Mary and four comrades survived and were imprisoned in Newgate prison until their story was picked up by influential people, such as James Boswell, who sought a pardon for her. In due course they were all freed and Mary returned home to Cornwall.

Another person who Ben came to know was Ann Inett, a convict woman who was serving her time living near Sydney with her two small children, Norfolk and Sydney. These two boys were the sons of Lieutenant Governor King, and Norfolk had been the first baby born on Norfolk Island. The Lieutenant Governor was anxious to acknowledge his responsibility for the two boys and believed that he was in a better position to offer them the advantages of life than their mother could ever be. He asked Ben to go and meet Ann and see if he could gently discover whether she would be content for the boys to live with the Kings on Norfolk Island.

He found Ann living with another convict to whom she was clearly very much attached. Together they ran an alehouse from which they sold such other necessaries as they could obtain. After a few moments' conversation, Ben was impressed at how realistic Ann was.

'I had a pretty good time on Norfolk Island. The governor looked after me well, as I looked after him. It was like being thrown together on a desert island after a shipwreck. We couldn't go anywhere. We were stranded and had to survive on what we had with us. There was no point in arguing about it. So I remember saying to Mr King, "How's about me doing for you, and making life a little better for the both of us." And he agreed.'

'So what do you think about the boys' future? Could Mr King play a part in it?'

'Well, he always said that he would see us right. My life isn't worth much here and I can't do more for my boys than keep them fed. If Mr King could see them educated, that'd be a wonderful thing. But they're very young still and I'd be worried about them being dragged away from what's familiar and being unhappy and fretting.'

As they talked Ben watched the three year old, Norfolk, playing outside with a girl who looked about nineteen or twenty years old and carried the little Sydney on her hip. All three were laughing as they played, a picture of carefree happiness.

'Who is that playing with your boys now?' asked Ben.

'That's Sally, my neighbour. She's had a pretty awful time of it. She was condemned at Aylesbury in 86. According to her she picked up a purse which someone had dropped in Stowe gardens, and was trying to hand it in at the inn where most of the visitors stayed. Before she knew what was happening she was being accused of stealing it. One thing led to another and she was condemned to seven years out here. She came out in the Lady Penrhyn which was lucky for her. Sally did alright.'

An idea was beginning to form in Ben's mind. It seemed a long shot, but it would be worth exploring.

'It seems surprising that a pretty young girl like that would not have been taken by a man. Presumably she is living with someone now, isn't she.'

'Well you'd think so, wouldn't you. She managed to keep herself to herself for a while but then she fell for a young fisherman. They got together and were living next door to us. But a few weeks back he was lost at sea out fishing, so I have been doing my best to look after her. She has really taken to the boys and they seem to be completely happy with her; she'll make a wonderful mother.'

'So here's an idea for you to think about. You are concerned that your boys may be upset to go off with Mr and Mrs King, although you know in your heart that is the best thing for them. The boys have formed a bond with Sally. Sally is looking for a new start. How would it be if I suggest to Mr King that Sally should come with the boys to Norfolk Island. She could help to look after them, and generally help Mrs King whose own child will be born in the next month or two.'

'Do you think the Kings would agree to that? It's a good idea and I'd be happy to know the boys have at least one familiar face. It'd be good for Sally to take her away from the place where she lost her love.'

'So that's agreed then,' said Ben. 'I'll ask Mr King if they'd allow Sally to come with the boys as nursemaid. I think you know Mr King well enough to know that he'll agree to that – he's always looking for ways to encourage people to leave their past behind and work hard towards a new life.'

A few days later Mr and Mrs King both visited Ann and offered to take the boys into their home, bring them up as their own sons, and give them an education and as much help as they could to get on in life. They readily agreed to the suggestion that they should take Sally too as nursemaid, subject only to Governor Phillip giving his permission for her to transfer to Norfolk Island.

On 25th October when the Kings and Ben embarked in the storeship Atlantic for the voyage to Norfolk Island Ann came to the landing stage with the boys and, with Sally, handed them over to the King's care before returning alone to her new husband.

The next stage of Ben's adventure had begun.

Chapter 10

The passengers aboard the Atlantic were a mixed bunch. Lieutenant Governor King and his wife, now very heavily pregnant, and the two small boys Norfolk and Sydney, nursed by Sally, were accompanied by William Chapman. Captain Paterson of the New South Wales Regiment and his wife were on board with part of his detachment, the remainder of which followed in a second vessel, the Queen. Mr William Balmain was an Assistant Surgeon in the colony who was moving to Norfolk Island to relieve Denis Considen who wished to return home. There were also thirty former marines who had asked to become settlers on the island and had been granted land with special conditions to enable them to establish themselves quickly and contribute to the economy of the island. Finally there were twelve former convicts who had also opted to become settlers on Norfolk Island rather than return to England.

As the Atlantic headed out to sea through the Heads, Sally was on deck leaning on the taffrail when Ben saw her.

'Don't lean too heavily against that,' said Ben, 'if it were to crack or break, you'd be straight over the side and that'd be the end of that.'

'Some might say that'd be a good end to a worthless life,' said Sally.

'How could you say that? You've survived, and look where you are now. A personal servant to a Lady and a Gentleman, engaged to care for their children. That's a position of trust and respectability, isn't it?'

'Yes, but I long for home. I'm ashamed that I let down my parents and family by being caught out as I was, and I can't tell them how sorry I am.'

'All the more reason for you to make a success of this stage of your life so that in a year or two you can go back home and prove to them that was just a slip. It's not what you are. You are, and will be, a great credit to them.'

'Oh but it was tough, Ben. I can't tell you how difficult it was to resist all the approaches of those beastly men, rough and crude they all were. Until I met George. And now he's gone just as we were getting to know each other. If there is a God why isn't he on my side; it just seems so unfair.'

'Mmm.' Ben was wondering how to reply. He looked at Sally and saw a prettily rounded face with fresh pink cheeks and fair hair. But there was a sadness in her eyes, and her shoulders slumped in a way which suggested that she was trying to carry the cares of the whole world on her back. Could he say something which would help her realise there was no need for her to worry; what was it in the bible which said that one should take no thought for the morrow, because it is all in the hands of God. But then if you felt that you had been let down before, it would be very easy to imagine that God was not doing such a good job for you.

'Well, do you know what I think,' replied Ben. 'I think that your luck is just about to change. None of what will happen could happen if you had not been through all those harsh and horrible experiences. I've got to know the Kings quite well over the past few months at sea. The Lieutenant Governor is a very strong and kind man. He's always looking for the best in everyone – even in the most hardened criminals. He believes profoundly in Christianity – I don't really understand the half of it but I've learnt some of the basics – that Jesus Christ was absolutely good and that His teachings and example show us how we should try to live our lives. We can't be as good as Him but we should at least try. And Mr King always said to me "Ben," he says, "there is something good in everyone, no matter how awful they may seem, and we should always start from the belief that we'll find that good thing, and encourage it to flourish." You'll do well with the Kings, I'm sure of it.'

Sally felt something in her heart. Was it a specially strong throb, a small ache, a twinge. No it could not be anything... and yet... She turned towards Ben and saw a hardened young face which had seen storms and winds, which had been in rough places and dealt with tough situations, a strong, determined and courageous man. And yet there was no harshness in his eyes, none of that hard look which so often warned her that this man was going to get what he wanted and that physical strength

87

was the only means of persuasion he knew. Ben seemed to be saying something different, something much more comforting and comfortable, more reassuring; kinder perhaps. Even George had not been quite like that.

'I hope you're right,' she said. She paused thinking that perhaps the conversation had gone as far as it could for now and that it was time to change the subject and focus on more practical matters.

'Do you know much about what we'll find when we arrive at the island?'

'I can only go on what Mr King has said about it,' replied Ben. 'It's a pretty small island, about three miles wide and five miles long, and most of the shore line is steep cliffs which are no good for anything other than the nests of birds. We will try to land on the south side where there is a small break in the reef. A boat can get through there quite well as long as the swell is not from the south, and up onto the beach. If there is a southerly wind and swell we may go around the north side to what they call Cascade Bay and go ashore on a stony beach there. Let's hope we can land on the south, then we can walk up the beach to where the houses are. Mr King says there is a Government House, but that it was built for him and Ann only and that he will need a larger house now with Mrs King, and three children, and some servants.

'What you will see at once is the enormous pine trees which were spotted by Captain Cook. Mr King says they look very fine, tall and straight, until you start to saw them up. They are perfectly good for timber planks, but quite useless for spars, other than very small ones, because of the way the side branches grow.'

'Can we expect to be hot or cold?' asked Sally.

'Well I think most of the time it is quite a reasonable temperature, though occasionally in January it gets very hot. At least we don't have to prepare for snow and ice like at home. I think we'll be more often too hot than too cold.'

The conversation could have continued for hours but was interrupted by the sounding of the ship's bell and the change of the watch.

'It's time for me to go and check on my charges,' said Sally. 'I don't think they will be bawling their heads off.' And she turned away and made to go below. As she reached the ladder, she turned to Ben and smiled; 'Thank you,' she said.

They arrived off the south of the island on 4th November and came to the anchorage in fine weather. Disembarkation was slow because everything had to be taken ashore by boat, and the passage through the rocks to the shore was not easy. William Chapman had attended the Lieutenant Governor as he landed in the first boat with Captain Paterson, whilst Ben prepared the King's and the Paterson's baggage. Boats plied to and fro carrying the soldiers and the settlers with all their kit and the large number of barrels containing all the other supplies needed on the island, and finally Mrs King and Mrs Paterson climbed down the gangway, with Sally, Norfolk and Sydney, and into a boat with Ben. The boat glided smoothly onto the sand and a reception party pulled it further ashore so that the ladies could step out without having to wade through the surf. Lieutenant Governor Ross who had been looking after the island for the past eighteen months was standing on the beach to greet the ladies and, with their husbands, he escorted them up to Government House which stood a little way inland looking out across the anchorage.

William and Ben found that they had been allocated a small house close to Government House. 'I hope you will find that satisfactory William,' said the Lieutenant Governor. 'You will of course eat with us whenever you wish to do so.'

'Thank you, Sir,' replied William. 'I am sure Luckett and I will get on famously. After all we are both here to do everything we can to support and help you and Mrs King.'

'First thing tomorrow we will begin a tour around the island to see how everything has got on in the past 17 months. You will both accompany me, please,' continued the Lieutenant Governor.

The house allocated to William and Ben looked reasonably well constructed of timber. It took no more than a few minutes for them to set down their sea chests and take stock of the place. The little dwelling consisted of a single room with a makeshift curtain dividing it into two.

But compared with what they were used to onboard ship it seemed quite spacious.

During the next few days Ben and William accompanied Lieutenant Governor King as he walked around the island. They started along the street at Kingston which was at the top of the beach. The huts were all very similar in appearance and size and each stood in a garden where vegetables were growing. Cabbages were obviously very popular and there were plenty of potatoes.

'Most of these are occupied by the convicts,' said the Lieutenant Governor, 'and I've always encouraged them to grow as much as they can for themselves. We'd only been here a short time when I allowed the convicts not to work on Saturdays so that they could tend their own gardens; that meant that they had time to do something entirely for their own benefit. Look at the difference between one garden and the next and you can see which of the convicts are the conscientious ones. They are the people who will make good and will turn the island into a supplier of wheat and other food to Port Jackson. But it is not as good as it was when I left – Lieutenant Governor Ross's martial law, which reduced the time the convicts have to themselves, may have something to do with it.'

They walked west along Arthur's Vale where the land had been cleared and fenced into plots of ten acres on either side of the stream. This was the area set aside for the free settlers where they could sow wheat and maize for their own use and for sale. Inland of the little settlement of Kingston and to the east, land had been cleared and was growing the government's crops. The Lieutenant Governor was very pleased with what he saw there, with the wheat growing well and promising a good crop.

'They have planted much more wheat this year, I am pleased to say,' commented the Lieutenant Governor, 'and it looks as though it will be ready for harvest very shortly. And the maize looks well, too. We had enormous problems in the early days with caterpillars and then with perroquets, which did their best to take everything.' The area under wheat and maize was now at least four times as great, but the population of the island had also risen to about 1000 people.

One day they set off in the early morning to walk to Queenborough. The road wound steeply uphill to start with but if you turned around you had a wonderful view out over the shoreline towards Phillip Island, a red mountain of rock about five miles away. The slopes were heavily wooded with majestic pine trees, some of them vast in size and very straight. The scrub was thick all around and occasionally they came across a pig happily digging around amongst the roots. Once up the initial slope the land was reasonably flat as they followed the pathway to the left along to Queenborough. There they found a street of neat houses, with the Superintendent's house and the guardhouse set aside and overlooking the street. They were shown around by the Superintendent, Mr D'Arcy Wentworth, and saw the seven acres of wheat which had been sown, and thirty acres of maize. Work was continuing to clear more land around the settlement but it was slow and hard. The scrub must be rooted out and most of the trees felled, and as soon as that had been done letting in light and moisture, weeds began growing in profusion which must be always cleared away before any crops could be sown.

It was evening before they returned to Kingston and the following day they were off again, this time to Phillipburgh. Again they set off winding up the steep hill but instead of turning west to Queenborough they veered slightly to the right and continued across the island to the north east. The road made its way through the woods and scrub, very little of which had been cleared until it began to go down towards the sea. For the last few hundred yards the path was very steep. As they passed the little village at Phillipburgh which consisted of a few huts standing on a flat space where a gully came down from the hillside, the Superintendent ,Mr Jamison, came out to greet them. He proudly showed off the land which was being cleared and detailed where he intended to sow wheat and maize after the summer.

'Thank you Mr.Jamison. And how are you managing when a vessel arrives for unloading?' asked the Lieutenant Governor.

'We know how to do it now, Sir; but getting the stores out of the boats is difficult because the beach is so rocky. If there's even a small lop there's a danger of stoving the boat in, and it's difficult to stand on the rocks when they're wet. There's nearly always an injury of some sort, and it's only a matter of time before we lose a man.'

'We'll have to build a wharf, if we can, and secure it somehow to that rock over there. We can then construct a crane on the wharf to lift the barrels, bales and cases out of the boats. That'd be much safer, would it not?'

'Aye, Sir, that it would. We have the timber and that man Nat Lucas, the carpenter, he's a right wizard when it comes to building. He's your man, not a doubt of it.'

'Well I shall consult the Master Carpenter, first, but thank you for the suggestion,' replied the Lieutenant Governor.

And the Superintendent mumbled so that the Lieutenant Governor could not hear, although Ben certainly did, 'Well better make sure you catch him in one of his few sober moments.'

'If we want to use this road regularly,' went on the Lieutenant Governor, 'we'll have to blast away part of the slope so that it's easier for bringing everything up from the beach.'

Between them they worked out what line the road should take. The job would require a working party with picks and shovels to strip off as much of the soil and loose rock first. The Superintendent asked if extra men could be allocated to him as his own men would not be sufficient to get the job done in good time. They would need to drill into the rock as far as possible and set charges to fracture it into pieces small enough to be moved. That would perhaps not be the best use of labour during the hottest months in December and January, but once the harvest was in and the days became rather cooler the work would need to be put in hand.

'How much do you know about mining and explosives?' asked the Lieutenant Governor.

'Not a lot, myself, but I daresay we can find someone here who has had some experience of it. Can I ask about?'

'Yes, by all means. And I'll ask Captain Paterson in case one of his soldiers has the right sort of experience. I daresay there's someone who knows a bit about explosives.'

'Mr Chapman,' he went on, 'I should like you to arrange the building of a store over here, in which it'll be possible to keep the provisions landed here. When it's built I wish you to become the storekeeper and to record all goods arriving and being issued, so that everything can be properly accounted for.'

'Aye, aye, Sir,' responded Chapman. Even though he was not a naval officer it seemed easiest to use the naval expression to acknowledge the Lieutenant Governor's order.

Over the next few days William began to make the necessary arrangements and to organise with the Superintendent for some convicts to be assigned to the work to clear the site and then support the stone masons. With the Lieutenant Governor's permission he went to live over there to be near to his work.

Meanwhile Ben was detailed by the Lieutenant Governor to get himself involved with the fishermen and to help them manage the boats which should go out every day when the weather was fine enough, to catch as much fish as possible for distribution to convicts and settlers in place of salt pork. On a good day they would be out for five or six hours and would come back with two or three hundred fish.

On 12th November as many people as possible gathered in the evening after the day's work, in front of Government House and Lieutenant Governor King read the commission appointing him, which had been signed by King George III himself. After the reading of the commission Lieutenant Governor King formally assumed command of the island from Lieutenant Governor Ross. They shook hands and proposed a toast to King George, followed by three rousing cheers.

Ben spotted Sally outside Government House during the proceedings and afterwards, as the crowd circulated and many of the settlers took the opportunity to congratulate Mr King and bid farewell to Mr Ross, they came together.

'How are you getting on?' asked Ben.

'Well the boys seem to have settled in well enough, and I really like Mrs King. She's quite charming and seems determined that Norfolk and Sydney shall be cared for as if they were her own children. And as you may have noticed she's getting near her time – only a few weeks to go,' replied Sally.

'What did I tell you? You're obviously becoming a favourite with Mrs King.'

'Yes, but it's all about her and the children, and I know that's important, but I'd like to have a life of my own as well.'

'Be patient, Sal,' replied Ben. 'Just let things settle down a bit and I'm sure something will work out. The important thing for now is to make sure that Mrs King – and her husband – recognise how much effort and commitment you're putting into looking after those children, and then, perhaps, when the time comes they'll be happy to give you a little more freedom – and eventually you'll be one of those emancipated convicts who'll be allowed home.'

Sally smiled sweetly at Ben. 'And how is it you have become such a gentle and wise man?' she asked. 'You're not a bit like most of the sailors I've met.'

The detachment of marines and New South Wales Corps which had now been relieved by Captain Paterson's detachment embarked aboard the transport vessel Queen on 22nd November and sailed for Port Jackson. The Atlantic had already departed with orders to go to Bengal and bring back urgently needed provisions, and supplies of other necessaries such as cooking pots and utensils, fabric for clothing, shoes and many other things which would provide a little comfort in a hard life.

As soon as his predecessor had left it was clear that Lieutenant Governor King was determined to make changes. He was firmly opposed to the martial law which Ross had imposed as soon as he took over from King in 1790. Perhaps it had been necessary then because of the large number of extra mouths to feed on the island resulting from the wreck of the Sirius.

Ben had heard about that disaster from John Mortimer, one of the convicts who had arrived with Lieutenant King in March 1788. It had been in March 1790 when the Sirius, the frigate under the command of Captain John Hunter, which had led the First Fleet out from England to Port Jackson in 1787, called at the island bringing provisions, and some additional settlers, marines and convicts to increase the labour force on the island. The little vessel, Supply, commanded by Lieutenant Ball, had arrived at the same time, so the activity at the Kingston landing had been frenetic.

'Then the wind shifted around to the South,' continued John Mortimer, 'and you could see how the ships might become trapped in the anchorage overnight, something they always tried to avoid. The Supply was first to weigh anchor and signalled frantically to Sirius to do the same. When Sirius did eventually get going she set off towards the west but could not clear the head and was forced to tack. She came around onto the starboard tack and hoped to make the gap between Nepean Island and Point Hunter, but she made too much leeway and must tack again. We were watching from the beach and you could see that when they put the helm over the ship didn't respond and began to fall off the wind. They tried a second time but again the ship would not come through the wind. By that stage there was not enough searoom to wear the ship without falling on the reef and it became inevitable that she would strike. Almost immediately the masts fell and the ship was a wreck. Then we had to try to get everyone off. All the boats worked as fast as possible to bring off as much of the stores as they could. But the sea was rising and the boats themselves were in danger of capsizing. Mr King immediately ordered some sheerlegs to be rigged and from there we managed to run a rope to the ship, with a traveller on it. Then one by one we hauled the people off the ship. They came splashing through the surf onto the beach until we were too exhausted to continue and darkness had overtaken us.

'The following day at dawn we set to again. The ship's company who remained onboard under the Bosun were frantically trying to get all the supplies from the hold. Some came off in boats and some on rafts. At the end of the day the last men came off. It was extraordinary that no lives were lost.'

'It must have been awful,' said Ben, 'All that surf and a swell making the reef dangerous and the landing place a great hazard.'

'Well it got better after that,' went on Mortimer. 'The following day the bosses, King, Ross and Hunter put on a show of handing over the command of the island and declaring martial law. I suppose that was because there were suddenly so many more people on the island and they feared losing control.

'After all that, there were two convicts, John Branagan and Will Dring, volunteered to go onboard and push the remaining animals overboard so they could swim ashore. They got onboard alright and some of the animals made it ashore, but the two lads decided they would stay and have a bit of fun onboard. They found the rum store and got themselves completely out of their minds. Captain Hunter ordered flares and rockets and guns to be fired to attract their attention but all that failed. Then Johnnie Ancott says he'll go off and fetch them. So he swings aboard using the rope to get him through the surf and he gets Branagan and Dring onto the traveller so they can be hauled over – it turned out that they had set fire to the ship, but either it burnt itself out or Johnnie put it out during the night. Branagan and Dring got what was coming to them. I can't really understand why they did that – if they'd just done what they went for and then come ashore they'd have been regarded as heroes, and if King had anything to do with it they would certainly have been given a tot or two for their pains. As it was they got fifty lashes each.'

'I suppose people who've experienced really tough lives with no benefits feel that when they see a chance they must take it, regardless of the risks of being caught and punished,' interjected Ben.

'Well I can't claim to be perfect,' said Mortimer. 'Me and my son Noah nicked a handsome piece of meat in Exeter. I suppose we thought we'd get away with it – and we were very hungry; everyone was nearly starving then. Well, we were picked up and jailed and then taken to Exeter assizes where the judge said we should hang, but we could take seven years transportation in Botany Bay if we preferred. We took the opportunity and I am right glad we did.   Both Noah and I picked up fifty lashes for something or other when we got here, but it was pretty obvious that we'd get on alright if we toed the line.   Mr King seemed to be a fair man and said he wanted every convict to be successful, and the way to that was through honest hard work, and not cutting corners by trying to pinch stuff off our mates.   I'm really glad he's come back and we might be able to get rid of that spiteful man Ross.   He's no time for anyone, and just wanted to grind us all into the dirt. We've got a year or two to go yet but we've a much better life here as convicts, especially under Mr King, than we'd have at home – it's never cold for one thing. We've got to being trusted now, and we work hard, right enough.   But when we get free and become settlers and get some land, by then we'll know how to make money from it.   More land, more food, more money, more comfort – and eventually we can stop working and pay someone else to work for us.   Sounds a good deal to me.'   At last Mortimer drew breath.

'So have you noticed a big difference between the King regime and Ross's?' asked Ben.

'Oh, yes.   Somehow King was willing to share the tough times with us. He wouldn't stand any nonsense, but you always knew he'd be fair, and if he could find a good reason to forgive someone he always would.   On paper the punishments were very harsh – 800 lashes, sort of thing – but he never allowed them to be carried out.   He'd rather let you off.   But there were one or two people who didn't get the message, and when they came back before the magistrates a second time they would not be forgiven.   There was one man who ran off into the wilderness on Mount Pitt; disappeared for several months.   Eventually he came back looking more like a skeleton than a man, completely naked as his clothes had rotted off him.   He could have been punished but Mr King said he'd suffered enough and he'd have learnt from his errors; gave him some food, got his strength back and then he could re-join the community and start putting in an honest day's work.   You can't get fairer than that.'

Chapter 11

Towards the end of November Ben reported to Mr King as usual at seven in the morning to be given the day's tasks. Mr King had clearly been working late and had a document in his hand.

'Luckett, today I am making a declaration of basic principles of life on Norfolk Island and I want to gather everyone together, at Kingston first and then at Queenborough and Phillipburgh, to read them out so that everyone will know where they stand.'

'Do you just have the one copy of the rules at the moment, Sir?'

'Yes, I finished writing them at daybreak this morning – not enough candles to do them last night. So I need some copies. Do you know whether Mr Chapman will be coming in this morning?'

'No, Sir. I don't know. Shall I go over to Phillipburgh and ask him to come back here to copy them for you. I can then alert Mr Jamison to call everyone over there together after work at four this afternoon to read them out. As long as I can find Mr Chapman it should be possible for him to be back here by mid-day. I can go on to Queenborough and warn Mr Wentworth there so that he can gather everyone at four as well. As I come back I will spread the word in Arthur's Vale that everyone there needs to come into Kingston at four for you to read them out here. Would that be a good plan?'

'Thank you Luckett, that will be excellent. You'd better get off right away, and spread the word as you go that everyone is to assemble at four this afternoon. I'll expect Mr Chapman at midday.'

'And Sir, excuse me for saying so, but I would be happy to copy documents for you. My hand isn't as good as Mr Chapman's, but I was able to practise a good deal under Captain Nelson.'

'Thank you Luckett. I'll certainly bear that in mind for the future, and it'd be very helpful if you were to make a copy or two when you get back here, especially if Mr Chapman should be delayed.'

'Aye, aye Sir. I'll get off to Phillipburgh right away.'

Ben set off at a brisk walk across the swamp and up the steep hill. He arrived at Phillipburgh just over an hour later and found William outside his hut discussing with the Mr Jamison the layout for the new store. As soon as Ben passed on the message, he gathered up a few pens and together they set off back up the hill towards Kingston. About half way he turned off to the right and followed the path towards Queenborough whilst William went straight on. Once he had passed the message on to Mr Wentworth he turned round and headed again for Kingston and arrived less than an hour after William.

There was very little space in Government House as the new and larger dwelling which the Lieutenant Governor had in mind had not yet been built, so William was seated at the one table in the house in the little room where Mr King had a small desk. There was a continual coming and going of people, including Norfolk and Sydney toddling around and very often being chased by Sally or Mrs King, so that concentration on copying a text was hard and took much longer than should have been the case.

'I wonder if it'd be helpful if we were to move out into my hut and finish the copying,' suggested Ben.

'We'd at least have some peace there,' replied William, 'and we might get the job done rather better than with these continual interruptions.'

So they gathered their things together and moved out.

'What's all this about?' asked Ben, as they walked across to Ben's hut.

'It's all about establishing some ground rules for the island. I think Mr King wants everyone to be clear about what they can and cannot do and what is acceptable behaviour. After all we have here a group of people from widely differing backgrounds. Quite apart from the people who were convicted for stealing, which they had done to earn a few pence to provide their starving families with food, there are all sorts here. Some are no more than labourers who have never been near a school, others are skilled craftsmen, and I discovered that there is at least one girl who comes from a very aristocratic house. So everyone has different standards.'

'Well, I can agree with that. I think it is much easier if you know where you stand. You might choose to do something wrong, which falls outside the frame, but if you do and you get caught, you know you'll deserve to be punished, and you can't blame anyone else. But who's the aristocrat?'

'She's called Olivia and is with a convict called Nathaniel Lucas. He's a carpenter – if you ever need a job to be done I hear he's by far the best; you see, Mr King will soon have him employed on his own house. But now we'd better get on with the job in hand.'

The two sat at the makeshift table in Ben's hut and wrote as fast as they could. When he got to the end Ben said, 'Well there doesn't seem to me to be anything very controversial in that lot. It's pretty much like a mixture of Christian teaching and common sense. Have I missed something?'

'No, I am sure you have not. But don't forget that many of the convicts are hardened criminals who have never recognised other peoples' property, so stealing has little meaning for them.'

'Pity they weren't all brought up in the navy. Onboard ship, stealing is one of the worst crimes because it completely undermines the trust that every man needs to have in his shipmates.'

Later in the day, the two delivered copies to the Superintendents and heard them read out with due solemnity.

In January 1792 Mrs King went into labour and gave birth to a son who was named Phillip Parker. Sally was kept especially busy helping to deal not just with the two toddlers but with a new baby. There seemed to be a perpetual round of washing and drying and the days passed very quickly for her, giving her little time to herself and none at all to reflect on the way her life was going. But time passed and gradually the routine became a little easier and she began to wonder about her future and whether she would have to remain tied for ever to someone else's children and a wash tub. Even the other convict women seemed to have more time off than she, and some of them had relationships of convenience, pleasure or passion. She wondered whether she would find herself cast out completely if she were bold enough to ask for some time to herself.

Meanwhile Ben was kept busy by Mr King, taking messages around the island and accompanying him on many of his visits. When a settler started in a new plot he was entitled to the assistance of two convicts for nine weeks to clear the thick undergrowth and scrub bushes as well as the mature trees. It was slow, back-breaking work using only saws, axes, spades and hoes; especially when summer took the thermometer into the nineties and the humidity reached an uncomfortable level. After that the settler was left to himself unless he could afford to employ someone to help him. Ben wondered whether he should apply to the Lieutenant Governor to settle, and thereby to be given some land. He would never have an opportunity to acquire land for nothing back at home, but truth to tell he was not prepared to make the necessary commitment and he wanted to be able to go back to sea, and eventually back home.

As January passed into February Ben seemed to spend more time around Government House and every time he caught Sally's eye he felt something moving inside him, a sort of excitement and joy. He asked her to visit him in his hut if she could take some time away from her charges, and so a relationship began. Though it was furtive at first, as if neither of them wanted to admit it was happening, over a few weeks it became almost routine, and a day which passed without them spending some time together would be a day of disappointment, only offset by the knowledge that all would be set right on the day following. The first meeting of eyes became a discreet touch of fingers and then a clasping of hands; an arm around the shoulder whilst they walked became an embrace amongst the trees above Emily Bay. A kiss on the cheek on departure became a meeting of lips and tongues.

Sally had been warned so often that men would seek only to use their superior strength to demand and secure the use of her body with callous disregard for her sentiment and feelings, and yet here was a man who always seemed gentle and respectful, who was sensitive to her reaction and seemingly reluctant to cajole her into something she was not ready for. But she grew bolder and found herself beckoning to Ben, encouraging him and caring little for the risks which might emerge for her.

'You seem a little distant, Sally,' suggested Mrs King one afternoon. 'I almost believe your mind might be somewhere else.' Sally hesitated before replying. Clearly she had been unable to conceal her feelings from another woman. Perhaps it would be better to admit what was going on in her head.

'I'm sorry Ma'am. I was just thinking of someone else.'

'Yes, I thought so. And it doesn't take a genius to know who that might be. Would you like to relieve the pressure on this house and move in with him? Norfolk and Sydney are very well settled now, and I'm sure they don't need you in the night as well as the day. Besides Luckett will benefit from having someone to keep house for him.'

'Thank you, Ma'am. I'm sure I could manage that and continue to work for you; I'll never be far away.'

That afternoon Sally met with Ben and reported her conversation with Mrs King. They sat together outside Ben's hut in the setting sun eating a few scraps of bread, enjoying each other's company until darkness overcame them and they went inside to their only privacy.

'How is it you can be so restrained, Ben? All the other men I have come across don't seem able to wait for anything, whereas you seem always to be waiting for me to make a move.'

'Little do you know, my dear. I reckon my feelings must be just as strong as all the other's. I want a relationship which will last as long as I do, which is based on ..... well, I suppose, mutual respect. If I start using my greater physical strength over you, I may win in the short term and feel wonderfully fulfilled, but that'll not make a strong foundation for the long term. Come here. Come close.'

The evenings and nights became occasions which Sally longed for. Often during the day as she went about some of her dreary tasks she dreamt of the evening and the night time, and she seemed never to be disappointed. Ben's caring tenderness inspired a growing and deeper love in her which, as each day passed, she wanted more keenly to express. Every day they both discovered things about each other which they did not know, and everything seemed to be good. Sally longed to hear more about Ben's home in Norfolk and the family he had left behind; she was intrigued by his tales of the sea and especially his stories about Captain Nelson in the West Indies. Ben wanted to know more about her family in Buckinghamshire and how she came to be at the Buckinghamshire assizes; he could not believe that she was guilty of having stolen that purse. It was true that her father and mother struggled to feed Sally and all her siblings, but at least he had employment on the estate at Stowe. Sally had never seen the Marquess of Buckingham who owned the estate but she had heard stories of how he was very important in the government and kept going to London. The person who dealt with all the employees was the agent, Mr Sharp, and he had always seemed quite reasonable even if he was very demanding and always expected more.

Meanwhile they always had news and information about the island to share with each other. Towards the end of January there were no fewer than five ships at anchor off the landing at Kingston. They brought with them some much needed provisions, especially salt meat, but also some rum, although the Lieutenant Governor was very careful to give instructions that the rum was not to be issued or sold except under very careful control since there was too great a danger of men becoming drunk and causing mayhem. As the ships Queen and Barrington were to go to Bombay, Mr King wanted to send reports with them to the Government in London, and Ben and William were kept busy copying out reports, letters and lists.

Several whalers had visited. The William and Ann came first, and the master, Ebor Bunker, had said that he would be looking for whales in the area of Doubtless Bay, in New Zealand. This was where several Maori tribes lived and from Captain Cook's observation it was clear that they knew very well how to turn the flax plants which grew there into good quality cloth. The same sort of flax grew wild on Norfolk Island but no-one knew how to harvest it and turn it into linen or sailcloth. Mr King asked Mr Bunker to see if he could find two Maoris who might be brought to Norfolk Island to teach them the process. Two other whalers, the Britannia and the Salamander, followed the William and Ann.

Ben was able to get onto the water often when the weather was fair to help the fishermen. Fish were very important for the people to survive, and some days they would bring in over 100 fish weighing on average six pounds. These were all distributed to replace the normal allowance of salt meat and enabled everyone to enjoy a change of diet. One of the greatest problems they had was a lack of cooking pots and it took great ingenuity to find ways of cooking fish without a pot.

More settlers had arrived in the Queen and required the allocation of areas of land where they could clear space to build a hut and begin to sow crops as quickly as possible. One convict had escaped into the undergrowth and lived there for some weeks before bursting in on the wife of a settler, beating her up, raping her viciously and then stealing from them and various other people nearby. Eventually the man was caught and tried. The magistrates declared that he should be sent to Port Jackson for trial in court there, but this would mean that the settler and his wife would have to go to Port Jackson to give evidence, leaving their own place abandoned, perhaps for as much as six months. Not only would they have suffered from the crimes, but they would then suffer from the remedy which would prevent them getting on with their work. The Lieutenant Governor decided that instead of all that, the convicted man should suffer the punishment of running the gauntlet. All the convicts were gathered together in two rows equipped with whips and sticks of one sort or another and as the criminal passed between them everyone had a chance to inflict a punishment. This was so severe a punishment that it was hoped that it would act as a deterrent to anyone else who thought that crime might provide an easier life. Ben had seen sailors flogged, and one flogged around the fleet, a truly brutal torture, and it always surprised him that there were some people who continued to misbehave despite the risk of being caught and subjected to a similar punishment.

There was much excitement towards the end of March when a ship was sighted working in to Cascade Bay. It turned out to be the Pitt from Port Jackson, bringing Mr Fane Edge, the Provost Martial, some more convicts, and a horse and mare. But even more importantly it brought a supply of goods for sale, some lengths of cloth, cooking pots, tea and coffee. Having goods for sale showed up a significant difficulty, namely that very few buyers had any money with which they could pay the

Master. To relieve the problem Lieutenant Governor King decided that it would be a good moment to inject some cash into the island's economy by buying as many pigs as possible from anyone who had pigs to spare. Every settler, including convicts who reached the end of their time but chose to remain on the island, had been given a pig and a sow to get them started. From this moment anyone who had pigs to spare could sell them to the government for cash and in this way a great many people were able to buy the goods on offer. Ben, who still had some cash, was able to buy Sally a length of cloth and some ribbons with which she could make herself a new dress. He also invested in some of the cutlery on offer, buying more than he needed in the expectation of being able to sell it later at a profit.

Early in April, Ben paid a visit to Queenborough and talked to the Superintendent there, D'Arcy Wentworth. He was a very intriguing character Ben thought, and after a few conversations he began to figure him out. He had been born in Ulster, the son of an innkeeper in the early 1760s, and was in some way related to the Earl Fitzwilliam who had become a senior politician in England, and who, in 1782 inherited the house and estate at Wentworth Woodhouse near Sheffield. Evidently D'Arcy considered himself far too good to succeed his father as an innkeeper and moved from Ireland to London. There he qualified as a surgeon, although it seemed that practising the profession was rather too humdrum and poorly paid to attract the handsome young D'Arcy. He told Ben, in confidence of course, how he had looked for easier ways to earn sufficient money to maintain the life of a gentleman, and had found that a good horse, a convincing disguise and a degree of contempt for people who kept their wealth for themselves, had led to 'One or two incidents.' He had spent much time at a fashionable tavern called The Dog and Duck, close to Southwark, south of the river Thames. It was well situated for getting to Blackheath which visitors to London from the South-east were obliged to cross.

'Finally I sailed a little too close to the wind, as you sailors would say,' continued Wentworth 'and I found myself charged at the Old Bailey. But I had a good lawyer and the judge was a decent fellow. During the trial I had a visit from my cousin the Earl with the suggestion that if I would go to Botany Bay as assistant surgeon, he would pay for my passage. The Judge was able to tell the court that I was booked onboard the Neptune and the jury declared a verdict 'Not guilty.' And here I am, not knowing whether I am being paid, having no money of my own, and just trying to do a decent job as best I can.'

'I guess you'll do your reputation no harm by using your Surgeon's influence to halt some of the floggings before they become too serious.'

'I hate the custom of flogging, especially of the women, although I suppose some sort of punishment is necessary. But you know while Major Ross was in charge, when Mr King went home in ninety, the whole atmosphere on the island changed. Instead of there being a sense of everyone being able to work for themselves and for the common good, it became a matter of getting away with as little work as possible, and avoiding being found out. No one can accuse Mr King of being soft, but at least he recognises that if you allow people to work for themselves, they will be less miserable when they have to do some things which are necessary but perhaps less pleasant. I know a lot of people are greatly relieved that Ross has gone; it's difficult to find anyone who has a good word for him.'

'You're quite well placed out here at Queenborough aren't you?' asked Ben. 'You have a good area cleared and I guess about ten acres in wheat which looks quite good and thirty of maize. How are the pigs? Have you enough yet to spare some for the store.'

'No, not yet. It'll be another year before the pigs have multiplied sufficiently. Besides the land up here is much less precipitous than near Kingston and Cascade, so we should be able to clear more land and grow plenty of wheat and maize. We just need the settlers and some convict labour.'

As Ben walked back to Kingston he pondered about why D'Arcy had got himself into his present position. Tall and handsome, well connected to an important family, qualified as a surgeon, and yet unable to secure a position in which he could earn an honest salary. He had obviously chosen to be a highwayman because it would be more exciting and might lead to riches; but the risk of being caught, tried and hung must be great. And that led Ben to wondering whether his chosen way of life as a seaman carried more or less risk. After all he might easily fall overboard, get shipwrecked, die of scurvy or some other dread disease, or even stop a cannonball. There must be risks in anything one chooses to do, but choosing to line your pockets with other peoples' money is, surely, dishonest and deserving of punishment. D'Arcy was paying for it now as he was not officially employed and there seemed to be little or no hope of earning great riches on Norfolk Island without a great deal of hard work.

Towards the end of May, Ben was accompanying the Lieutenant Governor to Phillipburgh when he began talking of his concerns about the quantity of wheat remaining in the stores, as reported by Mr Freeman the Commissary.

'According to his calculation we only have twelve weeks' worth of flour and maize at the current rate of issue. Within that time the new crop will not have matured and we cannot be sure it will not be eaten by grubs or locusts or some other pest. And we have no idea when we may see another ship bringing provisions for us. I hate the idea of cutting everyone's ration but we will look very foolish if we run out sooner than needs must. I think we can let the soldiers have some of the calavances we have just harvested; they may not like them as much as flour and bread but that cannot be helped. Can you think of any way of encouraging the military to help themselves rather more by cultivating their own gardens and growing some potatoes and vegetables?'

'Dare I say it, Sir, but some of those men are just plain idle and will always be so. They seem to think they are God's gift to mankind and more important than everyone else because they wear a uniform. You'd never believe how some of them speak to the convicts, or indeed the free settlers. And given half a chance they'd take a delight in giving a blow with the butt of a musket. From what I hear Major Ross encouraged that sort of behaviour.'

'I suspect that we'll have trouble from some of them, and Captain Paterson will have to make an example with some severe punishment. The convicts have suffered enough by being dragged half way around the world in the most horrible conditions. Surely to God we can give them a chance to recover their dignity as human beings and earn an honest living without being abused. Have you come across Lucas, the carpenter? He's amazingly skilfull and seems able to calculate the geometry of a building in his head and then cut timbers to an exact fit. His conviction was a dreadful miscarriage of justice from what he has told me. There is much good in that man and I'll encourage him and others like him to do all they can for their advancement.'

Monday 4th June was the birthday of King George, and the Lieutenant Governor declared that, as usual, there should be a celebration in his honour. The army detachment turned out at midday and fired a series of volleys in honour of the King, and then the officers and government officials all dined with the Lieutenant Governor. As darkness came on all the inhabitants of the island gathered at Kingston where a great bonfire had been built, and at a signal a light was set to it. There must have been about a thousand people gathered around, and then from somewhere came a great shout, 'Three cheers for King George.' Ben and Sally found themselves alongside Nathaniel Lucas and his wife Olivia.

'You've three fine children there,' said Sally, 'and a little darling as well,' she added, admiring the baby in Olivia's arms.

'They're doing well, aren't they,' replied Olivia, 'William's not quite five months old.'

'I could do with some more of him,' said Nathaniel, 'the sooner I can have an assistant the better I shall be pleased.'

'Mr King tells me you built his first house, and I know you are now on with the second. What's the next project?'

'Well there's a wharf to be built at Cascade; and I'll make a crane to lift things out of the boats. There'll never be a shortage of work here and it's splendid to have such a good supply of timber although sometimes it's touch and go whether Morgan can keep his sawyers going to supply fast enough.' Ben had seen Richard Morgan but had not yet got to know him; clearly he was a good friend of Nathaniel's, and an important one too as he was in charge of the sawyers.

'Do you ever long to be back in England amongst your family? We are a dreadful long way away out here, and even for a seaman it seems remote, I suppose because when you're at sea you're always on the move and at any time you might head for home. Here on Norfolk we're stuck until a ship happens along.'

'That's all true enough, Ben. But life was one hell of a struggle back in England. You never knew whether there'd be work or not, even close to Sheffield, and that meant you might not be able to feed your family. And the air was always foul with all the smoke belching out of the steelworks; and the cold and wet in winter; and the smallpox to threaten your children. No, I think I rather like it here; it's a bit hot and humid sometimes and food is not always very plenteous, but under Mr King's supervision it seems to be getting better as more land is cultivated. The biggest problems here are the few layabouts who can't be bothered to do any work and expect to survive by stealing from the rest of us.'

'Have you been granted any land yet?' asked Ben.

'Not officially, though many of us have been given a decent sized garden where we can grow plenty of vegetables. Mr King has always encouraged that since we first arrived. It took a turn for the worse under that dreadful man Ross, who seemed to think that men would work harder if you beat them regularly. But you can see how most of the gardens are well tended and producing lots of food. I'm growing potatoes, cabbages, turnips, carrots, beans, and in a year or so I'll be granted settler status and have ten acres to crop, and I'll be paid for my carpentry work. So for me there is plenty to like. I reckon that within a few years I'll have made far more money than would ever be possible back home in England. And my children will be far healthier too. Having said all that, I would like to see my father again and apologise for giving him all that worry on my account.'

Sally had been talking with Olivia and caught Ben's eye.

'We should be letting these good people get their children into bed,' said Sally, 'or they'll be good for nothing in the morning.'

And with that they parted with smiles, knowing that they would see plenty of each other in the months ahead.

'I'm not ready for bed yet,' said Ben once they were out of earshot. 'Let's take a walk up to Emily Bay.' So, arm in arm, they strolled away along the road which ran parallel to the beach, towards Emily Bay. The moon was up now and full, shining in a cloudless sky, the air cooler than during the day, of course, but pleasantly warm.

'There are many worse places we could be, right now,' suggested Ben.

'Mmm. There are. But I still miss my family dreadfully. My heart aches for them. I long to be able to tell my mother and father that I'm sorry putting them through all the worry they had about me, and the idea of me hanging – the shame.'

They continued along to the east end of the bay almost to the tip of Point Hunter. There the grass was short and Ben found a natural ledge just below the top of the slope. There they sat and enjoyed the clear evening air; and lay; and kissed, and joined together in pure bliss.

As they walked home Ben broke the silence, 'That was worth waiting for, wasn't it? And I wanted it to go on and on… for ever,' and Sally smiled but said nothing, hoping that he would say more.

'I know there are many couples on the island who share their lives and seem committed to each other, and I would like that. But I want more than that. I would like you to be my wife, before the law and before God. Only then would I be sure that I had committed fully to you for the rest of our lives. Sally, will you be my wife?' And as he said it, he turned and pulled her towards him and kissed her lips so that she could not respond at once, although her reaction to the kiss was one of welcome, of longing, of submission.

'Yes, of course. I thought you were never going to ask.'

By the time they reached Ben's hut they had excitedly begun making all sorts of plans, and when they finally fell asleep in each other's arms it was with contentment and happiness.

Chapter 12

Ben and Sally were duly married by the Reverend Bain. It was not long before Sally was complaining of feeling unwell most mornings, and she was aware of new life beginning to live within her. That knowledge enabled her to smile with satisfaction and joy tinged with only the slightest unease.

Ben continued to be much engaged with Lieutenant Governor King and was very pleased to feel that he was contributing to some of the creative work. In July of 1792 work began on improving the road to Cascade Bay. A huge amount of earth and rock had to be moved and Ben found himself helping to set the explosive charges needed to blast a way through the rock. When the road was finished the beach became much more accessible and the unloading of a ship, when next required, would involve less climbing up steep slopes with heavy loads. Nathaniel Lucas made progress with his new wharf which stretched out from the beach to the rock, known as the landing rock, some thirty yards from the water's edge. The crane which Nat had mentioned to Ben was there on the outer end of the wharf ready to lift goods out of boats, and sometimes to lift the boats themselves. Nat had also built several boats which were now ready to be launched from the crane, leaving them much less liable to damage from the rocky beach. When the Lieutenant Governor visited to see the progress of the works he was evidently much impressed, and Nat Lucas's reputation ran higher than ever.

After the Pitt in March many months passed without another ship arriving from Port Jackson, and the new season's grain was growing but not yet ready to harvest. The shortage of food persisted and people who had not been successful in tending their gardens and producing extra vegetables were often hungry. Mr King had been delighted when he dug up a crop of yams. He had brought a few from South Africa in 1788 but only one had survived and multiplied. The tubers were replanted in 1789 and in subsequent years, and this year he was able to harvest 2000 pounds which made a very welcome addition to the diet.

Several people who were feeling the effects of hunger tried to take matters into their own hands by stealing food. Some of the men who were threshing wheat, taken from the ricks, were filling their pockets before going home, and even the soldier, whose duty was to guard against such theft, not only turned a blind eye but filled his pockets too. But they were all found out and the soldier's crime was considered greater than the others since it was his duty to prevent the stealing. He was confined to the guardhouse until he could be sent to Port Jackson for Court Martial. The other convicts were found guilty; when their huts were searched, a store of wheat was found in every one, far in excess of what might have been legitimately issued from the main store. The Lieutenant Governor was clearly tempted to make a severe example of them but, rather than submitting them all to hundreds of lashes he decreed that their clothes should be marked all over with large letters R, so that everyone would know that it was they who stole wheat. In this way the thrashers would not be prevented from continuing their important daily work.

As the amount of food left in the government's storehouse gradually ran down the number of violent robberies grew and the jail and the penitentiary house were full to bursting. So Mr King and Captain Paterson and the other officers decided to send some of the worst offenders onto the barren Nepean island with the minimum of rations and some water, in the hope that this might act as a deterrent. The possibility of starvation was very real at this time, and only the regular catching of fish and the occasional killing of a pig could alleviate some of the pangs of hunger.

There was another tragedy during August when Nat Lucas set fire to two pine trees at some distance from his house, as an easy way of bringing them down. But for once his mathematical brain had got the sums wrong; he miscalculated the effect of the wind and the height of the trees, and when they fell the upper branches landed squarely upon his house, where his wife and children were. Very sadly the twins were killed outright, whilst Olivia was able to protect the baby which she was nursing, although one of her arms was broken in two places. She survived, although the pain was excruciating especially when Mr Jamison, the surgeon, pulled the arm straight and set it in splints. Nat was distraught to think that his carelessness had caused the death of his own two enchanting boys; how could he ever make amends for such carelessness? He turned more to his work and the rate of his output grew and the carpenters working with him were always being pressed for more.

The new Government House was nearly ready and Mr and Mrs King were longing to move out of their temporary house and enjoy the greater space which the new building would allow them. Sally was pleased at the idea that Sydney and Norfolk would have somewhere to play without getting under their father's feet, and she would not have to continue to tick them off for getting in everyone's way.

Later in August rations had to be reduced yet again although the Lieutenant Governor was hopeful that by early September the new crop of wheat would be ready to harvest and the full ration could be restored. And then, at last, a ship arrived. The Atlantic came from Port Jackson with six month's worth of stores onboard, to everyone's relief, and the normal full ration was issued. The soldiers were particularly pleased because some rum arrived especially for them. The new wharf and crane at Cascade proved very useful and on some days as many as 400 casks or bags were being landed. Many of the settlers felt well rewarded as the Lieutenant Governor issued them all with an extra two week's worth of stores. This would make up for the fact that their rations had been cut back more because they had their own potatoes and vegetables to fall back on, whereas the military did not. The Lieutenant Governor had kept faith with them; he was as good as his word. Nonetheless only a few days later the Judge Advocate received a letter from the settlers demanding that everyone who was not a free settler should be prevented from growing their own vegetables or rearing stock, in order to secure the settlers' market. The Governor made it clear that he could not do this, for the situation on the island was such that everyone must be encouraged to grow as much as they could no matter what their status. Mr King commented to Ben that the settlers seemed to think that he should discourage the work of others, military and convicts, in order to line their pockets, which was hardly consistent with his philosophy of encouraging everyone to work hard.

During October Ben accompanied Mr King on visits to every part of the island to review the crops and the state of clearance of the land. The lack of food which had been experienced before the arrival of the Atlantic had very clearly reinforced the need to be self-sufficient. Mr King frequently demanded the Deputy Commissary Mr Freeman to calculate how much food remained in the stores and for how many weeks it would last. But many of the settlers were now producing enough for their own needs and probably sufficient to contribute to the stores.

'One of the difficulties,' said Mr King as they walked, 'is that I have no instructions whether I am permitted to spend Government money on buying wheat or pork from settlers. If I do so without authorisation I may find that the Government then tries to make me pay the money back from my own pocket; but if I do not the settlers will not grow enough to ensure they have plenty for themselves and spare to help us all through another difficult period. Damned if I do and damned if I don't. You know, Ben, sometimes I think life at sea would be far simpler.'

'How can you manage the fact that gradually all the money we have on the island will accumulate in the hands of the most industrious of the settlers?'

'That is certainly a problem. We can draw Bills of Exchange which can be used as currency so that a settler who has, say, fifty pounds in money can swap it for a Bill which at some point in the future he could take to the payer and turn it back into money. But this is complicated and requires complete trust in the government and the banking system. No-one has thought to provide any instructions about this and always at the back of my mind is the fear that if I were to advise someone to draw a bill on the Treasury in London, for example, someone there will dispute it and come after me for the money. Unlike some senior people I simply do not have that sort of money and I would be ruined.'

'That's unreasonable. Isn't that part of the risk that the government should have recognised when they sent you and Governor Phillip out here?'

'You might have supposed so, indeed. Unfortunately governments don't work in that way and even those who you would expect to be entirely honest and correct seem to see things through different eyes, especially when they're on the other side of the world. Besides, we don't know and can't predict the sort of pressures under which they'll be working in nine month's time when the first bill might arrive in London.

The country might be at war again; the King might have died, God bless him.   All I can do is what I think is right and then hope that by recording my reasons and the circumstances which led me to my conclusion I'll eventually be found to have acted correctly.'

Ben felt thoroughly relieved that he was not in the same position and did not have to make decisions which would have a serious effect on the lives of many others.   He would serve as best he could, and pray to God that all would turn out right.

During the last few months of that year Ben and Sally got to know not only Nat and Olivia Lucas but also Richard Morgan.   One evening Ben and Richard were sitting at the top of the beach looking southwards towards Phillip Island, enjoying the setting sun.

'I could just do with a large mug of ale, right now, and life would be nearly perfect,' ventured Ben.

'A few years ago I might have said the same,' replied Richard. 'But then I discovered that the effects of drinking rather too much were not just a sore head, but finding that I had been cheated and defrauded by the most insufferable scoundrel I ever met.'

'That must have been pretty unpleasant.'

'Well, it is what eventually ended up with me being here.   I had been one of the city of Bristol's best gunsmiths, making muskets for our boys fighting the American colonists back in the early eighties.   Then the war ended and no-one wanted muskets; I was laid off but found myself work in a rum distillery, maintaining the pipework and other machinery.   The owner was a mean swine, but at least I had something to live off and keep my wife and son.   Whilst doing the maintenance I came across some pipework which should not have been there and I realised that it was taking off a good proportion of the spirit and running it through the wall.   I discovered where it was going, and after watching and waiting saw the owner, his foreman and some foppish gentleman removing the spirit which would then clearly avoid duty.   I went quietly to the Excise men and reported this fraud which would have been enough to have all three of them hung.   Within a month or two, my wife died, my son disappeared in strange circumstances and I took to drinking more than was good for me. In a drunken haze I was seduced by a very attractive French girl who, when I think about, it must have been in the pay of the foppish, supposed gentleman. I moved in with the French girl and then discovered her in bed, stark naked below the waist, with the fop, who invited me to accept his bill in compensation. Stupidly I agreed, and he left, leaving his pocket watch behind, which I slipped into my pocket meaning to return it to him later.

'Ah, how foolish one can be when one is not thinking straight as a result of a few too many jugs of rum. I was arrested and thrown into jail. And what made it worse was that this foul crook engineered for the case to be heard at Gloucester rather than Bristol. He knew that in Bristol I was known and the judge and jury would have been inclined to take my part. In Gloucester I was a stranger.'

'So the case was completely fabricated against you, then?' asked Ben.

'Completely. And what made it worse was that I had to stand in the dock and hear the outrageous lies put forward by this evil fop without being given the chance to cross question him under oath, or even to put my own case. My side of the story was never heard – I longed to be cross-questioned by the cleverest lawyer in the land. Anyway, the outcome was to be sent out here for seven years, and the way I am thinking right now, I'll do better to end my days here than go back to that stinking cesspit of Bristol. The weather is better here, and the air cleaner. The work may be hard and the threat of starvation never far away – but so it was in Bristol. I'll tell you what, Ben; I can live without that drink, and there's nothing for me to go back to which is the least bit attractive.'

'I can see that. Wouldn't you like to have the opportunity of getting your own back against the supposed gentleman who put you away?'

'Of course, nothing would give me greater pleasure than to see him rot in jail or, better still, swinging from a gibbet somewhere and being pecked to bits by the crows. But the risks of returning home and trying to devise some scheme to get even with him would be very great. So I have decided in my heart to have nothing to do with him, to put him out of my mind and let God take care of him at the final reckoning. In any case it's more than likely that eventually he'll over-reach himself and he'll fall to pieces. I'm not ready to forgive him, for he's shown no remorse or penitence, but I will forget.'

'I envy you the certainty,' said Ben, 'and I almost wish I was in the same place. Although I'm heartily glad I didn't have to go through the same horrendous process to get here. My Sal is certainly longing for her family and will, I'm sure, want to get home as soon as she reaches the end of her sentence next year. As for me, even now I long to get back to sea; there must be something about it that gets into your bones and blood and though life can be pretty hard it beats being stuck in one place on land.'

'I wish you well of it,' said Richard, 'and you certainly need to look after young Sally and I hope that you two won't have my experience; me and Peg, we lost our Mary to smallpox. Peg never really recovered, and one day had a fit and died, and I was left with little William Henry who became the core of my being. But then he disappeared. Many said he had drowned in the river, but his body was never found. And the rest of my story I've told you.'

How could life be so hard, wondered Ben later, as he walked home. How can one explain such terrible injustice? And yet, despite their misfortunes and the injustice they have suffered both Nat and Richard seem to be at ease with themselves, confident that things would turn out alright in the end. How was it that they had such great personal strength?

Through the later months of the year Sally grew larger and, to Ben at least, seemed happier and more attractive than ever. Ben put up with the insects which seemed to eat up everything they could find, so that the vegetables he had tended seemed to struggle to survive. But the sun shone, Sally was happy, Mr and Mrs King were wonderful people to work for and whilst Norfolk and Sydney rushed around happily as small children will when they feel confident in their surroundings, the baby Phillip was sitting up, beginning to crawl, and would soon be up on his feet.

A few days before Christmas the Philadelphia arrived with news from Port Jackson.

'Not good,' said the Lieutenant Governor to Ben, 'Governor Phillip's gone home. Apparently his health had begun to fail and the pressures on him at Port Jackson became more than he could bear. I suppose I should be thankful that my responsibilities are rather less than his. The trouble is that he's to be succeeded immediately by Lieutenant Governor Grose, and I know that his views about how a convict colony should be run are quite different from Governor Phillip's and mine.'

'Will he have so much influence over what goes on here, now that we're more or less established?' asked Ben.

'Oh yes. After all, he can issue any order he likes and I'll be obliged to obey, however much I disagree with it. The greatest problem is likely to stem from the fact that he sees all convicts as sub-human and therefore as legitimate objects to be abused, insulted and beaten. And moreover he counts on his right to enrich himself whilst he is out here to the greatest extent possible, and at the expense of anyone who he can cheat or exploit.'

'That sounds rather like the sort of person who did for our chief sawyer, Morgan. He was telling me how he was defrauded by an unscrupulous scoundrel.'

'At least I can prevent profiteering here,' said theLieutenant Governor. 'If any ship comes in which has items for sale I shall ensure that the Master doesn't sell everything he has all to the same person or class of people. If need be the government will buy everything and sell it on at a modest margin so that everyone can benefit. Life is difficult enough without profiteers. But as far as Lieutenant Governor Grose is concerned I suspect we may find life getting rather more tiresome.

'In the meantime, Luckett, we need to get on with applying some amended instructions which Governor Phillip has sent me respecting the settlers and the form of land tenancy they are permitted to enjoy. He evidently received instructions from London that no one on Norfolk Island is to have more than 15 acres granted to them; they can see how well we are doing and how fertile the land is and seem to be worried that some hard-working settlers may create too much wealth for themselves and not pay enough tax. Typical government, and just the sort of problem which led to the American colonies walking away and deciding to set up their own state.'

Christmas was upon them and the drink of the season was rum shrub, a mixture of rum and lemon juice imported from India. Even Richard Morgan was seen to enjoy a sample to celebrate Christmas and the end of another year, and the general atmosphere in the island was one of contentment despite the thermometer going well above a hundred degrees on one or two days.

As the Philadelphia left in the New Year, bound for India and carrying despatches and mail bound eventually for London, so the first plague of locusts arrived. They landed one day in Arthur's Vale and began eating everything they could find, but fortunately for the crops, they moved up the hill where they would do less damage, and after a couple of weeks suddenly they were gone.

It was early in February 1793 that Sally gave birth to her baby, a beautiful boy who Ben decided must be called Thomas after his own father. The women living in and around Kingston had all rallied around to make the birth as uneventful as possible but even so Ben had been distraught as he heard the groans and cries through the thin walls. He wanted to be there with Sally, to share, in so far as a man can ever share, the whole event. But convention dictated that men were kept away, for they could be of no practical use and would be more likely to get in the way of what was necessarily women's work.

But in due course he was allowed to hold the tiny human, part of him and part of Sally, whose wrinkled face and tiny fingers and toes were such a stunning example of the process of creation which God had ordained for mankind. Baby Thomas would henceforth embody the love between him and Sally, and, God-willing, would become their immortality.

A few days after that significant event, a ship called Kitty arrived from Port Jackson bringing a new detachment of soldiers. The King's good friends Captain Paterson and his wife would return to Port Jackson, depriving him and Mrs King of their closest confidantes. What made matters worse was that Lieutenant Governor Grose had not sent a Captain with the new detachment, apparently because no-one of that rank was available at Port Jackson, and command of the unit would rest with a young and relatively inexperienced Lieutenant. William Chapman and Ben talked about the prospect

'Like so many things we experience here,' said William, 'it's less than ideal. But Mr King's response on hearing about it was, we shall just have to accept it and do the best we can. He's already written to Lieutenant Governor Grose to ask that a Captain be sent out as quickly as possible, but I rather think he may be short of volunteers because the army in Port Jackson know that as long as they're there they can line their pockets at the expense of the settlers and the convicts – and, I daresay – of the government. They know that on Norfolk Island that's not possible.'

'Why is it,' asked Ben, 'that when men get into positions of power they almost always abuse it – and mostly for their own benefit? And yet those same people so often claim to be inspired by Christian beliefs of love and charity. How can people live that sort of double, hypocritical life?'

'Well I'm nowhere near enough of a theologian to answer that. But Mr King has been pretty clear about where he stands. He put out that order last December saying that the convicts had as much right to the protection by the laws of England as anyone else. Do you remember he said 'no person whatever will be allowed to beat any convict on pain of being prosecuted as the law directs?' He is quite clear about it and I am sure he starts from the belief that everyone, no matter what they have done, has good in them. Give them a chance, encourage them to reform and many, probably most, will get along fine and be an asset to the rest of us.'

'But against that he and Captain Paterson sent those men to Nepean Island because they would not show any signs of remorse for their crimes. They stole because they were desperately hungry like the rest of us. Surely they should be given a chance to reform.'

'True enough; but if everyone was allowed to steal when they felt hungry you'd have anarchy. You and I were hungry, but we didn't steal. Anyway they're back from the island now and the ones who were not sent to Port Jackson in the Kitty are being given the chance to go straight – and if they don't, I guess the magistrates will return them to the island. It must be grim to be there – no food or water other than what's provided, the minimum of shelter, and the knowledge that if you try to cross over to the mainland you will likely be carried away by the tide, or dashed to pieces on the reef.'

'So who will be in command of the soldiers when the Captain leaves?' asked Ben.

'I think it will be Lieutenant Abbott. He doesn't seem to be a bad officer, but I suspect he's rather inclined to get a bit too close to the soldiers.'

'I remember when I served under Captain Nelson in Boreas that I sometimes wondered whether he was on too familiar terms with the sailors. But somehow he just had the knack of knowing how far he could go, and he could quickly turn off the familiarity and become the leader we all looked up to, and who we would follow; to death if needs be.'

'Let's hope Mr Abbott learns that same knack.' And after a pause William went on, 'Another person who came in the Kitty is Zechariah Clarke. He has come as Deputy Commissary to replace Mr Freeman who is off home at the end of his contract. Let's hope he is an understanding and diligent person, as Mr King must rely upon him for keeping all the records and ensuring that the right people get issued with the right amount of food and the stocks of food are kept in good order, otherwise we shall all starve.'

'And didn't I hear that a new Master Carpenter has arrived too? I wonder how Nat Lucas will take to that. The new man will have to be good if he's to win as much respect as Nat has.'

The conversation could have gone on but both young men had work to do and they would have plenty of chances to talk again. William was continuing to live at Phillipburgh but came over to Kingston to take his meals with the Kings in the new Government House, a much larger and more substantial stone building than the original wooden one. William was so popular in the house that Sally had heard him referring to the baby Phillip King as 'my little brother.'

121

Having experienced very few visits by ships in the previous year the island did not have to wait long after the departure of the Kitty before two more arrived, the Chesterfield and the Shah Hormazear. They brought more provisions, and some of the other items which made life a little more bearable, tea and coffee, clothing and shoes; but there were no tools, which caused considerable concern, as hoes and spades, saws and axes, cooking pots and knives were all becoming very worn and needed replacement.

The Shah Hormazear had also brought some ewes and rams which delighted Mr King. The only sheep on the island were the remains of those he had bought in the Cape. They had not thrived and the ewes were now useless because the only ram had died and the flock was gradually diminishing. But with two new rams there was hope that the ewes would again flourish. Mr King had decreed that the new sheep would remain in government ownership. As he said to William, 'If anyone else could get hold of them, like as not they would have them chopped up in a trice and on the dinner table.'

Most significant of all was the arrival aboard the Shah Hormazear of two young Maori men, who were to prove to be fascinating people with whom Mr King established a strong relationship which ultimately endured far beyond their lives.

Chapter 13

When they first landed at Cascade Bay the two Maori men, Tooke and Huru, looked frightened. It was only later that anyone realised that their great fear arose from the belief that they were about to be killed and eaten, for that was the custom in the Bay of Islands in the north of New Zealand where they came from, when one tribe captured the people of another.

Mr King immediately took charge of the situation and approached them with his hands open and his arms outstretched to demonstrate that he was carrying no weapon. He smiled at them and stretched a hand towards them. He spoke softly and reassuringly although, of course, they understood no English. After a few minutes he had achieved a smile from one of them and after a few more minutes he had persuaded them to walk with him towards Kingston. Once they had arrived at Government House he took them in and showed them to his guest room and by gesture invited them to make themselves comfortable. And there he left them for a time, not confined by lock or closed door, and quite free to come and go as they pleased.

Very soon he issued a general order to the effect that these two men were to be treated as honoured guests of the Government, and were, under no circumstances, to be verbally abused or physically attacked or injured in any way. Every day with the help of William Chapman, and the other officers, he would patiently talk with them, and gradually he began to build up a dictionary of Maori words, nothing very complex or profound, but enough to create some understanding and confidence. He was worried to see that quite regularly they would retire into separate corners and huddle down weeping profusely, and on one occasion one of them indicated very obviously that he wished to commit suicide. Happily he was dissuaded.

The arrival of the two men had been conceived at least two years previously when Mr King, still in England, had written to the authorities to express his belief that the wild flax growing on Norfolk Island in profusion would, if processed in the way the Maoris had been seen to employ, be able to clothe the whole of the colony of New South Wales at minimum cost. Captain Cook himself witnessed the process and had suggested that the flax could be used for sailcloth for all the ships the British would need to deploy in that part of the world. This assertion was supported by a young naval Captain, George Vancouver, who had sailed as a Midshipman with Cook in 1778 and seen the flax and cloth made from it in New Zealand. Vancouver had risen to Captain and been given command of the Discovery and the storeship Daedalus with which he was to round Cape Horn and explore the west coast of America more thoroughly than Captain Cook had been able to do on his final voyage. King and Vancouver had met again when the Gorgon was in Capetown and King had asked him, if he had the chance, to arrange for two Maoris who knew the flax process to be brought to Norfolk Island to demonstrate their methods.

Vancouver, after reaching the north west coast of America had sent the Daedalus on this mission in 1792 and the two men had been enticed onboard with the lure of acquiring tools and other artefacts which they wanted. They had been utterly distraught when they realised they had been kidnapped as the Daedalus headed for New South Wales. There they arrived in March 1793 and were immediately transferred to the Shah Hormazear which was about to sail for Norfolk Island.

One of the first hurdles to be surmounted on Norfolk Island was the departure of the Shah Hormazear with an explanation that the ship was going to India and then to England, not to the Bay of Islands, and that therefore there was no point in Tooke and Huru being on board. Mr King ,with William's help, drew pictures to show the relative positions of all these places. He made a promise to them that they would go home in six moons. When the Master of the Shah Hormazear and his wife came ashore to bid the Lieutenant Governor and his wife farewell the two Maoris made it very obvious that they were sorry to see them go.

As he got to know them a little better Mr King and William began to introduce questions about flax and by slow degrees they learnt more about Huru and Tooke's status and lives. Huru was son of a chief and Tooke of a priest, and they came from neighbouring tribes. It was never quite clear whether Huru would succeed his father as chief, but Tooke would definitely become the chief priest when his aged father died. Both men had wives and children at home who, they hoped, would be waiting for their return. Both clearly longed to be at home with their families and would stand on Flagstaff hill and look out to the southern ocean in the direction of home. Gradually the attention they received and the obvious goodwill of those around them began to make them feel more comfortable and secure in their strange circumstances.

'I think we may be winning them over,' said the Lieutenant Governor to William, 'although I would feel a little happier if they had not told me of their custom of committing suicide when they are feeling sad. We must count ourselves lucky to have found two very bright and intelligent young men who are quickly learning English, and that alone will make our communications much easier. I must admit to being surprised that their manners and disposition are so much more pleasing than I'd ever have imagined from a native of New Zealand.'

'They're feeling easier with us now; that much is very clear. I think we've convinced them that we wish to be friends and that we're not going to harm them. It's quite unpleasant hearing them try to explain the tradition the tribes have of eating their enemies when they defeat them.'

'That's a major concern, for when we find a ship to take them back home I fear that a lazy master might simply put them ashore in the most convenient place and that might be in the midst of their enemies. Then they would just be put to death and eaten and we'd have done nothing to re-assure their fellow men that white men from across the world can safely be treated as valued friends. When the time comes I feel that I must go with them and be absolutely satisfied that they're landed amidst their friends.'

'Shall I try to get them to draw a map of where they live, and then perhaps we can match that against our own charts and locate their homes?' asked William. That became his major project for the next few days, and Tooke's drawing did eventually show a good resemblance to the charts of Captain Cook.

It was soon clear that in New Zealand flax was dealt with entirely by women and the two young men had never had any practical experience of doing the work. But they were able to describe some of the important elements, how, for example, the women ran a thumbnail along the hard central stalk leaving the side part of the leaves. Then they held the leaf strips in a particular way and used a mussel shell to scrape the soft part of the leaf away from the fibres. If it was to be used for weaving cloth it was washed repeatedly in water to separate the individual fibres which could then be spun to the correct thickness before being woven. But neither Tooke nor Huru was practiced in the use of the mussel shell and it took hours of practice before the convict flax dressers developed the necessary skills. Even when they had produced some reasonable thread they had no loom on which to weave, and they needed the ingenuity of Nat Lucas to build a weaving frame which would enable them to make something useful. No7 sailcloth, Ben reckoned, at best.

Looking after the two Maoris became a daily task involving Mr and Mrs King, William and Ben, as well as some of the other officers, and as the days turned into weeks the two seemed happier and more settled. But the occasional black moods continued when swore that they were about to commit suicide if they were not immediately allowed to go home; then all the skills of Mr King and his small team were needed to persuade them to laugh it off.

It was Mrs King who pointed out to her husband after one of these traumatic episodes, 'They certainly seem to have some very strong beliefs. You know how we say that such natives are lacking in culture. Well I think what we have learnt is that they have a very well-developed culture; they are intelligent people, and the only fundamental difference is that their culture is different from ours. When you look at some of our own less agreeable people it is not so hard to rank Tooke and Huru as our equals as human beings.'

Mr King was very happy to agree with his wife. 'They're our honoured guests and I'm certainly very happy to have them living in my house – in fact I'd rather have them than some of my own countrymen.'

'Should we write to Mr Wilberforce and explain some of our experiences with these two? It might help him in presenting his case for more humane treatment of the African slaves in the Caribbean and Southern States of America.'

'That might be a good idea, my dear,' replied Mr King. And he went on, 'We certainly have very clear evidence that these two are as much God's people, as we are, and whilst they may not have recognised the fact it is surely our Christian duty to treat them as children of God, even though they have not had the good fortune to know the love of our saviour Jesus Christ.'

In addition to the care of these two important people, the business of the island had to continue and especially the struggle to produce food. In June of that year some of the newly emerging wheat was suddenly eaten to shreds by a plague of caterpillars. By good fortune Mr King noticed one of his chickens eating a caterpillar with apparent delight and he conceived the idea of letting all his chickens loose where the caterpillars were most plentiful. They did a fine job, and so he collected 300 more chickens from around the island and bought them for government. The caterpillar problem was dealt with and the wheat began to grow as it should. But up at Queenborough a ground grub was causing havoc by eating just about everything green. D'Arcy Wentworth set as many of his men as he could to pick the grubs off the plants and observed that it took only ten minutes to fill a three gallon pot. But even then the grubs did not disappear; they particularly liked the maize and despite every effort ravaged about sixteen acres. So it was decided to sow the maize crop later in future years when it should still have time to grow and yield well.

In August Mr Balmain, the Assistant Surgeon and a magistrate, persuaded his friends that it would be a good entertainment to put on a play. It should not be too difficult to arrange and it would provide a little intellectual stimulus after a day's work. Ben and Sally had heard about this but 'I couldn't do that Sal; it is just like pretending one is someone one is not. It takes me time and effort enough to know who I am anyway. Besides I'm not one for standing up in front of a crowd and showing off. We could go together to one of their performances, perhaps. You would come wouldn't you?' The plays were duly performed amidst much laughter and gaiety and were reckoned to be a great success.

'Well William,' said the Lieutenant Governor after the second performance, 'at least that went off without the sort of bawdy and licentious behaviour often associated with playhouses in London.'

William though it better simply to agree rather than to ask Mr King whether he had found the play amusing and funny.

Through the months of August and September buildings seemed to be going up very fast and it was a great comfort to see the settlements taking on a more permanent look. At last there was a proper stone bakehouse, a far more suitable place to keep an oven going than a wooden building, and a secure stone granary had been completed. The Superintendents now all had stone chimneys to their houses. Boat builders had completed a new five-oared boat for Cascade Bay, which would help with unloading but which would also be used for fishing.

In October two trading vessels stopped by the island in order to land a convict who had got onboard unnoticed in Port Jackson. As they had not expected to call at the island on their way to Bengal they had no letters. But the Lieutenant Governor was able to send off a report direct to London. This showed that there were now over 1250 acres cleared and under cultivation and the prospects looked quite favourable for good crops of wheat and maize.

As the two vessels set sail Tooke and Huru looked out from the beach with tears in their eyes, desperately sad that once again they had been unable to go home.

'I promise I will take you home', said the Lieutenant Governor to the distraught visitors, 'but I cannot easily order a ship to change its plans for your benefit. I should get into dreadful trouble and probably find myself charged a lot of money to compensate. But I will eventually find a way. At least the Governor in Port Jackson knows that you have to be taken home.'

Only a few days later on 2nd November the Britannia came in sight and anchored in Sydney bay. Mr Raven, the Master, came ashore with Captain Nepean of the New South Wales Regiment who was on his way home. The wind had set in at North and, when combined with a full moon, there was a very strong reason to believe that it would blow from that quarter for at least two weeks.

'Welcome to you, gentlemen', said Mr King, as he greeted the new visitors, 'have you brought despatches only or some provisions as well?'

'We are on our way to India,' began Mr Raven in explanation, 'on charter to Major Grose and his fellow officers to buy general stores for sale in Port Jackson so there is a certain amount of pressure on us to keep the time down to a minimum. What these soldiers don't understand is that when the wind blows in the wrong direction a ship cannot make progress. And with this wind there is not much point in setting off now since we will not make any headway to the north'.

'That gives me an idea. How long would it take to get to the Bay of Islands at the northern end of New Zealand?' asked Mr King.

'Not more than three days if the wind holds', answered the master.

'So if we set off quickly we could easily be back here within a fortnight, probably ten days, and still have time to drop off my two New Zealand guests at their homes. They've given us all the information they can about processing the flax and I've promised to take them home. They've been here a full six months now and we're getting to know them well, although communications are still a little difficult. Would you take me and them down there whilst this wind blows from the north and in ten days drop me off here on your way to India'?

'I don't see why not; I can't go north so I may as well spend a few days going south and by then the wind will perhaps have changed and we'll be on our way – little or no time lost'.

At that Lieutenant Governor King called his wife and told her of his plan. He then sent for Ben and William and while he was waiting for them he spoke with Captain Nepean.

'Captain, I should be very grateful if you would accept a commission to act in my place for the next few days; would that be acceptable to you'?

'If that is what you wish, Sir, I shall be honoured. 'Tis a soldiers duty to obey the orders of his superior officer which will depend upon circumstances. But do please tell me why you would not entrust that role to Lieutenant Abbott who is normally second-in-command on the island and who would expect to succeed you in case of an accident.'

'I shall inform the acting Governor Grove when I report to him that the reason for asking you to remain here is so that there are sufficient officers to call a Garrison Court Martial should that be necessary, and given that you are here and available and senior in rank to Lieutenant Abbott it would be perverse if you were not in command.'

'That seems very reasonable and correct; and clearly there is no possibility of consulting with the acting Governor so we must act to our best ability for the good of His Majesty's Service.'

'But', went on Lieutenant Governor King, 'There is another reason why I am not entirely confident of leaving the command with Lieutenant Abbott, and that is that I received a complaint a little while ago which intimated that he had refused to discipline properly a member of the detachment who had abused a settler. Overlooking such a matter may appear trivial but in a very close community like this one it is the little things which soon escalate out of all reasonable proportion and create the most dreadful tensions. Furthermore I came to hear about another complaint made by a settler against a soldier which Lieutenant Abbott should have brought to my attention; he has not done so, and that does nothing for my confidence in him. But he's a young man and I'm sure experience will gradually serve him well'.

'Yes, that I can see too. It has sadly become a feature of Port Jackson that the soldiers can get away with almost anything and they abuse the convicts most terribly – and quite unnecessarily.'

'I've issued an order here that expressly forbids soldiers or settlers of any description from beating or verbally abusing any convict. That way leads only to conflict and resentment. The convicts have been through the most horrible experiences to get here and surely suffering the ignominy of transportation and the forced separation from their homes and families is more than enough punishment. Subjecting them to such terrible conditions in the transports on the way out here was further punishment. So the least we can do is to treat them like God's children, with respect and decency so far as we can and so far as they comply with the rules and orders designed to serve the community as a whole.'

'You give me an excellent briefing, Sir, as to your philosophy which I shall do my utmost to preserve during what I hope will only be a very brief absence.'

'Well, on the whole, everyone is very orderly and the vast majority understand well the need to work hard for the survival of us all. There are so many things we would still like to do to make life more agreeable but first of all we have to make sure we have enough food. Will you take Luckett to show you around and introduce you to the key people; he is a good man and will give you a very true picture of how things are.'

'Thank you Sir. I appreciate that. In the meantime will you be seeing Lieutenant Abbott to inform him of your arrangements?'

'Indeed I will. And I look forward to seeing you for a meal later.'

Captain Nepean left the Lieutenant Governor and found Ben waiting at the door.

'We will do a complete tour, Sir, if you are happy about that, starting here in Sydney and going up to Cascade and Phillipburgh and then back to Queenborough and down into Arthur's Vale by way of the dam.'

Ben walked briskly along with the Captain pointing out the neatly arranged houses and how fortunate it had been that Mr King had ordered all the trees to be felled just before the hurricane struck and rooted up so many of them across the island. They walked along to Turtle Bay and then back on the other side of the swamp along the path which ran at the edge of the low ground. They passed the barracks and Ben pointed out Nathaniel Lucas's house, neat and tidy, with some small children in the garden. Then they turned up the hill along the road to Cascade Bay which had been properly established while Mr King had been away. Ben kept a good pace up the hill and the Captain noted that none of his soldiers at Port Jackson would have been fit enough to keep up with him; a clear sign that the diet on Norfolk Island was far healthier than the scarce provisions which could be provided in the parent colony.

They reached the slope down to Cascade, passing by the few huts which made the settlement of Phillipburgh and Ben pointed out the Landing Rock and wharf. They turned and looked in at the flax manufactory where about twenty women were stripping the flax leaves. Ben was always surprised at the amount of noise which accompanied this work for the women were always talking and vying with each other, apparently, to be heard.

They passed from there back up the road and on the top they took a right handed fork towards Charlotte's Fields and Queenborough. Huts were being built up there and they came across Nat Lucas supervising some carpenters as they fitted together the boards which formed the walls.

'We're just finishing off some of these huts before starting on a new granary up here, which will be on stone foundations, and about 24 feet long and 12 wide.'

'Why do you choose those particular dimensions?'

'Well the sawyers cut six foot lengths because it is very difficult to handle a tree trunk which is any longer than that. Six feet long, one foot wide and one inch thick. We generally make all our buildings in multiples of those – simpler and quicker.'

'I can see that, and now that you tell me it is quite obvious', replied the Captain. 'Thank you Mr Lucas. And Ben pointed out your house to me; you have two very bonny children.'

'I would have two more had I not been so foolish as to misjudge the fall of a tree and drop it right onto my own house. But Mrs Lucas is a wonderful woman and is about to give me another child.'

'I would like to know what you most lack here, Mr Lucas. I am on my way back to England and will have a chance to make representations to the authorities in London so it would be good to hear it from you? Do you need more food or what?'

'No we can just about manage for food now and there is still plenty of land to be cleared. We need tools. Our saws are in a dreadful condition and it is only because of Richard Morgan and his supervision of the women sharpeners that we are able to get anything done. You will see vegetable gardens growing very well and the cereal crops are coming along nicely but we could do so much more if we had a few oxen and ploughs, or horses. All the tilling of the field must be done by hand. You should talk to Mr Wentworth as well while you are up here'.

'Thank you Mr Lucas, that is very interesting and helpful.'

They did not have far to go before they found D'Arcy Wentworth, certainly not far enough for Ben to be able to give the Captain an account of his colourful history and aristocratic connections.

'We're making progress', said Wentworth in answer to the Captain's question, 'though we could do with more tools and more people. Pigs are multiplying very successfully and we'll soon have plenty to feed ourselves and be able to salt it down to send to Port Jackson and elsewhere. Most days I can walk down to Sydney and find there are fresh fish to eat which is wonderful, although there are many on the island who won't touch it for some reason. You'll see the dam on your way down to Sydney and before too long we hope to have a watermill there, if Nat Lucas can make it work'.

'So you say you could do with more people as well as tools'? asked Nepean.

'Yes indeed; but preferably only those with relevant skills – carpenters, stonemasons, flax dressers, weavers, farmers and gardeners. But above all not in the condition of those poor wretches who came out in the Lady Juliana and the Neptune. So many of them were near dead and it took months before any of them was able to do a proper day's work – but I hope that message has already reached England. It must be very difficult for the people over there to realise what it's like to start a new settlement from nothing, even when there are no hostile natives and the land and climate are generally pretty favourable'.

'I share your sentiments entirely, Mr Wentworth. I saw myself the state of those poor people in the Lady Juliana when Port Jackson had already almost run out of the things needed to enable them to survive and recover. That was why Governor Phillip decided to send so many of them over here – he knew that life was not very easy here but reckoned that it was probably a little better than at Port Jackson.'

The discussion could have continued but Ben felt it was time to set off back to Sydney and they strode off towards Charlotte's Fields before turning down to Arthur's Vale.

'Richard Morgan's house is over there, set back a little way from the road', said Ben as they descended, 'He's a very private sort of man and doesn't welcome having too many others around him, but he works every day at one or other of the sawpits taking a turn on a saw. He says a man can soon get lazy if he does no work, and he can very quickly show a new sawyer what standard he expects. He's meticulous in supervising the sharpening too and all the women who are now doing that job know very well that he can do it better than they. And he's a master gunsmith, but although there is not a great deal of call for that skill, he always attends the Saturday morning firings to make sure that the muskets are firing as they should.'

'Shall I be able to meet this extraordinary man'? asked the Captain.

At that moment they came to a sawpit at the head of a wide valley where he could just see some of the houses of Sydney in the far distance. It was covered with a roof, and sawyers were working at a massive twelve foot diameter log, the upper sawyer standing barefoot atop the tree which had been stripped of bark, and rhythmically pulling the saw from calf level to chest as the teeth ripped into the timber.

'Good day, Mr Morgan,' shouted Ben to be heard above the noise of the saw.

'Stop', ordered Morgan as the saw rose to his chest level, and he jumped down.

'This is Captain Nepean of the New South Wales Regiment, on his way home to England in Britannia, and Mr King asked me to introduce him to all the key people, Richard'. The Captain saw a large and clearly very strong fit man, above forty years old, with dark hair and an intelligent look in his eye.

'Thank you for stopping by Captain. I've just about done my turn on the saw so if you bear with me for a minute or two I'll set things moving again and walk on with you.' So saying he gave some orders to the men standing by and they quickly set the saw going again.   Morgan picked up a rag and wiped the sweat off himself before putting on a shirt and his shoes.

'So what is your secret, Mr Morgan?' asked the Captain as they set off.

'Take every opportunity as it comes along, watch and learn, and look after yourself', replied Morgan, rather tersely.

'You appear to have been able to apply that to become proficient in many skills,' replied Nepean.

'Well, Captain, my father was a victualler and I grew up in a public house and there I learnt a good deal about life as well as being able to help with all aspects of the trade.   And when Bristol was down, in the American war, I was offered an apprenticeship with a gunsmith who had a contract to supply muskets for the army.   One of my cousins was a sawyer and I was able to help him by applying some gunsmith skills to sharpening his saws for him.   And I was lucky enough to be taught to read and write, and develop an interest in many other aspects of life.   That gives me more than enough to occupy myself without having to resort to rum or wine, or to womanising, which other men seem to regard as necessary to them – and it invariably gets them into some sort of trouble'. A complete life history in just a few words.

'If you'll excuse me, Sir, I'll break off now and go to visit one of my other sawpits.' He was not ill-mannered, thought Captain Nepean, but extraordinarily dedicated to his work and determined to allow nobody and nothing to get in the way. He could see just why Lucas, Wentworth and Morgan were so important to the settlement and to the Lieutenant Governor.

As they walked alongside the fields from which harvest had been partly gathered, Ben pointed out the dam which had been created by Mr King, and the site of the watermill which everyone expected and hoped for, with enough capacity to grind corn for the whole island.

That evening the Captain dined with Mr and Mrs King and Tooke and Huru, and they talked about the island and the people that Nepean had met during the day.

'I think I shall enjoy my short stay here,' said the Captain.

'Good, I am very pleased you happened to be aboard Britannia at this moment. You know how anxious I am to return our two friends to their homes. We've very much enjoyed their company and learning their language and customs, but the manner in which they were taken was abrupt and cruel and they need to be returned as soon as possible. Besides, from what they tell me the tribes which are neighbours to them are sometimes at war, and if a war has started since they've been away it'd be a disaster for them to be dropped off in the wrong place. I now understand more of their language than anyone else and feel it's my duty to make sure they are landed correctly. Besides, there'll be many advantages to His Majesty's service if we establish a good relationship of trust with the people of those islands. I hope I can rely upon you to report to the Government the state of affairs here and, in particular, why it's necessary for me to absent myself for a few days. I would ask permission of the Lieutenant Governor in Port Jackson except that would delay matters even more, and, in any case, in the navy we are always expected to take initiative when authority is too distant.'

'I am afraid that's not quite the same as the army,' replied Nepean. 'We're invariably rather closer to higher authority and when faced with a situation outside our orders or commission it's usually quite easy for us to ask higher authority before we take action. I can certainly make that very clear when I get home. But right now I must ask you how Lieutenant Abbott took to my presence?'

'Ah', replied King, 'not so well as I had hoped. In fact to begin with he flatly refused to accept my plan. When I told him that it must be possible to hold a Garrison Court Martial during my absence, and especially so should I be detained for some unexpected reason, he understood but refused to accept. I told him to go away and reflect upon what he was doing and to return this evening. So I daresay we can expect him any time now.'

A few minutes later there was a knock on the door and Lieutenant Abbott entered.

'Ah, Mr Abbott, a glass of port perhaps? I don't think you have had the pleasure of meeting Captain Nepean since his arrival on Norfolk Island'. Abbott was a little taken aback by the warmth of his welcome given his earlier conversation with Lieutenant Governor King, his superior officer.

'Thank you Sir….and how do you do Captain?'

'Well now. You have a glass of port in your hand, which I'm sure will do you a power of good. Have you reflected upon our earlier conversation?'

'Yes Sir, I have. I can't say I like your decision since I believe that I am second in command on the island and should therefore deputise for you in your absence. However, I do understand the desirability of taking advantage of another officer to make a Garrison Court Martial should one be needed, and I also acknowledge that Captain Nepean is my superior in rank within the regiment. I will therefore accept your decision and place myself, during your absence, under Captain Nepean'.

'Thank you, Mr Abbott. I'm grateful to you for taking that point of view, which makes it far more likely that we can ensure that our two friends here are returned to their homes in safety and a spirit of friendship. I believe it would be right if we were to stand and drink a toast to His Majesty, and then to Tooke and Huru, so that they may always recall our respect and gratitude to them'.

Chapter 14

Lieutenant Governor King stepped into the boat with Tooke and Huru and, waving to everyone on the shore, set out to the Britannia anchored in the roads.   A platoon of New South Wales Regiment had already been embarked with Ben and William Chapman, and ten sows and two boars which would be given to Tooke and Huru's tribe.   Mr King had also confirmed with Mr Raven, the master, that there was a good stock of beads, mirrors, ribbon and cloth onboard which could be used as gifts for the Maori tribes.

There had been a tearful departure for Tooke and Huru who had shown much emotion in bidding farewell to Mrs King, their hostess for the past six months, and to many of the other inhabitants who had shown them much real kindness and affection.   Although both men were relieved to be on their way home at last, they had become markedly attached to the people they had met and clearly their treatment had removed much of the natural fear they had felt when they were captured and removed so swiftly from everything familiar and dear to them.

As soon as they were onboard the master gave the order to weigh anchor, the sails were shaken out, and Britannia gradually gathered way towards the south.

Just three days later land was in sight and the ship moved slowly towards the group of islands and inlets, directed in part by Tooke and Huru who recognised some of the landmarks.   As they closed with the shore they saw some canoes heading out towards them and in due course both Tooke and Huru gave out shrieks of delight as they recognised some of the people in the canoes.   Within minutes they were alongside and the New Zealanders began climbing onboard.   Tooke at once knew a close relation of his mother from whom he began to gather news about the rest of his family and his tribe.   Lieutenant Governor King was fascinated by the facial markings on some of the people which he knew from what Tooke had told him distinguished the more important deputy chiefs, and to these he began handing out some of the chisels and hand axes he had brought for the purpose.   Very soon a trade started in which the sailors exchanged scraps of iron for flax cloth and various less useful mementoes and keepsakes.

By seven in the evening as darkness fell the New Zealanders all left to return home. But then another smaller canoe arrived with four men who fearlessly jumped on board and were quickly engaged in a negotiation to sell their canoe to Mr Raven. During the evening they were able to reinforce all that Tooke had been told earlier and they told stories about local happenings which at some points left Huru in tears. At one point he heard how a neighbouring force of thirty men had attacked his tribe and killed the Chief's son, whereupon he took himself into a corner of the cabin consumed by grief and vowing revenge.

The following morning a massive canoe with 36 paddles came out to them carrying a very important looking chief, named Ketoheka. He must have been about seventy years old and the whole of his face was covered with spiral lines. He first embraced Tooke in the most affectionate manner and when Tooke introduced the Lieutenant Governor the ceremony of rubbing noses, called ehonge, took place and the chief removed his cloak and placed it on the Lieutenant Governor's shoulders. He in turn called for a large length of green baize cloth which he gave the Chief.

More canoes soon appeared and so many people came onboard that Tooke asked that the poop should be reserved for the Chief. The wind had dropped and Lieutenant Governor King became concerned that Britannia would not be able to deliver Tooke and Huru to the right spot. However Tooke then came to him and assured him that it would be alright for them to go with Ketoheka who had promised to deliver them to their homes by the following morning. Nonetheless the Lieutenant Governor still had a fear that Ketoheka might be tricking them in order to get them into his clutches; but Tooke said with absolute confidence that 'a chief never deceives'. So Tooke, Huru and King went into the cabin with the old chief and with Tooke's help King explained that he was very grateful to him for taking his two friends back to their home and that he would give some gifts to mark his gratitude. However, he also signified that he would come back with some more gifts in three months' time which he would give the Chief only when he knew for certain that Tooke and Huru had been returned to their homes safely. Kotoheka said nothing in return but went up to King and clasped the sides of his head gently but firmly between his hands, indicating that King should do the same to him and they drew their noses together remaining together for a good three minutes, during which time Kotoheka seemed to be reciting some sort of prayer which King could not understand. He then went through the same process with Tooke and Huru in turn. Tooke then told King that Kotoheka had now become their father and would personally ensure their safe delivery to their homes.

The New Zealanders were evidently very keen to know what Tooke and Huru had been doing whilst they were away and they gathered in a circle around them while they told their story, describing what they had seen on Norfolk Island. At one point Tooke leapt out of the circle and dashed to the poop, picking up a cabbage which had been cut from the King's garden four days previously. He then asked the Lieutenant Governor to give a demonstration firing of the soldiers' muskets and the ship's cannons. Before doing so King was anxious to explain that these fearsome weapons were only used in the most extreme situations and that he wished to reassure Kotoheka of his hope that they would never be used against any of his countrymen. So the platoon of soldiers was lined up and went through their musket drill, firing three volleys into the sea, before two of the cannon were fired, one with round shot and the other with grape. King was keen that they should observe how far away from the ship the shot landed.

After the shooting display the wind was beginning to get up from the south and King felt it was time to begin the farewell process which was likely to be protracted. Tooke and Huru proceeded to embrace nearly everyone onboard and made King promise to visit them again as soon as possible. Kotoheka embraced King yet again and tried hard to pronounce his name – something like Kingi. The last of the canoes cast off with more gifts including of course the ten sows and two boars, and Britannia shook out the sails and began to pick up the first of the light breeze.

'Well, Ben', said the Lieutenant Governor, 'We've only been here eighteen hours or so and yet I feel that we have made a tremendous impact. What do you think?'

'Yes Sir, I am sure you are right', replied Ben, 'it was wonderful how relaxed Tooke was when they came to bid farewell and I have to admit I was rather sorry to think that we will probably never see them again. I suppose we can only hope that British ships visiting in the future will treat them correctly and not undermine all your good work. If Europeans ever wanted to come to live here it would be essential that peaceful relationships were maintained.'

'I suspect I shall get criticised by Lieutenant Governor Grose who is unable to see anything beyond the end of his nose. I reckon his horizon is no further away than tomorrow. And I am really sorry that I shall almost certainly be obliged to break my promise to return within three moons. If I were able to return and live as their guests for a few months we would really establish a lasting relationship. But sadly I can't see that happening.'

It took them five days to sail back to Norfolk Island and the Lieutenant Governor was relieved to find that during the ten days of his absence everything had continued in an entirely orderly fashion. Britannia stocked up with provisions for her voyage to Calcutta and two days later King thanked Mr Raven and Captain Nepean, to whom he gave some despatches to deliver in London, as they embarked and set sail to the north.

Ben had much to tell Sally about the trip and gave her a Maori club which he had been given by Huru as a mark of friendship.

'They're really lovely people', he said, 'and seem so contented with their way of life. It's very different from ours; they don't have as many possessions as we do, but they're happy. It shows that you can be happy and contented without possessing lots of wealth and things, and I can't help wondering if perhaps the pursuit of riches and power is one of the reasons why wars happen. Relationships and values are much more important'. Ben paused wondering if he had over-reached himself and embarked upon a whole concept which was too far beyond his and Sally's comprehension. He decided to bring things back onto a much more personal level and continued by asking Sally directly 'Are you happy?'

'I'm glad to see you safe home, Ben, and I'm very happy to have a roof over my head and to know that I'm loved. There are two other things I'd like just now; the first is to know from the Governor that I'm now free, for I've served my seven years; and the other thing is to see my parents again and tell them how sorry I am to have brought shame upon them by what I so innocently did. Can you fix that for me? And now come here, come close and love me'.

The harvest was coming in well and Christmas was approaching; life on the island was almost as good as anywhere else with enough food for everyone to keep healthy, and considerably more than most working people had in England. The diet was quite well balanced with some fresh bread, potatoes and rice providing the carbohydrate, fresh pork and fish giving protein, and a wealth of green vegetables grown in everyone's garden – cabbages, cauliflower, many types of beans. Fruit was also available with some bananas and guava apparently growing indigenously and pineapples which had been brought for planting from the Cape. Salt pork and beef remained in the stores and was not generally issued unless fresh meat was temporarily unavailable.

In the very hot weather leading up to Christmas the last of the harvest was brought in, and the Lieutenant Governor was able to announce that there would be an extra issue of fresh pork and enough flour for everyone to have plenty to bake for Christmas Day. There would be an extra day's holiday and beer would be issued for everyone without limit. It was as happy a day as anyone on the island could remember.

Ben had approached the Lieutenant Governor about securing Sally's ticket of leave which would confirm to everyone that she had served her sentence and was now free.

'I'm more than happy to give her her ticket', said the Lieutenant Governor. 'But are you both sure that you want to go back to England. After all I can grant you 60 acres here which is more than enough for you to live off and raise a family, and is much more than you'll have back in England.'

'Yes Sir; that's certainly something we have considered. But I know that at heart I'm a seafarer more than a farmer, and much as I've enjoyed being here and serving you, I hope satisfactorily, I really would like to get back to sea. And besides, having married Sally, I know she'll be much better able to cope with my absence at sea if she's somewhere near to her family. None of us can tell the future but with the navy now in a war with the French again there'll be opportunities for me I'm quite sure. Perhaps in due course I might even get a commission. I don't want to be ungrateful to you, Sir, for you've been very generous but I would like to get back where the action is and see what I can make of it. Who knows, perhaps you yourself will return home and command a frigate.'

'That'd be good, but over the past six years I've lost precious sea time and many of my contemporaries will already be in their second or third lieutenant's appointment, getting ready to command. I'd have to return and then start in a second lieutenant's position in order to get well noticed – I've no one in the navy to pull any strings for me.' King was confident that Sir Joseph Banks, the naturalist and polymath, who certainly had the ear of people in high places of government, would be prepared to recommend him, but his words would have more weight in a colonial context than in a purely naval one. Banks had no standing with the leaders of the navy who were in the position to give him a worthwhile appointment at sea.

'If you're really sure', said King, 'I'll arrange a ticket for Sally, and write to Lieutenant Governor Grose to confirm that you're married to her and wish to take her with you when you go home to volunteer for further service in one of His Majesty's ships. I'll recommend most strongly that you both be found a passage on the next available ship to the Cape, or to India if there's none going all the way home. You'd then be able to take passage in an East Indiaman – you might even be able to work your passage as I daresay they're often short of experienced seamen'.

'Thank you Sir. Sally and I will be most grateful if you could do that. And in the meantime we'll be very happy to continue to serve you in any manner you think fit.' And with that Ben saluted the Lieutenant Governor and withdrew.

Christmas was a happy occasion, but there were some evil clouds beginning to appear on the horizon which finally created a storm. Some of the soldiers of the New South Wales Regiment seemed determined to find an excuse to pick a fight with the convicts, and even with the freemen.

Ben and Sally were having a Sunday meal with the Lucases early in the New Year when Ben and Nat raised the subject.

'Did you hear that Willy Dring has been on a charge for thumping that awful so-called soldier, Charles Windsor? Where do they find people like that for the army; God help us if they're ever faced with a real enemy.'

'There are some very stupid men around, in the navy as well as the army, who seem to think that everyone else owes them a living and that because they're in uniform they can help themselves to whatever they like, and that someone else has a duty to feed and clothe them.' Ben spoke up. 'They resent being here as jailers, or law-keepers, but if they were sent home and required to fight the French most of them would be completely ineffective.'

'Do you know what happened to Willy and what the governor thinks about it all?' asked Nat.

'He's in a difficult position because he must uphold the army, however much he scorns it. And you know he's had some doubts about Lieutenant Abbott. That said, Abbott did forbid Windsor from going anywhere near Willy or Ann. Windsor clearly arranged for Ann to be sent a message to meet someone on the Queenborough road. She assumed it was innocent, told Willy where she was going, and he followed her at a distance. When she got to the appointed place, there was Windsor who immediately grabbed her in a very provocative manner. Willy saw it all happening and, hardly surprisingly, pulled them apart and proceeded to give Windsor a bit more than a light punch on the nose. There can surely be no doubt that Windsor invited some sort of violence by behaving like that – any man would have stood up for his wife and his own honour. He was court martialled for disobeying the Lieutenant's order but I don't know what the outcome of that was. Willy was found guilty of striking a soldier, of course, but the Justices imposed a fine which he'll pay when he's sold some wheat to the stores; and old Wilbur Smith gave security for the fine'.

'I suppose the soldiers think that he wasn't punished enough and therefore that the governor doesn't support them. From my point of view it's the soldiers who should be disciplined; perhaps they have been and we just don't hear about it.'

Subsequent events showed that relationships were not at all as the Lieutenant Governor would have wished them to be. The increased numbers on the island, the higher proportion of sick convicts who could not work, and the fact that Port Jackson had sent a number of their wickedest and most incorrigible offenders to the island, all contributed to tensions. An important factor was the change from a marine detachment who understood naval ways to the New South Wales Regiment which had recruited a large number of scoundrels who had volunteered only to avoid a jail sentence. During his first spell as Commandant of the island King would have described three different categories of people: military, settlers, and convicts. Now as the population had grown the categories were different; there were the workers, both free and convict, who gave a fair day's work and were truly productive – whether as farmers, carpenters or labourers; there were the sick and disenchanted convicts, who were either unwilling or unable to work; and finally the army detachment who believed themselves superior to everyone else, entitled to live off everyone else's labour, and, which was worse, subject to a different set of standards of behaviour under a different law. Of course there were exceptions; there were certainly some soldiers who cultivated their own gardens and contributed to the island's essential food stocks. And one must be sympathetic to those convicts who had such a dreadful passage from England and were too weak to work – many of them had already died. The Lieutenant Governor longed for the happy family atmosphere where everyone worked hard for the community and for themselves. He must do his best to enable the workers to thrive, for that was the only way to produce enough for the community to avoid starvation, but he must also be prepared to punish those who transgressed, after sentencing in the appropriate civil or military court. He hated the very idea of approving sentences of hundreds of lashes for, though it was considered an acceptable punishment at the time, it removed the recipient from the workforce for weeks, perhaps months, and did nothing to encourage the notion of redemption. The Lieutenant Governor's belief in the fundamental goodness of every one of God's beings was being very sorely tested. Sometimes he could not help feeling that God was definitely against him, especially when he suffered an attack of gout which would leave him weakened through excruciating pain and confined to his house for days or weeks on end. Keeping everyone safe was his top priority and that meant producing enough food, and to spare, so that no-one would starve whatever unforeseen storms and plagues might visit them.

The small detachment of about fifty soldiers, however skilled and brave they might be – and there were plenty of doubts about that – could not defend him from three or four hundred determined settlers and convicts. Somehow he had to ensure that the majority would feel happy and comfortable, and adequately valued under his regime, whilst the soldiers were not too jealous and resentful of the wealth being accumulated by others. Emancipated convicts had been rewarded by grants of land, whilst others had earned sufficient to buy plots, clear them and farm them productively in order to earn significant money in return. How could a soldier earn anything beyond his small wage unless he was able to corner a market in something. In Port Jackson the army had cornered every market, and especially rum with which nearly everyone wanted to drown their misery. There the garrison had no thought about the superhuman effort needed to carve out a new successful colony, but were quite happy to line their own pockets without the slightest consideration for the wider impact on everyone else.

On Saturday 18th January, there was some excitement and anticipation because a play was to be produced by a group of enthusiastic actors directed by Surgeon William Balmain. A playhouse had been erected by Nat Lucas and his carpenters on the flat area close to Government House. People began to gather sitting together in family groups and with their friends; some who arrived early reserved adjacent seats for the rest of their party. At the start the atmosphere was festive and friendly; Ben and Sally were there looking after Norfolk and Sydney King as well as their own baby; the Lucases had their children with them; John Mortimer and his son Noah were there with their family; Richard Morgan the Superintendent of sawyers, usually strong and silent, looked as though he expected some intellectual stimulus. D'Arcy Wentworth had come down from Queenborough.

Then an argument seemed to develop in the front row where a soldier was trying to barge in and take a seat which had been reserved for the family of a settler. Angry words were exchanged.

'Move out of the bloody way; you're only a convict and I'm quite entitled to move you on; move over and make room for a proper man'.

'We're at the play and I'm just as entitled to a seat as you and there's nothing to prevent me keeping a seat for my husband, if only to avoid having to sit next to a filthy smelly scum like you'. The man she was addressing was not in uniform, although he was a soldier; he was in a filthy check shirt and was unshaven – not a good advertisement for the military.

'Watch your fucken words, convict whore. We could easily murder the whole fucken lot o' ye starting with the fucken Guv'nor'.

At that moment the Lieutenant Governor came in with Mrs King, two year old Phillip and the eight-month old baby Maria. There was a bit of a general hush but when someone said to the soldier at the front, 'Shhh, the governor's just come in', replied 'Damn the governor and all of you together; it's my own officers that I am to mind.' But then things did quieten down and in a few minutes the play began.

At the end of the performance the applause was long and sincere; the audience had evidently enjoyed being transported into a different world for a little while and were impressed by the effort that had been made by everyone who had taken part. The Lieutenant Governor and Mrs King left and returned the few steps up the slope to Government House where Mrs King took the children inside. Mr King stayed outside in conversation with Surgeon Balmain, whom he was congratulating on the whole organisation of the event.

'It sounds a bit rowdy over there now. Had I better go over and see what's up?' said Balmain.

'Well, I don't think there is anything to worry about', replied King, 'they'll very soon disperse I'm sure.' So the surgeon went his way along the seafront back to his house at the east end.

The Lieutenant Governor walked up the slope towards his house and heard more shouting and argument so he ordered Sergeant Whittle to go down and disperse everyone. A few minutes later the shouting and profanities were continuing even louder and the Lieutenant Governor heard a man in a check shirt shouting with real venom, 'Damn my bloody eyes, kill every bugger of them'. At the same moment he saw a party of soldiers with bayonets fixed running across from the barracks.

Ben had appeared at that moment and said to the Lieutenant Governor, 'You'd better come quickly Sir, it looks as though they're all intent upon murder'.

He marched smartly down to where the disturbance was happening and went straight up to the man he had seen shouting and swearing before, who was still yelling the most fearful obscenities, and approaching him from behind took a firm grip of his shoulder.

'Sergeant Whittle, take this man, whoever he is and lock him up in the guardhouse while he cools off; do you know who he is?'.

'Bannister, Sir', and turning to Bannister he ordered firmly, 'Come away with ye, now!'

John Fleming, an overseer, came up to King. 'Excuse me Sir; you should know that I saw Cowper there strike out at Bannister and land a firm blow upon him'.

'Take him off to the jail then and the justices can deal with him in the morning', ordered King, 'and tell everyone else to get off home directly'.

As they walked back towards Government House Ben noticed that Lieutenant Abbott was directing twenty soldiers back into the barracks. He said 'That was almost a disaster. If you'd not been there, Sir, to strengthen Sergeant Whittle's position it might have turned really nasty. It looked as though, once you were there, the other soldiers responded correctly to Lieutenant Abbott who seemed to have lost control before'.

It was only on the following day, Sunday, that Lieutenant Abbott reported to the Lieutenant Governor that there had been a mutiny of the detachment on the previous evening, that about twenty soldiers had rushed out of the barracks with their bayonets fixed and contrary to his own specific order to desist. It was only when they reached the playhouse where the other arguments were going on that they were persuaded to return to their barracks, that being the only way to avoid significant and unwarrantable bloodshed. The Lieutenant Governor and Lieutenant Abbott agreed that for a short period the soldiers' weapons must be removed and that to keep order a small militia of the most trustworthy citizens, mostly former marines or sailors, should be formed. A decree was issued to that effect on Sunday afternoon. Various investigations took place over the next few days and these led Lieutenant Abbott and his fellow officers to conclude that there were only five soldiers guilty of mutiny, and that the others had simply been carried along fearing a reprisal if they did not. Amongst the bravest and most principled of the soldiers was the drummer, Coulson, who first reported to Lieutenant Abbott about the mutiny, risking a beating from his fellows.

About a week later things seemed to have settled down and Ben and Sally were sitting outside their hut with the children asleep inside.

'I suppose all that just shows that things are not perfect here', said Sally. 'I feel very sad for the Lieutenant Governor who so desperately longs for everyone to get on with each other and behave sensibly'.

'Well, yes', agreed Ben, 'It's just as well he's a man of such strong principles who's prepared to take charge of a serious situation with great determination. Many officers would have huffed and puffed and let things be, sentiments would have festered. At least what he did was clear and decisive and everyone knew who was in charge. I daresay the military will be upset about being disarmed although I gather that all bar five of them have their arms back now, and apart from those five they have all once again sworn their loyalty to the King'.

'It's the right time for us to move on; you've said that you long to be back at sea, and I long to see my family and introduce you and Thomas to them'.

'You have your ticket of leave which declares you are a free person. Mr King has written to the Governor in Port Jackson. All we can do now is to wait for a ship to arrive'.

The following day the Lieutenant Governor responded to Ben's question saying;

'Well, Luckett, I have an unpleasant feeling that the affair of the mutiny and the steps I took to regain control, will not be approved by Major Grose. He sits in Port Jackson supposing that everything here is exactly the same as there; he has no idea except that the whole enterprise is a complete waste of effort and that his actions should therefore be focussed simply at enriching himself and his fellow officers. He doesn't even understand the basic principle of treating other people like human beings, recognising that sometimes they fail, often through no fault of their own. Above all he can't see that many of his officers and soldiers are themselves drawn from the scum of the earth and only escaped being convicts by volunteering as soldiers. And he cannot understand the concept of delegated authority – or certainly not in the way the navy sees it. He will probably judge that I should not have left the island to return the New Zealanders, without his prior permission, never recognising that communication between here and Port Jackson is irregular and unpredictable. We have to take our chances. He probably thinks that I should have asked his permission before taking steps to deal with the riot and mutiny. What a stupid, narrow minded and selfish man'.

'I've said more than I should have done, Luckett; but I rely upon your discretion as usual. My gout leaves me in almost permanent pain and recently I've been suffering from some severe stomach pains as well; it doesn't improve my temper. Now I'd better get on with those letters before something else intervenes'.

Ben withdrew, expressing his, and Sally's, thanks to him. He was due on the beach to help launch the boat, scheduled to go out fishing, and then he must go to Queenborough so that he could report to the Lieutenant Governor about the harvest and how the ground was being prepared for the next crop. He would pass by two of the sawpits on his way and would, probably, find Richard Morgan pulling the saw in one of them; but it would be good to find out how the supply of timber for building was – although there were just about enough houses for everyone, many were in an unsafe condition after five years, as timbers embedded in the ground had rotted, and in any case there was a school and orphanage to build, and a watermill, and a larger jail and penitentiary.

On 9th March the schooner Francis arrived and Ben was on the beach to welcome Lieutenant Townson who stepped first out of the boat. Ben saluted and asked the Lieutenant to follow him to Government House.

Mr King was at his most affable in greeting the Lieutenant. It was only later when Ben reported again to the Lieutenant Governor and saw the look of fury in his eyes that he learnt of the despatches brought by the Lieutenant.

'It is much as I had feared', he said to Ben. 'Townson has gone to the barracks to tell Lieutenant Abbott that he is taking over, and as if that were not outrageous enough, he has Grose's orders to commandeer any house he chooses and to demand that I allocate any cleared and cultivated twenty acre plot he chooses. That man has simply no idea about how to generate and sustain the sort of relationships between the military and the freemen without which our little society will fall apart. If you wanted to foster resentment this is a very good way to do it. Get your bags packed Luckett and be ready to sail with the Francis to Port Jackson; with any luck you can get away from there within a couple of months. And one of my letters will be to request my replacement and permission to return home for my health, though there is no hope of receiving a reply in less than a year'.

Definitely time to be moving on, thought Ben as he left the enraged Lieutenant Governor and went home to tell Sally to start packing their belongings and bid farewell to the good friends they had made during the previous two years.

But on the following day everything changed again. The Lieutenant Governor explained.

'I am afraid, Luckett, that amongst the despatches from Port Jackson I have a direct order from Grose telling me that I must allow no-one to leave the island without express permission from him. A few months back I would have been quite happy to let you go, as I have many others who had served their time or who were already free. But now that man has got it into his head to make everyone, regardless of their status, a prisoner at his behest, and I am afraid I simply cannot make an exception even of you. What I will do for you, though, is that I'll write to the Advocate General, the chief legal officer, and put your case to him in legal terms and ask him to be kind enough to press your case and secure approval. After that we can only wait for another ship and hope that you can secure a passage. I think Mr Collins might be helpful – he is a marine officer at heart, so he knows how a sailor's mind works and

I'm sure he will be sympathetic to your request to return home and get at the French'.

'Thank you, Sir. I will inform Sally that we'll stay put for the time being and hope to get away in the next ship'.

Chapter 15

Disappointment gave way to resignation as Ben and Sally settled back into the routine of life on the island. So often in life expectations are built up, perhaps as a sudden opportunity seems to offer the lucky break one could only hope for, only to be dashed by solemn reality forcing one to draw on all one's resources of resilience.

'It's no good feeling sorry for ourselves', said Ben to Sally. 'The fact is that we can't go now, so we may as well settle down and make the most of things here while we wait for the next chance. Who knows, it could be in the next month or two. And, anyway, let's not forget that we're quite reasonably comfortable here; it's definitely better for Thomas than being at sea and possibly better than being back home in Buckinghamshire'.

'But I am so anxious about father and mother and the rest of the family. I'm sure they'll be worrying about me, as I worry about them, and I fear that if I don't go home soon I may never see them again, and they will've died believing I'm some sort of monster'.

'You worry too much my love. Let God carry the weight of your concerns; serve him and go on loving your friends and neighbours – and me and Thomas – as you so obviously do, and all will be well'.

Life continued much as before and Ben was kept busy by the Lieutenant Governor, visiting the other parts of the island and acting as his eyes and ears as he sat at home suffering increasingly from gout. Sally looked after Norfolk and Sydney King as much as she could, whilst baby Thomas, now over a year old, was growing fast. And in February Sally was confident enough to tell Ben that she was pregnant again and that he could expect another child in October.

The flax manufactory at Phillipburgh continued to make progress as the women who worked there became more adept at stripping the leaves and exposing the fibres, using the edge of a shell which was sharp and light enough to be effective. But weaving remained a significant problem and they could still only make very poor quality canvas. The wharf at

Cascade had been washed away and rebuilt a second time with a more effective crane, designed by Nat Lucas so that it could be removed when not in use, and it had proved its worth in making it much easier to lift casks and bales out of the boats. William Chapman had proved himself a rather disinterested storekeeper and there were always rumours of things going missing or being incorrectly counted. He spent most of his time with the King family and was clearly a firm favourite with Mrs King and with the young Phillip. D'Arcy Wentworth at Queenborough took every opportunity to make it clear that his role as Superintendent was really far beneath his dignity and that he only continued to do it out of respect for the Lieutenant Governor. Everyone knew that when a sentence of flogging had been handed out he, as Assistant Surgeon, would invariably make sure that the punishment was stopped after only a few lashes.

Apart from the wharf at Cascade Bay, Nat Lucas had built a system for a mill to be powered by six men operating a cranked handle, but this had proved very inefficient and he began working to design and build a waterwheel. He had discussed with the Lieutenant Governor how to make use of the head of water which had been created by the dam at the top of Arthur's Vale. He had never seen a water wheel but imagined how it might work and after a certain amount of trial and error he built a small prototype, five feet in diameter, which the Lieutenant Governor described as an overshot mill. He built a channel for water to be released from the dam, falling some ten feet into the cups of the wheel. When he was satisfied that the design would work he built another wheel seven feet in diameter which was then linked to a millstone and eventually enabled enough wheat to be ground for the whole community. It did away with the need to use the hand powered querns which had been the only alternative up to that point.

The Lieutenant Governor was always worried about the amount of food in the various stores and was determined to have at least six month's supply secured. He arranged to buy surplus wheat and maize from the farmers and as the supply of salt beef ran low he bought pork to issue instead. Pigs were a very good source of meat and gradually the number on the island grew. A volunteer agreed to go with his family to Phillip Island with some pigs and to look after them there. They very quickly multiplied and provided further security for the meat supply.

The northerly gales of May and June did some damage, but the crops were planted well and promised to yield a good harvest, if only the weeds could be kept down. The acting Governor in Port Jackson had ordered that Lieutenant Townson as commanding officer of the detachment should be allocated ten convicts to work his land, and other officers five each, so the number available to work the government land was reduced, and a greater proportion of the overall supply of wheat for the government's store would need to be bought from the officers and free settlers.

In July the schooner Francis returned to the island and brought both good and bad news. The bad news for the settlers was that acting Governor Grose ordered that the government should not pay for the 11,476 bushels of wheat purchased by Lieutenant Governor King with a view to supplying Port Jackson. Clearly the acting Governor's army friends in Sydney wanted to protect the lucrative business they had established by importing from India and selling in Port Jackson. Mr King had immediately to issue an order to inform everyone that no further purchases of wheat would be possible which caused great disappointment and frustration. The good news was that convicts who had served their time could be permitted to return to Port Jackson. Here was the chance which Ben and Sally had looked for, with the hope that they could persuade the acting Governor in Port Jackson that they should be allowed home so that Ben could fight the French.

On 22nd July, Ben and Sally duly bade farewell to all their friends on Norfolk Island, with much sadness at the parting and a hope that perhaps one day some of them might meet again. Sally knew that it was not only other convicts to whom she owed a debt of gratitude, people like Olivia Lucas, who had helped her during the past two years, but also Mrs King who had been so understanding and sympathetic, without being puffed up or pompous. She had always made it clear to Sally that she cared for her as a person, but also that she expected a fair day's work from her and a clear commitment that she would be responsible for Norfolk and Sydney. Leaving those two boys behind was one of the most difficult partings for they had grown to love Sally and she them, and she cared very much for their future. But life is full of partings and she had to remind herself that she had Thomas upon whom she could still lavish attention and focus her love, and they, Norfolk and Sydney, would have each other and would be given a proper education by their father so that they could get on in life.

There were others too who they were very sorry to leave. Nathaniel Lucas, of course, was such a fine example of a steady and reliable character that it was a mystery how he ever came to be in court, let alone found guilty and transported, and his skill with plane and chisel was a true joy to see. Richard Morgan, a silent man, but as good a friend as any could want, looked after himself quietly and with dignity whilst caring deeply for those who had shown him friendship, and if you watched him re-set a saw or strip and re-build a musket you knew you were seeing a real professional at work. John Mortimer had arrived at Norfolk Island with resentment for his treatment and an apparent determination not to submit, but had recognised that there was an easier way to live and that reasonable hard work, far from being harmful, provided the means to self-improvement and financial gain, which was much less painful than breaking law and convention and being caught. But above all both Ben and Sally felt a profound sadness at leaving the Lieutenant Governor. Mr King was perhaps rather prone to fits of temper and he did like rather too much port, but he was an honest man who believed passionately in the underlying goodness of everyone. They knew that he had so often given people a second, or third, chance to lead honest and hard-working lives, and it was easy to hear his frustration when a particular person proved incapable of recognising the opportunity he or she had been given. He had a deep sense of what was right based on his very strong Christian beliefs, redemption through Jesus Christ, love of all people, regardless of their status in society or their colour, and many people would see that as weakness in a senior officer. Nonetheless he had shown himself quite capable of acting in a decisive, principled and firm way, for example, in honouring his commitment to the Maoris despite the possibility of rebuke from Port Jackson, and in dealing quickly and firmly with the mutiny which could so easily have got out of hand. Ben and Sally, like the others who were able to see him in his true colours, were profoundly grateful to him, respected him and would follow and support him without question. Now they were stepping back into the unknown, trusting in their own resourcefulness, and taking total responsibility for their own and their children's lives.

'I know it was me who insisted that we head back to England', said Sally, as they settled into the small space they had been allocated aboard the Francis, 'but I must admit that I'm a bit scared at what might lie ahead. We've an awfully long journey and goodness knows what we'll find when we get home. Perhaps England will have been invaded by the French or something dreadful'.

'We've been very lucky, you and I', replied Ben, 'for we'd never have met if you hadn't been transported, and that your first husband drowned, and that you met Ann and her children, and that I happened to have come out with the Kings. That is a very long set of coincidences – if only one of them had not happened we wouldn't be here together, loving one another and being blessed with our child. Call it luck, if you like, but I would prefer to think that the hand of God has a lot to do with it – that he actually does love us and know what's best for us. Stick to his laws of love and he'll look after you even though it may feel a bit cruel at the time, like when the judge in Aylesbury sentenced you to seven years. And, right now, pray for His further loving guidance and protection'.

Ten days later they arrived at Port Jackson and faced the immediate prospect of finding somewhere to stay. They knew that Mr King would never suggest that they get close to the acting Governor, Major Grose, but he had suggested that they should make contact with the Advocate General Captain David Collins. He was likely to be more sympathetic to a sailor than Major Grose or any of the army, and his position of Advocate General might enable him to ensure that nothing was put in the way of Ben and Sally returning to England so that Ben could help fight the French. Ben took Mr King's letter and found himself being very warmly received; temporary accommodation was found.

Having settled Sally and Thomas, Ben went exploring the ships in the harbour, to see whether he could find some work there. He might be able to sign up as a seaman in a ship which would take them back to England, work his passage, and save himself and Sally the cost of the voyage. Down in the anchorage he found Britannia which he had been aboard when she sailed from Norfolk to the Bay of Islands with Tooke and Huru. There he found the Master, Mr Raven, who greeted him warmly, expressing surprise at seeing him in Port Jackson. Ben told him of his intention to return home and asked what Mr Raven's plans were.

'My next trip will be to the Cape to see what I can buy there to sell here. I would be delighted to take you that far but you would have to take pot luck from the Cape to England, although there are usually a good number of sailings of East Indiamen'.

'How soon are you likely to sail?' asked Ben.

'As soon as I can, and in any event within the next month', replied the master.

'I think that might not work for us. Sally is likely to give birth in the next two or three weeks and I would prefer that to happen ashore than at sea. Do you know about the movements of any of the other ships?'

'The Speedy won't be much good to you. Mr Melville has told me that he's going on another fishing trip and is unlikely to be going back to England for a while yet – and anyway you would be very uncomfortable aboard a little ship like that. I have heard that the Daedalus may be away in the next few months. Lieutenant Hanson the naval agent told me the Governor wants them to go to Norfolk and back before making for home'.

Ben thanked Mr Raven for the information, wished him well in his next venture and departed. He headed for the Daedalus and asked to see Lieutenant Hanson.

'What can I do for you, Luckett?' asked that officer.

'I was hoping I might do something for you, Sir', replied Ben. 'I am a seaman of some experience having served under Captain Nelson in Boreas and more recently with Captain Parker in Gorgon when she brought Lieutenant Governor and Mrs King back from England in 91. I have been acting as one of Mr King's assistants on Norfolk Island for the past three years and I am now anxious to get back to England and help deal with the French. What chance might there be of working a passage aboard the Daedalus with my wife and, I hope, two children?'

'That is indeed an interesting proposition. I daresay I could prevail upon the master to fit you in. I believe he is somewhat short of skilled seamen. How would Bosun sound'.

'I should do that, as I have always done, to the best of my ability, Sir'.

'I'll speak to the master shortly. A wife and two children you say?'

'Well only one at the moment, Sir, but a second is like to be born any day now'.

'Fine. We'll be sailing for a round trip to Norfolk before setting off for home. Probably in the next week or two, so we would need you aboard as soon as you can. Can you be here tomorrow? Come down with your kit and in the meantime I will see the master. It'll be good to have another skilled seaman onboard'.

'Aye, aye, Sir. I'll be back with my kit tomorrow. Thank you'. And with that Ben departed, feeling that he had achieved as good a deal as he could have hoped for.

Sally was not best pleased to lose him so soon but realised the benefits of him working their passage. She would miss him when their child was born, but it would be more important to have some sympathetic women around her to act as midwives. She had to admit that a skilled seaman was probably more use at sea than in a nursery.

The Daedalus sailed, with Ben aboard, on 26th September by which time he had got to know the rest of the crew. As Bosun he would be keeping watches opposite the mate so he needed to be thoroughly familiar with how this particular ship sailed and how much sail could be carried in any particular wind. Apart from being loaded with provisions for the island and a small amount of clothing and tools, they were carrying a detachment of 51 privates of the NSW Regiment, with three corporals and a subaltern.

Ben was able to talk to the subaltern about life at Port Jackson. 'It's very boring for us, and pretty pointless', answered the subaltern. 'There is no real enemy to fight and we act more like policemen than soldiers. There is not any chance of earning a decent amount of money whilst we're here either, although Lieutenant Macarthur seems to have wound things up a bit. He's organised for the officers to have a monopoly in the supply of rum. Every ship that arrives is visited first by him and he buys everything onboard which is for sale. He'll then sell it on for two or three hundred per cent profit – he's getting rich.'

'But what about the settlers and the convicts?' asked Ben innocently.

'Well no-one cares about the convicts anyway – they're only here to rot. And as for the settlers, well they have to take their chance; they pay the price or go without.'

'And I suppose the next thing you're going to tell me is that all they end up buying is the rum, they get drunk out of their minds and then do things they subsequently regret'.

'Yes, that's about it. I bought ten acres off one settler who'd got into debt because he bought too much rum. Now he works for me, doing the farming, and I pay him as little as I can get away with – just enough to encourage him to do the work. He buys grain and meat from me and I sell the surplus. It looks like being a nice little earner for me; and he's getting all the rum he wants.'

'Well you'll find things very different on Norfolk Island. Lieutenant Governor King encourages all the convicts to work for themselves as well as for the government and some of them have become very important, especially those with a trade. And the settlers get fair prices for anything they buy which comes ashore, and now I know why there's so little. MacArthur has bought it all in Port Jackson before it gets a chance to reach Norfolk'.

'Well, fortunately, I'm not staying on Norfolk Island; I'll return to Port Jackson. I see it a bit like a jungle – survival of the fittest. As long as I can stay alive and don't get some horrible disease or find myself at the wrong end of someone's knife, I want to be able to go home with money in my pocket and a good number of bills that I can call for payment back in London'.

'At least you know what your priorities are; I'll grant you that', said Ben, 'but I can't accept that way of life, where you are prepared to walk over anyone who gets in your way. A proper life is better than that – it may not end with great riches, but it is more likely to be happy and content'.

That was the end of that conversation and it was clear enough that the two men were going to agree to differ. The refusal to pay for the maize which Mr King had 'bought' from the settlers had caused an enormous upset and had been a great blow to the morale of the settlers. 'What's the point', they all said, 'if we can only grow food for ourselves and never sell any surplus. How can we clothe ourselves? How can we ever have any enjoyment? How can we buy tools and cooking pots?' Several of the former marines who had chosen to become settlers had now decided to sell up and enlist in the New South Wales Regiment.

The Daedalus discharged the provisions which had been sent and then began loading up with a quantity of timber, some of which had already been made into oars, but mostly beams and planks for building. In due course 42 soldiers were embarked together with 50 emancipated convicts and a few others. Lieutenant Governor King had completed a bundle of despatches for Port Jackson and had entrusted Ben with a box of papers and samples for him to deliver in London, whenever the ship might arrive there. After just a month anchored off the island the weather looked fair and the Daedalus weighed and set sail for Port Jackson.

After another uneventful voyage, happily much shorter and calmer than when Ben had last left Norfolk Island, the Daedalus entered Port Jackson and came to anchor off Bennelong Point. The soldiers and other passengers had to be disembarked first before Ben could get ashore to find Sally and Thomas. He was very happy that both were in fine form and that baby Sarah had arrived just two weeks previously, and seemed to be a very happy little soul, feeding well and putting on weight as rapidly as one might hope. Sally was relieved to see Ben again and their embrace was warm, loving and close. This was a real man, thought Sally, he smells good, and feels good, and raises my spirits so that I feel wonderfully happy that he is here; how fortunate I am.

Life aboard Daedalus was very busy over the next three weeks as everything was prepared for the voyage back to England. Supplies were laid in and partitions built to allow at least some privacy to the passengers. But Ben was able to live ashore with Sally and began to get to know Sarah, but there was little time to make connections with the people living in and around Port Jackson. They did manage to find Ann Inett who had married a convict called John Robinson with whom she was running an inn in Sydney. Ann was delighted to see Sally and to hear about her own two sons and how they were getting on in Norfolk Island.

By 15th December the Luckett family was established onboard the Daedalus and the acting Governor Major Francis Grose came aboard as a passenger, with Mr Bain, one of the chaplains and Mr Laing one of the Assistant Surgeons. The ship weighed anchor at midday and made sail down the harbour and out into the Tasman Sea through the Heads. Sally thought back to the time she had first entered the harbour, locked below in the Lady Penrhyn, at the end of a dreadful voyage. This time it would be different; she was free, and could move about the ship provided only that she kept out of the way of the working of the sails.

The master had decided that he would take the route south from Port Jackson heading at once for the westerlies of the southern ocean to carry the ship around Cape Horn. It was cold and rough but they kept up a good pace and avoided any mishaps. Ben decided that he would focus firmly upon his duties and make no particular attempt to engage with the other passengers with the exception of Mr Bain. He was nervous about finding himself in any discussion with Major Grose, knowing as he did the antipathy which existed between him and Lieutenant Governor King. In any case in such spare time as he had he was keen to engage with his little son Thomas and encourage him to understand a little of the way of life at sea.

They called briefly at Capetown to take on water and some fresh food and continued northwards hoping to avoid any French or Spanish privateers. Their luck held and at the beginning of June 1795 Start Point was sighted and they had a fair southwesterly to take them up channel to the mouth of the Thames. A few days later they were berthed comfortably at Deptford and the passengers were able to disembark. Ben was paid off and given a ticket of leave and he and his family set off quickly from Deptford to avoid any risk of an over-enthusiastic press-gang capturing Ben before he had seen Sally and the children back home.

The first stop was Westminster to enable Ben to deliver Lieutenant Governor King's box of despatches to the Admiralty. He needed also to contact Mr James Sykes, Mr King's agent, and give him some letters, and enquire whether Governor Phillip was in London.

At the Admiralty Ben asked for the office of Mr Evan Nepean, the Secretary. He felt somewhat out of his depth in such a grand place where all the decisions about the navy were taken and he was very conscious of the bustle, and coming and going of officers in uniforms, mostly Captains and Admirals, looking very much as if they owned the place. Eventually he was taken into a waiting room and seemed to be in a queue of people apparently waiting for Mr Nepean. He was a little surprised to be called forward more quickly than he had expected and was ushered into a comfortable room with a large desk. Mr Nepean, he supposed, stood up as Ben entered.

'Good day to you, Luckett. I hear you have some papers for me from Commander King'.

'That's right Sir; I have this box which Mr King entrusted to me before I left Norfolk in Daedalus. He asked me to hand it to you and give you his warmest compliments'.

'Thank you very much for that, I shall take great delight in finding what he has sent me, for I feel sure there will be some samples of Norfolk Island produce as well as papers. But tell me, how is Mr King'.

'Well, Sir, he manages very well despite suffering considerably from the gout which causes him a great deal of pain, as you may imagine. But Norfolk Island under his management is a fine place where everyone can thrive and have a role to play. The climate is quite pleasant except for the occasional gales, and the soil is wonderfully productive so that even a sailor like me can soon have a garden with cabbages, beans and potatoes. I've found him to be a very fine man to work for and I hope perhaps I may one day have the privilege of serving under him again'.

'That's good to hear. So do we need to bring him home to recover from the gout or will he stay?'

'That's hardly for me to say, Sir, but if I may be so bold, I daresay you may find amongst those letters a request from him to return home on account of his health, but I know he's such a man as would never wish to seek special favours'.

'Thank you Luckett, you've put that very well and kindly. And may we expect further service from you in this war?'

'Yes Sir, absolutely. I hope at once to take my wife and family to her home in Buckinghamshire and then to seek a position in one of His Majesty's ships. I would most like to serve again under Captain Nelson who I was with in the Boreas. He taught me much and gave me great encouragement and it was only the peace which took me to Botany Bay in 90'.

'Well your friend Nelson is commanding Agamemnon in the Mediterranean at the present time, and I have no doubt that if you find yourself a passage to Leghorn he'll be very pleased to see you. As you'd expect, Nelson doesn't stay idle for long. But there are many other ships out there so you'll have no difficulty in finding a berth and I'm sure any captain will be delighted to have onboard a man of your experience'.

And with a further shake of the hand it was clear that the interview was over.

From the Admiralty it was only a few minutes' walk up the Strand to Arundel Street, where Mr Sykes had his office. The letters were delivered, Mr Sykes asked after Mr and Mrs King, and Ben gave a complimentary report with a brief description of how matters stood upon the island. He then asked Mr Sykes whether he knew the whereabouts of Governor Phillip for he had letters from Mr King for him. Sykes thought for a moment and then said that he had a feeling that he had moved to Bath which was a favourite place for naval officers to go to recover after a period at sea or abroad; he suggested that Ben should entrust the letters to him and he would undertake to make sure they reached Captain Phillip.

'That's very considerate of you', replied Ben, 'but Mr King specifically asked me to go to find him. I think he wants me to talk to Captain Phillip and give him a first hand account of how things are and tell him some things which Mr King could not write about.'

Ben went on to ask Mr Sykes about the war against France and how things were with the navy's role.

'The greatest threat at the moment is that the French might try to invade, and to prevent that we have to keep control of the Channel. We also need to keep as many of the French ships as possible blockaded in their ports. So the Channel Fleet spends a lot of time at sea guarding the French port of Brest, while the Mediterranean fleet is blockading Toulon. We have about 80 ships of the line either at sea or in the dockyards preparing for sea which presents a huge supply problem, and keeping the sea-lanes open is vital. In Britain we don't have enough timber, flax, hemp and tar to sustain the fleet, so we have to protect the sea routes to be sure of receiving enough of such vital commodities. It's a massive task and the government is always complaining about having insufficient money to pay for it all and therefore the need to raise taxes'.

'So there shouldn't be much difficulty for me to get back to sea?' suggested Ben.

'Not at all. In fact if you were to hang around the docksides here in London for too long you would very quickly be picked up by one of the Press gangs and find yourself aboard some ship or other'.

'Well, I'd far rather choose which ship to serve in – and which Captain. I was with Captain Nelson in the West Indies and would follow him to the end of the earth. He may be small but there's just something about him which is hugely inspiring. He'll talk to everyone and even as a lowly sailor you felt that he was genuinely interested in you. In fact in my case he arranged for my schooling and it's through him that I learnt to read and write, and the basics of navigation. If I could get into his ship again I would be a happy man'.

'I believe he's out in the Mediterranean now commanding the Agamemnon. He had hoped, they say, for a second rate, but he did not impress the Admirals when he was in the West Indies, so they've held him back. Having said that I daresay, given his reputation, that he'll have made the Agamemnon one of the most efficient and happy ships in the fleet. You might be able to find a way of working a passage out there aboard one of the schooners or transports which sail regularly from London, Portsmouth and Plymouth'.

'I'll take my family back to their roots first and make sure they're established there and then get out to the Mediterranean and see if I can find Captain Nelson or someone else like him. Thank you very much for your time and advice. And just in case I should ever have need of an Agent would you be willing to act for me in that capacity?'

'Any friend of Mr King is a friend of mine. Please write to me at any time and I will be glad to act for you to claim prize money or negotiate bills and the like'.

Ben departed feeling that he had fulfilled at least a part of the mission he had been set by Lieutenant Governor King on Norfolk Island. He would need to travel to Bath at some point, and then, hopefully, he could find a commission which would take him out to the Mediterranean.

But first he must take Sally and the children to Buckinghamshire.

Part Three - Mediterranean Romance

Chapter 16

Chackmore is a small village a little to the south of the great Stowe House. The green rolling fields and woods of Buckinghamshire were a contrast to the world of sand dunes, marsh and creeks with the smell of the sea where Ben had grown up. The village was a collection of small houses, many built of wattle and daub in the old fashion and then in brick around a timber frame, and the most modern ones entirely of brick. This was where Sally had been born and spent her childhood. The whole village belonged to the Marquess of Buckingham, the owner of the big house, who was a friend of King George and a member of the House of Lords. He had been Lord Lieutenant of Ireland, acting there for the King, but by 1789 had become rather unpopular and had returned to England. The great house at Stowe had been built a century earlier but had been repeatedly modified and enlarged by the Marquess's forbears so that it was now one of the greatest houses in England. The gardens at Stowe had been laid out in the early part of the century and visitors had come to enjoy it since 1717. The Head Gardener was a very important person at Stowe and he controlled and managed about 70 under-gardeners amongst whom was Sally's father, who had grown up at Chackmore and worked in the gardens all his life.

The joy with which Jack and Sarah Grover greeted their daughter was wonderful to see. After so many years during which they had received no news her arrival home with two beautiful children and a husband who looked strong and intelligent, was an event wholly beyond their wildest dreams. The tears of surprise and happiness which flowed from mother and daughter dissolved the potential for tension between them after so long away, while the two men formed an immediate bond despite their very different backgrounds and life experiences. Within a few days it seemed as though Sally had never been away, and Ben fitted in as a member of the family within the little community.

But he was immediately restless. He knew he must travel to Bath and seek out Captain Phillip, and must then fulfil the commitment he had made to rejoin the navy and fight the French. He was quite confident about leaving Sally and the children at Chackmore even though they would be obliged to live for the time being with her parents. He was determined to return from the Mediterranean with enough prize money to enable them to have a house of their own. He was thrilled too that Sally's third pregnancy was proceeding well and she looked a picture of health and happiness.

One day early in the New Year of 1796 Ben was in the garden helping his father-in-law when they were approached by the Head Gardener.

'Good morning, Luckett', he began on seeing Ben, 'I am grateful to you for lending a hand. We never seem to have quite enough people to get through all the work and make sure the place looks good, as well as providing all the fruit and vegetables for the house.'

'I am always keen to learn new skills,' replied Ben, 'and welcome the opportunity to do something useful at the same time'.

'Well, I'm glad to have found you anyway', continued the Head Gardener, 'Mr Sharp, his Lordship's agent, was saying only this morning that he could do with finding a naval man to take some of his Lordship's letters out to the Mediterranean. I told him you were here and seemed a pretty solid sort of a sailor. So I suggest you get up to the house and find him and see what he wants'.

'That sounds very interesting. I'll be glad to get in out of the cold and delighted to be on the move towards the warmer climate of Spain or Italy'.

Ben went off to find Mr Sharp who he ran to earth in a small office in the basement of the house. He was a large and rather florid man who looked as though he was quite accustomed to good living and avoided all exercise if he possibly could.

'So you are Luckett, are you?' he began.

'Yes Sir'.

'Tell me a bit about yourself and why I should entrust his Lordship's letters to you'.

That was an opening to which Ben was very pleased to reply, and he recounted his career, emphasising how much he had been taught while serving under Captain Nelson, and how he had sailed to Botany Bay with Lieutenant Governor King and had served as one of his most trusted assistants on Norfolk Island.

'I still have letters from Mr King to deliver to Captain Phillip, who was Governor in New South Wales, and I have been puzzling how to get to Bath where I believe him to be. If it suited you, Sir, I could perhaps visit Bath and then continue down the west road to Plymouth and pick up a schooner or trading vessel there. But most importantly I shall need a pretty strong letter or passport to make sure I can avoid the interest of the press gangs in Plymouth'.

'Excellent', replied Mr Sharp. 'How soon can you start? If you go to Buckingham you will be able to pick up a carriage going south or west. I'll arrange for you to have sufficient funds for your transport and for your passage. And while your wife is living on the estate we can make sure she's properly looked after too; Grover's a good man. But I haven't told you where I want you to go'. He paused for moment as if he needed to re-fuel for the next few sentences. 'You're required to find a ship called Inconstant, a frigate, commanded by Captain Thomas Fremantle. We don't know exactly where she will be, of course, but she's most likely to be somewhere near Corsica, Leghorn or Naples. The British fleet is blockading the French in Toulon so if you take passage on one of the vessels going out to the fleet, you will quickly discover where to find Inconstant and Fremantle. You should be aware that the Fremantle family has been very helpful to his Lordship, especially when he was Lord Lieutenant in Ireland, and he's anxious to continue to be of service to them. Once you've found him I suggest you offer him your services as I've no doubt he'll be able to make use of another experienced sailor in some capacity'.

'That sounds excellent and is just the sort of thing I was hoping for. I don't need much time to prepare as Mrs Luckett has known all along that I shall be going away at some point. How about me setting off the day after tomorrow if the weather doesn't look too bad'.

'Good. Come to me in the morning and I'll have the package ready for you and a letter to show any press officer, to allow you to continue. And we can deal with the money then too'.

'Thank you, Sir'. And with a light heart Ben left and headed for home to tell Sally and her mother the news.

There were protests, of course. Ben had expected those. But he and Sally had talked about something like this many times before, so it was certainly no surprise. Over the next 24 hours Ben made sure he was as well prepared as possible and that the kit he already had was in good order with all repairs completed, and he walked up to the house to find the agent. The business was done and a bag of letters was handed over to Ben with some coins and some small value bills which Ben would be able to change for money at a suitable banking house over the next few years. By ten in the morning he had returned to Chackmore on his way to Buckingham. He called at the cottage, kissed his two children, politely shook the hand of his mother-in-law and embraced Sally giving her a long and lingering kiss which he hoped they would both be able to remember until his return. Then he hoisted his kit bag onto his shoulder and set off at a brisk pace down the road to Buckingham.

He knew the coach was due to depart for Oxford at midday and to reach its destination about four hours later. He expected from there to be able to connect with another coach to Cirencester or perhaps even the whole way to Bath.

A few days later Ben reached Bath, the weather having been reasonably kind for the time of year. After a little detective work in the city he found that Captain Phillip had moved to live in Bathampton a mile or so outside the city. The Phillip household was busy when he arrived since after a period of illness and recuperation the Captain had finally been given a command and he would be leaving very shortly. Nonetheless he found the time to see Ben and receive the package of letters from Lieutenant Governor King about whom he asked affectionately. Ben re-assured him that he had left the Kings in good heart with two children, and that although King's health was not good he was determined to remain in post until duly relieved.

His duty done in Bath, Ben took to the roads again and began the journey down to Plymouth. He had not been there for more than a few days before he found a small trading vessel due to sail for the Mediterranean with supplies for the British fleet, which the master expected to find off Toulon blockading the French, or possibly at Leghorn.

Once again Ben was at sea, heading for a new destination and another adventure.

Chapter 17

Some weeks later the little ship in which Ben was a passenger reached the Mediterranean and headed north-east towards Toulon to find the British fleet which, the master had been informed, would be blockading the French. After unloading the supplies and delivering mail to the fleet she was ordered back to Gibraltar to collect dockyard supplies and fresh water. Ben had found no sign of the Inconstant with the fleet and no clear advice as to how he might make his way in her direction wherever that might be. But after the second visit to the blockading fleet Ben's ship was sent to Leghorn.

She arrived in the Italian port in early June of 1796 and found the place a hive of activity. British ships were coming and going, supplies being landed and then often quickly trans-shipped to be taken out to the fleet. Warships came in from time to time, especially frigates bringing in the French coastal traders which they had captured. Ben made contact with the British Consul in Leghorn, John Udney, who treated him with great kindness and consideration.

'I am delighted to welcome you to Leghorn', he said. 'I know Captain Fremantle well; he's one of our best customers. I feel sure he'll not be long arriving here and I've no doubt he'll be very happy to see you'.

'But look out', he went on, 'the French are coming and it won't be long before they get to us here in Tuscany the way things are going at the moment. I've asked for as many ships as possible to come here to take away all our British people and stores before the damned French arrive'.

It was quite true that there seemed to be hundreds of ships in what was not a very large port. As soon as one ship was loaded it was cast off and sent to anchor out in the harbour mouth until a convoy could be made up. Within a few days a frigate arrived which Ben soon realised was Inconstant. His expert eye ran over the rigging as she came into harbour and he watched the performance of the topmen as they furled the sails, and he concluded that this was an efficient and well-run crew.

As soon as opportunity arose he went onboard with his bag of despatches from Stowe.

'I have despatches to deliver to the Captain', he declared as he stepped onboard. One of the Midshipmen came forward and gestured him to follow.

'What is your name?' asked the young man.

'Luckett, Ben Luckett', answered Ben, 'Seaman, most recently from Stowe in Buckinghamshire but previously from Norfolk Island in the Pacific. Served under Captain Nelson in the West Indies, and a Norfolk man'. Ben had given an outline of his life in a few brief words. They arrived at the Captain's cabin where the marine sentry barred their way. The Midshipman knocked on the door and was replied with a lively 'Come in'.

'Wait here a moment', said the midshipman to Ben as he went inside. A moment or two later he came out and invited Ben to step forward. Ben entered the cabin and came face to face with Captain Thomas Fremantle. He was a man of medium height with a roundish face which smiled in welcome, well built but not fat, and he had sparkling alert eyes which immediately captivated Ben and made him think that this was someone who meant business.

'Good day Mr Luckett', said Fremantle, 'I hear you have some papers for me'.

'Aye, Sir, I have. And I have also come to offer myself as a volunteer if you can use my services'.

'We're always short of good men', said Fremantle, 'so I expect we can find a berth for you. What have you done until now'.

Ben embarked upon a slightly longer version of his career than he had given the midshipman emphasising the fact that he had served under Captain Nelson where he had learnt the basics of navigation, and had then gone to Norfolk Island to serve Commander King who became Lieutenant Governor of the island.

'I think perhaps I could rate you Master's Mate while we see what you can do. Do you seek a commission?'

'No, Sir. I have never thought of myself as an officer, but if I can serve under a fine officer and enable him to do even better I shall be very satisfied. It was an enormous privilege to serve Mr King, as fine a gentleman as I ever came across; he inspired everyone who was prepared to work hard – and it was hard on Norfolk Island, as you never knew what to expect. And those who would not work hard got the thick end of his tongue and quite often rather more. He was always having new ideas, and encouraging everyone else the same'.

'Sounds very much like me. Can't stand an idler; too many things to do for anyone to sit around doing nowt. So get along and find the First Lieutenant and tell him we've met. Then see the Master and get going. I'll see you again before long I don't doubt'.

'Aye aye, Sir,' replied Ben as he turned and left the cabin. He returned to the gangway and soon found the First Lieutenant, Mr Hutchinson, was directed to the Purser's office to draw his hammocks, and to the Master to report for duty. It all seemed entirely familiar to him, as though he had come home. He had been taking in the appearance of the ship as he went around, noticing how few frayed ropes there seemed to be, how well everything had been stowed, how clean the decks were, and how little it seemed to smell between decks, despite the warmth of the weather.

At the first opportunity he went ashore and collected his bag and paid off his lodgings, pleased to note that he still had a few pounds left from the money he had been given at Stowe. Over the next few days he got to know other crew members especially the Bosun and the Bosun's mates. He talked to everyone he could find who could tell him something about the way the ship sailed, what sails it could carry under what conditions of wind, how close to the wind it could sail, how it worked in a sea, trying to learn as much as he could so that when at sea for the first time he would have a good idea how best to make Inconstant sail well.

Late on 23rd June the Captain warned the ship's company to expect even more activity on the following day since orders were being given for the evacuation of British citizens from Florence. People began to come onboard early the following day, directed to the ship by the Consul. Here was a gentleman, slim and good-looking, but quite elderly, with his wife who was elegant and a little haughty with rather darker skin than would have been customary had she been a native of Norfolk. And there were four daughters, the older two were in their late teens, he judged, and there was not a man onboard that didn't look up as they arrived, smiling, laughing and joking about something which clearly only they understood. The other two girls were children of around 12, high-spirited for sure but lacking the elegance and beauty of their older sisters.

A little later Ben was summoned again into the Captain's cabin.

'Ah, Luckett. I'd like you to meet Mr and Mrs Wynne and their daughters. They have just arrived from Florence which they left last night in rather more hurry than was desirable and they are taking passage aboard Inconstant. Will you please ask the First Lieutenant where he can create a cabin space for them and then help them to get comfortable. Make sure all their baggage is accounted for and that they have everything necessary for their comfort. We don't yet know how long they will be with us.'

'I apologise', the Captain went on, addressing Mr Wynne, 'that we're too small a ship to be able to offer you spacious accommodation, but you'll always be welcome in my cabin and will, of course, dine with me. And perhaps a little later we'll have occasion for some music and dancing'. As he said 'dancing' he smiled directly at the oldest of the four girls. Ben noticed that her smile in return contained a look of wonder which seemed to suggest that she saw the whole escapade as a huge adventure, with the Captain as the dark-eyed handsome hero who had rescued the ladies from the enemy in the nick of time.

Within a few minutes Ben had found the First Lieutenant.

'The carpenter is putting up some extra partitions for'ard of the starboard side cabins. Make up a couple of cots for the lady and gentleman and draw hammocks for the girls. You'll need to show them how to get in and out of them. They look fit enough so I don't suppose they will have too much trouble. That's all their kit, over there, in a pile.

Find out which of the bags they need and we'll stow the rest in the hold. Did the Captain say how long they'd be onboard?'

'No Sir he didn't. But surely it will not be more than a few days as we should be getting at the enemy not being a passenger vessel. Leave it to me, Sir and I will set them aright'.

And Ben was off again. He took a close look at the pile of baggage which consisted of four or five trunks; they might contain belongings which would not be needed but they would make useful tables or seats, and it would be better to keep everything out of the hold if possible as it would be less likely to get lost or damaged on the maindeck. He then went to see how the carpenter was getting on and find how long he expected to take; it should not really be more than a few minutes because the partitions were kept readily available and could be set up or taken down in a few minutes. If the Captain were to give the order to prepare for action, all partitions would be struck down to the hold with chests and suchlike which would get in the way in case of a fight. Once he had confirmed that the carpenter had nearly finished he returned to the Captain's cabin to collect the family and show them where they would be sleeping.

In reality it was only a few strides from the Captain's cabin to their quarters where he showed them how the cots could be slung. There would not be a lot of space, once the luggage had been brought in.

'This looks wonderful, doesn't it Mama', said a girl's voice behind Ben, 'I am sure we can make ourselves quite comfortable, don't you think?' Mama did not seem to be quite so sure, and only nodded assent.

'Betsey and Eugenia, will you please go with Luckett and tell him which of the bags is most necessary for us to have here and which can be sent below. I shall need my writing desk of course but not much else'. That was Mr Wynne, exerting a little authority over his family, although Ben thought he did not seem to be a particularly assertive gentleman.

'Follow me please, ladies, and we will find your luggage'.

As they went forward they passed through a welter of sailors rushing in every direction without any apparent order or logic, although the looks on their faces suggested that they all knew what they were doing, where they were going and why. They climbed the companionway to the upperdeck and Ben looked behind him to see how they were getting on in their long dresses – not an ideal garment for climbing up a steep stairway.

'When it comes to going back down again', said Ben, 'You will see that us sailors all go down facing forwards, but you will need to turn round and go a bit slower and backwards'.

'Can you teach us more about how the ship works and what everyone is doing, please', asked Betsey.

'Yes of course, but we need to get all this stuff stowed first and then I will show you around. Now which are the most important of the items for you to have to hand?'

'There's Father's writing desk', said Betsey, pointing to a rectangular wooden box made of nicely polished wood with a handsome brass handle at each end. When you looked closely you could see hinges on one of the long sides and a lock on the other so that it could open up to be used; it would need a table to stand on which did not seem to have been brought along. Then they identified four other boxes which they certainly needed to have with them; one of which was of a good size to make a seat or table.

'I think we could take one more large box', suggested Ben, 'so which shall it be?'

Betsey chose another box and Ben called on some sailors to give him a hand in taking the selected luggage below. Within a few minutes he had set it all down in the Wynne's new space, and they could begin to work out how best to arrange things.

'If you'll excuse me, Sir', said Ben to Mr Wynne, 'I'll go and secure the remainder of your things in the hold so that they're all together and can be found easily if you move elsewhere. I'll also get the cots and hammocks you'll need and bring them back to set them up'.

Ben was quickly off again and Betsey turned to her father, looking hugely excited. 'Isn't it wonderful, Papa. It is so far preferable to being with all those Italians who are always just a bit too charming, don't you think? Isn't Luckett a dear! And it is so clean everywhere. I always understood ships to be smelly places but this doesn't seem so at all'. The words poured out of her like water rippling along in a hillside stream. Clearly Mr Wynne was less convinced.

'I agree that we have been well-received so far', he said, 'but we will find it all rather more cramped than it was in the palazzo in Florence'.

'Yes, for sure. But I can't wait to get out to sea and feel the wind driving the ship along, and even trying to understand how it works and what all those miles of rope up there are for. I'm sure Luckett will tell us – he's very helpful and knows everything. Perhaps he will be our tutor which will be better than Mr Jaegle's lessons, don't you think Eugenia? And we'll be away from the clutches of Count Montenari, stupid man. Aren't you glad of that?'

Ben was back shortly with a large bundle of canvas, some mysterious pieces of wood and a length of rope. The girls watched intently as Ben put together the cots, and arranged for them to hang alongside each other from hooks in the beams above their heads.

'Will you show us, please, where we may go in the ship and how it works? Where can we see what is going on without getting in everyone's way?'

'With your permission, Sir', said Ben, addressing Mr Wynne.

'As long as you don't let them be a nuisance to you – or anyone else', he replied. So with the two younger girls, Justinia and Harriet, Ben led his four charges up again into the fresh air. First they went aft to the quarterdeck where Ben stood them by the ship's side and began explaining something of a sailor's language.

'You must know that bow and stern mean front and back. Larboard is left and starboard is right when facing the bow, for'ard'. And Ben continued to explain the names of the masts and the sails, halyards and braces, sheets and stays. He told them that the bell would be rung every half hour, and that at eight bells the watch would change and the cycle would start again. They looked at the wheel and the binnacle which held two compasses so that the helmsman could see the course to steer, whichever side of the wheel he stood. He told the girls that the best place for them to watch the ship's activities would be close to the ship's side and just abaft the mizzen mast.

A cry was heard, 'Luckett....' Ben stopped in mid-sentence to note where the call came from and saw the First Lieutenant by the gangway.

'Excuse me, ladies. It seems I am wanted by authority. I will catch up with you as soon as I can'.

The First Lieutenant wanted Ben to take two new arrivals, Miss Pollard and Miss Hood, below and organise for the carpenter to put up more screens for them.

That evening, as the activity slackened a little, music was heard from the Captain's cabin, with some singing and plenty of rippling young laughter. Mr Udney had sent a harpsichord onboard and it turned out that Betsey was able to play very nicely to amuse the Captain and his guests.

The following day was Sunday and once again the Inconstant was the centre of activity. The Wynne family and other guests dined with the Captain at 3 pm and he then informed them that they should transfer to a merchant ship, the Achilles, where Captain Parrish would take care of them. A convoy would sail at 3 the following morning and would take them to Corsica where they would be much safer. There they could stay until a passage could be arranged for them to return to England.

Ben was again involved in helping the family pack up again and transfer to the Achilles which lay close by.

'Do we really have to go, Papa? This is such a lovely ship and everyone is so wonderfully helpful and welcoming', said Betsey to her father. 'Could you persuade the Captain to let us stay'?

'I think not my dear. After all Inconstant is here to defend the convoy so she may have to fire her guns and so on. We would all be an incumbrance in that situation. We will go to the Achilles and hopefully will not have more than a day or two before we can disembark and be comfortable again at Ajaccio'.

'If you say so Papa. But shall we ever see Captain Fremantle again, he's so charming, don't you think?'

'Charming I'm sure', put in Mrs Wynne, 'but don't think any more about him. He is far too busy to have time for us; and he has a job to do to defend us from the French. Let him get on with it'.

'Well I hope I do see him again', said Betsey, 'whatever it is he has to do'.

Ben helped to carry the baggage across to the Achilles and see the family settled in an even more cramped space there. But Captain Parish seemed a civil kind of officer and clearly they would be as well looked after as possible.

French privateers were waiting outside the harbour and after the convoy sailed at four in the morning the wind dropped and made it impossible for the naval ships to defend the convoy, and two of the smaller ships were taken. With no wind no-one was going anywhere.

During the early morning the Inconstant remained alongside as some final stores were brought aboard. Sailors were standing by to slip the berthing ropes quickly; the longboat was in the water, fully manned, so that it could pull the ship off the quayside if that should be needed. As the middle of the day approached musket fire was heard from the edge of the town and the captain gave the order to cast off. The upper deck was cleared for action, the guns loaded with grape shot, and the marines were formed up ready for battle in case any French troops should attempt to make mischief from the quayside.

Sails were set and the helmsman steered to try to pick up the afternoon breeze. The Inconstant sailed amongst the convoy and as she passed the Achilles, Captain Fremantle hailed them with his speaking trumpet, confirming that all was well and expressing the hope that the passengers were being made comfortable. Two days after leaving Leghorn the wind got up and the 48 ships of the convoy began to make better progress, although the passengers found the movement enough to make some of them seasick. The wind rose to storm force and the Captain of the Achilles decided to take shelter in the Bay of Mortella off the little fishing port of San Firenzo in the north of Corsica.

Meanwhile the Inconstant took advantage of the strong easterly wind to join the main part of the British fleet off Toulon. Fremantle reported to Admiral Jervis about the departure from Leghorn and received new orders to find all the ships which had left there and make sure that they gathered in Ajaccio to form a convoy for Gibraltar. He was given orders for Captain Lord Garlies in the frigate Lively to escort the convoy.

'What should we do with the passengers, the Wynne family?' asked Fremantle.

'Is there something special about them which would prevent them from going to Gibraltar and then onwards to England?' asked the Admiral.

'It's only that they seem to belong as much in Italy as in England. The two older daughters are uncommonly fine-looking ladies and very accomplished. I believe they are fluent in languages and have many social attributes. I wonder if they might not be quite useful to us out here, perhaps in Naples.'

'What's this then, Fremantle? Are you again hinting that your inclinations towards the fairer sex should be colouring our judgement?'

'Of course not, Sir; I would never suggest such a thing. Although I do admit that Miss Betsey does seem to be very charming and will be a good influence on some fortunate man. In any case I cannot even contemplate becoming a family man before I have made significantly more prize money'.

'Ah, I see a crack in your defences! I will bear that in mind and see if I can't put you in the way of some prizes. After all there are plenty to be had from the coastal traffic from France towards Italy. For now, go and find the Wynne family and take them onboard again. Settle the formation of the convoy for Gibraltar and send Garlies with it. Call on Sir Gilbert Elliott – did you tell me he is now at Bastia? – and talk with him about Elba. We need to prevent the French from getting established there so he needs to be persuaded to order an invasion force.

There is unlikely to be any proper opposition. And when you have done that return to the fleet and the Wynnes can move aboard the Britannia. I'll fix it with Foley who can look after them while I give you something else useful to do'.

The Captain returned aboard his ship with a letter for Sir Gilbert from the Admiral, and issued orders for a course to be set for the northern cape of Corsica. From there he would locate the vessels which had left Leghorn and would be sheltering from the easterly gale.

On 2nd July the Inconstant dropped anchor in Mortella Bay and Ben was soon taking the Captain over to the Lively. They arrived in the middle of dinner and found Lord Garlies holding forth in his cabin with a great party of people which included the whole Wynne family. Ben held back as his captain stepped into the cabin but he could not help noticing a broad smile on his face as his eyes met those of Betsey. Of course he could not feel her heart beating but from the smiles on her face it took little imagination to sense that she was not just a little excited at his arrival.

It was at least an hour before Captain Fremantle appeared again and he seemed to be very content.

'That's all fixed. Luckett', he said, 'Lively is going to collect all the vessels out of Leghorn together and take them to Gibraltar. The Wynnes will move out of Achilles into Inconstant in the next day or two and we'll take them back to the fleet. The misses were rather more in favour of that arrangement than, I suspect, was Mr Wynne, so we'll need to take good care of them. In the medium term the idea is to find them a nice comfortable ship to take them back to England, although that might mean stopping for a while in Elba or Naples until one is available'.

Ben assented to his captain who continued, 'I've invited them all to a ball in Inconstant on Monday. In the meantime I have to go to Bastia to find the Viceroy. I'll go back aboard and collect some things and brief Mr Hutchinson. Will you please go ashore and find me a good horse and a reliable guide to take me to Bastia.'

'Do you wish me to accompany you? I had some experience on horseback in Antigua with Captain Nelson'.

'Thank you, but not on this occasion. I should like you to look after the Wynnes for me and see them settled onboard. All being well I'll be back Sunday evening. If I'm delayed please transfer the Wynnes on Monday and get them settled so that we can be ready to sail if necessary'.

Ben returned to the Inconstant after seeing the Captain off on horseback and reported to Mr Hutchinson who had only time for a few very brief words with the Captain. They agreed that the Wynnes would move on board on Monday morning and that there would be a dance on Monday evening.

On the Monday morning the wind was still strong and the water in the anchorage quite choppy. Nonetheless Mr Hutchinson told Ben to go ahead and transfer the passengers.

'We must be ready to sail in a hurry when he does arrive,' ordered the First Lieutenant.

The transfer process was rather wetter than would have been agreeable as the ladies and gentleman were brought across through the flurries of spray. Everyone got wet. The family was again set up on the maindeck for'ard of the other cabins. But there was no sign of the captain except for a message which arrived mid-afternoon to say that he was detained and would return on Tuesday.

When he arrived onboard on Tuesday morning the Captain immediately called a conference of the officers during which he told them that he had been discussing with the Viceroy a plan to take Elba. 'For the present the Inconstant will remain here,' he said. 'Sir Gilbert is arranging for the army to provide sufficient soldiers to land on Elba, which is only very lightly defended, and some transports to carry them. When he has everything ready he will send for us, which will be in a couple of days. Until then everything must continue as normal. I don't want any hint to get out that we are going anywhere but it would be a good idea to drill the men in small arms, and check over all the kit as part of the routine. If anything gets out it may alert the French and make the project much more dangerous.'

So determined was the Captain that no hint of the impending operation should leak out that he ordered preparations for a Ball that very evening. And after dinner when the dancing started the Captain was by far the most lively of all the officers, making sure that he took the floor with each of the ladies in turn. Careful analysis of his movements might have revealed that Miss Betsey had more of his attention than the others but he was clearly doing his best to give nothing away. The dancing continued through the night and into the morning watch so that the ladies were rather late rising. At dinner the following afternoon the Captain received a letter and immediately gave the order to weigh anchor. Within an hour the anchor was up and they had turned north and then east to round Cap Corse.

While still some miles short of Bastia late the following afternoon the gig was launched to take the Captain ashore. In the southerly wind it would make a faster passage than Inconstant itself.

'Where has he gone now, Luckett?' asked Betsey, 'It looks as though they are going towards Bastia. Won't it take an awful long time to get there.'

'Yes indeed, Miss Betsey, I doubt they'll arrive before eight of the morning watch. And I am sure he'll want to be back onboard as quickly as possible'.

'Well I'm glad to hear that. Somehow the ship seems to go flat when he's not here; do you feel that as well as me?'

'Most of us know when the Captain's not around', he replied, 'but we have to get on with the day's work just the same. No doubt he's left orders with the First Lieutenant and the Master'.

The following day Inconstant was still some distance from Bastia when a transport vessel was sighted and as the ships closed, it was clear that the Captain was onboard. He was soon rowed across and began giving orders to sail for Elba. The rendezvous position with other naval ships and transports had been established and the Inconstant must be there at the correct time.

It was not long before Betsey and her sisters were looking out towards the city of Porto Ferraio in Elba. There was a great flurry of activity with sailors preparing the ship's main armament and arranging muskets and cutlasses where they would be immediately available if required. Boats loaded with soldiers and small cannons were being rowed ashore from the transports. A large warship had also joined them and Betsey had counted 37 guns on each side.

'What's that ship?' she asked Ben.

'It's the Captain', he replied, 'with Commodore Nelson onboard. He and our Captain have worked well with each other before. I heard how they ran the siege of Bastia together a couple of years back and both of them got knocked off their feet by a ball from the city – it was pretty careless'.

'Do you know what's going on?' asked Betsey.

'No not really. But we have to prepare for action in case the Tuscans in there choose to open fire on us, which they might do. We need to be ready for anything which is why all the boats are in the water and the arms are prepared'.

Tension remained high during the night although there seemed to be no reaction from anyone ashore. The following morning it was possible to catch an occasional glimpse of groups of people moving ashore and closing in on the fort. As far as one could see the people in the fort were doing very little but going about their normal business. In the afternoon the Captain returned and gave orders that the following day the ships would all enter the harbour. He invited the Wynnes to venture ashore for a walk with him; all had apparently been amicably settled between Tuscans and British. The British would provide military security to ensure that the island was defended against the French whilst the Tuscans would provide the civilian government.

Ben was coxswain of the boat which took the party ashore the next day, and although there appeared to be little conversation between them he could not help thinking to himself that the Captain and Miss Betsey were both experiencing a sense of attraction. When they returned an hour or two later after their walk ashore all the Wynne girls were bubbling with excitement and chatting about how beautiful the scenery was and how clean and tidy the city and fortress were. How remarkable it was that the Tuscan and English troops seemed to be such good friends.

Having returned onboard in the evening the order was given to weigh anchor, but the ship did not go far before running onto an unexpected sandbank. The Master had misjudged the amount of leeway which Inconstant would make under a rising wind. Ben was quickly in a boat taking a kedge anchor off astern to pull the ship clear and after plenty of heaving and effort she came off and was able to sail clear.

On the quarterdeck next day Ben was drawn into conversation by the Captain.

'We had an easy ride in Ferraio, Luckett. The Tuscans seemed to be very willing to accept our offers of protection. I think they wanted to avoid the fate of their friends in Leghorn who have been properly beaten up by the little Corsican Napoleon. Now I've a far greater problem which is going to be less easy to resolve'.

'Walk aft with me, Luckett', he continued. 'I told the Commodore that you had joined me and he recalled at once that you had served together in the Boreas. I also learnt from him that he had found you to be someone of great discretion in whom confidences might be shared with the certain knowledge that nothing would go further'.

'Thank you, Sir. Captain Nelson and I often talked about matters he could not share with anyone else. It was sometimes a little awkward because others onboard tried to get out of me what was going on, but once they realised they would get nothing that ceased to be a problem'.

'I'm sure you have noticed that Miss Betsey seems to take an uncommon interest in me. I sense in how she looks at me that she feels something. And I own that I too find her unusually attractive. In her company I seem able to relax; I tease her and she laughs; I complement her and she smiles; I chide her and she responds positively. She dances beautifully, appreciates music and so on'.

'It took no great skill on my part to notice there is something between the two of you', replied Ben. 'What then is the difficulty; you both seem to acknowledge the attraction, so why are you nervous about it?'

'Ah, well. Put it this way; I've not always been such a paragon of virtue as I suspect she imagines me to be. Like so many of us I've found pleasure in many different women – you probably didn't notice the lovely Adelaide who was on board when you arrived here; she's been a delight to Captain Nelson as well. I'm not sure that I'm ready to be faithful to just one. And besides in my position I'm expected to be able to show I've enough money for her father to believe that I can look after her well enough; and there I fall far short. That's the real sticking point. If I don't stop it now it will all come to tears when I tell Mr Wynne that I have but half a farthing to my name and cannot be sure to keep his daughter well, unless my naval career becomes markedly successful. So I think I must nip it in the bud. Stop it now. It'll be easier when we join the fleet and we can transfer the family into a ship where they can be less cramped'.

'If you're really serious about that, Sir, you must act sooner rather than later. And I will, if I can, do my best to soften the blow. Might I suggest, Sir, that when they move into another ship, you send me with them as a sort of sea daddy. That way I can keep an eye on things for you'.

'So then I lose you too, Luckett. That doesn't seem such a good deal, though there are some attractions to it'.

'If it all blows over I can transfer back to you whenever you wish. But if you remain of the same mind in a couple of months it'll be easy for the two of you to pick up where you left off. You get the best of all worlds'.

'In the meantime I guess I'd better have a conversation with the parents and warn them that I've no fortune and that they might therefore regard me unsuitable as a suitor for their daughter. I've never given a moment's thought to the possibility that I might seriously fall for a girl'.

'I had a similar experience in Port Jackson. Meeting Lieutenant King and finding myself close to his family brought me into regular contact with the girl who was looking after his two illegitimate children. I was hooked and am glad of it; it's given me a new purpose in life'.

'Thank you. I'll speak with the Wynnes directly and we'll transfer them when we join the fleet. You go with them and look after them and in a few weeks I'll get back from whatever the Admiral has in mind for Inconstant. You'll remain on my books and I'll have you back – I'm not letting any fellow Captain lure you away, now that you're here'.

Chapter 18

On 14th July Inconstant came up with the fleet and the Captain left at once to call upon Admiral Jervis in Victory. The Admiral asked the Captain about his passengers and found that the younger man was remarkably frank about his sentiments, especially in view of his reputation in the fleet for enjoying himself in female company. His orders were clear; he was to take Inconstant to Ajaccio first and then cruise in the waters north of Corsica to pick up some prizes from amongst the French ships re-supplying Napoleon's army in Tuscany. He was then to sail to Constantinople, call upon the Sultan, and escort a supply convoy back to the fleet. French merchant vessels and privateers should be taken and any other nationality's vessel if it was believed to be carrying goods for the French.

'In the meantime', went on the Admiral, 'you can transfer the Wynne family into Britannia. Foley will take good care of them and they can use the Admiral's quarters at least until another Admiral is appointed. I'll think about how to get them back to England in due course; but for now we'll enjoy their company here – it'll do us all good to have some pretty faces around whilst we are on this tedious business. Now, go and get yourself some prize money'.

Fremantle was delighted to have been given such a wide brief enabling him to range through the eastern part of the Mediterranean looking for Frenchmen. As soon as he was back onboard Inconstant he sent for the First Lieutenant and Ben and told them of the plan. He turned to the Master and said 'Make for the Britannia and lay close alongside'.

The Wynnes were soon climbing down into the boat with the Captain and Ben and setting off towards Britannia a cable away. Captain Foley welcomed them all with warmth; it would greatly enliven the dull days on blockade duty to have some good looking young ladies onboard. Another boat arrived shortly afterwards with the Wynne's belongings and within an hour Inconstant's sails had filled again and she heading away to the east.

Betsey soon found a way of cornering Ben on the quarterdeck. She was looking visibly downcast and miserable.

'Oh, Ben, how can life be so cruel. As soon as we begin to get to know something about each other, he's wrenched away from me. We'll never meet again. I'll never see that lovely ship of his again, or enjoy the company of his officers. Suddenly there's nothing to look forward to'.

'You shouldn't see it like that – it's just one of the ups and downs of life. If you don't have some difficulties and hardship, you never really appreciate the good times. And if you want my opinion, Captain Fremantle will be back here, asking after you, as quick as he possibly can be'.

'I see there's some sense in that, but I've to get through the time between. I shall have to be bright and cheerful to everyone, when my heart is nowhere nearby. I don't want to find lots of others thinking they can fall in love with me'.

Over the following few days Captain Foley was very attentive to his guests. Every day he would receive Captains from the other ships rowed across whenever the sea was sufficiently calm. The parties in the great cabin were invariably enjoyable as the Captains got to know and understand each other, and the Wynnes provided a focus for conversation which was not about ships, battles and the enemy. Lord Garlies from Lively was often there, and Ben Hallowell from Courageux, who had an excellent ship's band, and Captain Grey from Victory. D'Acres came from Barfleur, and Sir Charles Knowles from Goliath, and young Charles Ogle from Minerva, Samuel Hood from Aigle which had just returned from the Levant, and Tom Troubridge from Culloden and many others. It was quite clear that one of the reasons they were all so keen to visit Britannia was to be able to enjoy some female company. Captain Foley often obliged them all by arranging a ball, which his own officers were also able to join. Ladies were, of course, in short supply which meant that the Wynne girls found themselves dancing with a great many different partners.

Early one morning a letter was received by Mr Wynne from the Admiral inviting the whole family to go to Victory to dine with him at 3pm. Fortunately it was a fine day and the sun was shining on them as they were rowed across to Victory.   Admiral Sir John Jervis received them with great affability and with a kiss for all the ladies, young and old alike. They were soon joined in the Admiral's cabin by a number of other Captains who were each required by the Admiral to kiss the ladies as they entered.   At dinner the Admiral had placed himself between Mrs Wynne and Betsey.

'How delightful it is to have you aboard, Miss Wynne.   You know how tedious and dull we get on this blockade duty, never being quite sure when the French may try to break out and make a run for it, but most of the time having nothing much to do.   Your company is most welcome; it brings new life to us all'.

'I am glad to hear you say that Admiral.   We're very well cared for by Captain Foley.   But I found Inconstant such a very fine ship and Captain Fremantle made us extremely comfortable and welcome.   I was sorry to have to leave'.

'I know Fremantle enjoyed your company, and would like more of it.   I have sent him off on a mission which will put him in the way of some prize money.   That might sweeten your next meeting, don't you think?'

'He's given me a ring to keep until we meet again.   But he told Mama that he couldn't think of being engaged to me because he has not the means.   I can only dare to hope that he'll take enough prizes to convince Papa.   I feel that my heart is mine no more'.   Betsey realised that she had said far more than she should have done to the man who held Captain Fremantle's future.

'You make your feelings quite plain and I'll do my best to ensure that the gentleman concerned is fully acquainted with them when I next see him. And in the meantime I can perhaps ensure that others don't entertain any hopes'.   Betsey smiled in appreciation but thought that it was time to change the subject if she could.

'Papa is very concerned that we should get back to England as soon as may be possible so I've no doubt he'll be asking you to allow us to take passage aboard a suitable ship which is returning there'.

'Inconstant is probably the next frigate to go home', said Jervis, 'but that will not happen until I have another ship to replace her. I'm afraid I can only ask you to be patient'.

'I'm sure I'd be delighted to take a passage again in Inconstant although I suspect Papa may be concerned that it would place me rather too close to Captain Fremantle for too long'.

'By the time he gets back with his pocket full of prize money I doubt your father will have anything to complain about. I can see you've nailed your colours to the mast; I'd better speak to Foley and tell him he must haul down his battle ensign and look in due course for another port. I daresay he will moan that he's never met a young lady with such fine attributes, or something like that'. And with that the Admiral turned to his right to engage Mrs Wynne's attention leaving Betsey to turn to her left where Lord Garlies was looking somewhat deserted.

'How is the Lively, Lord Garlies?' asked Betsey to open the conversation.

'We go on quite well, thank you, Miss Wynne, though I cannot say that acting as messenger for the fleet is as exciting as the mission your man has been sent upon'.

'And what do you mean by 'my man' exactly?' rounded Betsey, not wanting to admit that she knew exactly who he was referring to.

'Why, Fremantle, of course. You must know that he has always enjoyed flirting with every pretty girl he meets and his affairs seldom last more than a few days. He's a typical sailor with a girl in every port and a peculiar inability to be faithful to any, despite all his protestations'.

'Thank you for the warning Lord Garlies, but for the time being I shall continue to believe what I see and feel and avoid seeking any other approaches. We may dance, for there is little alternative and we are so totally outnumbered, but I will not engage'. Betsey was relieved that the Admiral pushed his chair back and rose asking that the young ladies might perhaps perform a duet for the company and when the applause had ended after the second song he thanked everyone for their company, wished them a good evening and retired.

Ben was in the boat which waited to take them back to Britannia and they were very shortly on their way. As they passed Courageux they could hear Captain Hallowell's band playing on the quarterdeck.

'Can we stop and listen to them, they play so beautifully and it is a very fine evening?' asked Betsey of the young midshipman who was in charge of the boat.

'I see no reason why not', he replied, 'if you are all happy about that', looking directly at Mr Wynne, who said nothing but nodded in assent. So the oars were shipped and the sailors, like the passengers sat and listened to the band's concert which played many of the popular tunes of the day. After about an hour, bobbing around, the concert ended and they returned to the Britannia. There they found many of those who had been dining in the flagship who hoped to continue the evening with some dancing. A ball was hastily arranged and the ship's band played for them until well into the night. Ben watched for a while but having decided that nothing untoward would happen to his protégé he turned in. It was time for him to dream of his own Sally and the two children, to hope and pray that all was well with them.

A week later another message came from the flagship asking Betsey and Eugenia to come to Victory to help with translating some documents into German. They were rowed across and Admiral Jervis explained the problem.

'This young man who has come onboard is a German, wanting to get away from the French and offer his services in King George's army. We can have him swear the soldier's oath of loyalty except that he does not understand any English at present so we need to translate the oath so that he can swear it and sign up'.

Betsey and Eugenia took the document from the clerk and at once set about translating it into good German, in which both were fluent. They wrote out a fair copy and presented it to the German who was able to sign it, thus solving the problem and recruiting him into the army. While the ladies were working, Victory had sailed quite close to the shore and then the wind dropped leaving them just about within range of a fort. Fortunately the fire was not accurate and the balls fell some distance short, and Victory was soon towed out of danger by its boats.

'What's it like in battle?' Betsey asked Ben at the next opportunity.

'I can only guess', replied Ben, 'as I've never been in one. But I have, of course, been part of exercising the guns. After the first broadside the whole ship is filled with smoke. People have told me what it's like when you take a hit from an enemy ball. The worst thing is the splinters. Even if the ball doesn't get through the ship's side what happens is that splinters fly off the inside where the ball hits. They travel very fast, like arrows, and if they hit you they will do a lot of damage. You never see it until it's too late to get out of the way. And after a few minutes of action everyone is quite deaf from the noise'.

'What happens when someone gets wounded?' asked Betsey.

'First of all they get pulled out of the way so that the others can keep on fighting. If they're lucky there'll be some spare hands who will take them down to the orlop deck, below the waterline. That's where the surgeon works, and he's helped by any women onboard and by the Chaplain, all by lamplight. Most surgeons deal with people in the order they are brought down regardless of their rank. The best of them can cut off a leg or an arm in about two minutes; they work very fast'.

Days passed with a similar routine until a week of August had passed. Meleager arrived from England bringing the news that war had broken out with Spain, making Gibraltar a very unfriendly and uncomfortable place to be. Any ship bound for England would have to pass through the Straits and continue home without stopping. And, Betsey heard, Meleager would not be staying long, so any hope of a passage to England seemed to have receded, and the question was raised where the family should go, 'We can't stay onboard indefinitely,' commented Mr Wynne, 'and I'm ready to set foot onshore for a while'.

August passed, and September, and the Wynnes remained onboard Britannia. Betsey spent much of the daylight hours on the quarterdeck looking for the arrival of new ships, hoping against hope that each one might turn out to be Inconstant. Captain Foley had found an occasion to speak quietly to her and express his admiration for her. 'But', he said,

'I fear at 42 I'm too old for one so young and lovely as you. Besides I know well of your attraction to my friend Tom Fremantle and I'm sure he'll make a fine match for you'.

'Thank you for being so frank, Captain Foley, and for being such a generous host to us for so many weeks. You must be ready for us to move on, although I don't believe Papa really knows where he wishes to go. He doesn't like Naples and we can't return to Florence whilst the French are there'

After another two weeks of anxious waiting and boredom at the repetitive nature of the blockade, the Admiral announced to his Captains that he had received orders to leave the Mediterranean. Clearly the government priority was the defence of England from invasion by the French across the English Channel and they wished to make sure there were enough ships there to deter the enemy.

Gradually the blockade of Toulon wound down to a few ships. Britannia was ordered with a few others to return to Corsica and meet the Viceroy to find out his requirements. There would be stores and people to be removed from Corsica and also from Elba. Britannia and Blenheim came to anchor in San Firenzo bay early in October enabling Captains Foley and Bazeley to call on the Viceroy at Bastia. Betsey continued to spend many hours looking for new arrivals to the fleet. She was with the rest of the family dining onboard the Blenheim when Fremantle brought Inconstant to anchor close by. Ben noticed, of course, and had not long to wait before Fremantle arrived at Britannia. Ben met him at the gangway.

'Good afternoon, Sir', he said

'Good afternoon, Luckett. Now tell me what has befallen Miss Wynne. Has she fallen for old Foley yet?'

'No, Sir. We've taken good care of that and Captain Foley has made clear he's not interested, and professed the hope that Miss Wynne would find happiness with you'.

'Ah, well, that's a relief. Where are they all now?'

'They're dining in Blenheim today. I'm sure Miss Wynne will be more than a little excited to see you, Sir. She's been pining for you ever since you left'.

'I shall go there at once. Is Captain Foley there as well?' The Captain sounded rather animated as if he might charge into Blenheim's great cabin like a bull at a gate, prepared to take the lady from under the nose of a fellow-suitor.

'I believe so. But, Sir, if I might suggest, I think you can afford to take things very gently, rather than creating a monumental scene. Captain Foley is no longer a competitor. And when she sees you I suspect Miss Wynne will be overcome, probably speechless, and very likely tearful. Calm down and you will easily win'.

'Ah, Luckett, you have seen through my own excitement. I have been anticipating this moment for three months and I fear that if I appear too relaxed she will be unconvinced of my sincerity. But you're right – I will be gentle'.

At that the Captain disappeared over the side and in a moment was being pulled lustily across to Blenheim.

Fremantle entered Captain Bazely's great cabin unannounced and stood at the doorway for a moment taking in the scene. Next to Bazely was the person he most wanted to see, and he was pleased to note that Foley was several places removed from her. It was some moments before anyone noticed him; Betsey dropped her fork onto her plate, put her hand to her mouth and was lost for words. Conversation stopped suddenly like a ship hitting the rocks. Into the silence Bazely threw some words.

'Welcome Fremantle. Come and join the party and tell us all where you've been and what you've found. We've all been missing your company. Mr Long please make space on your right for the Captain'. Mr Long was one of Blenheim's lieutenants who had found himself placed very agreeably next to Miss Wynne. It was with a little reluctance that he moved his chair to make space for Fremantle.

Betsey recovered from the shock of seeing again the person she had most missed these past three months. Would he still be the same? Perhaps he had changed his mind.

'It is indeed very good to see you again Captain Fremantle. We had all begun to wonder whether you were intentionally avoiding a return to the fleet. Perhaps you will tell us what has kept you away so long'.

'I'm pleased to see you looking so radiant Miss Wynne. I had feared that all the sea air you've had might have damaged your complexion and health. We sailors get accustomed to the restricted diet we have to live on at sea, but it's not very agreeable to those who are accustomed to live well ashore'.

'There is no need for you to be concerned on that account', replied Betsey. 'We've done very well and enjoyed the sea air, although I would relish a walk ashore to see if I can still stand up when the floor is not rolling like the deck'.

'Will you do me the honour of accompanying me ashore tomorrow and we can take a walk together like we last did in Elba. And if you say 'yes' we had better then stop monopolising each other now and I will tell a wider group about my exploits'. Betsey looked delighted and, of course, at once nodded in the affirmative, with a winning smile. As she looked away she caught Eugenia's eye and the sisters exchanged a look which others might have had difficulty noticing or interpreting, but which they both understood exactly.

The remainder of dinner passed with Fremantle telling the company about his experience with prizes and his visit to Constantinople and to Smyrna. He had clearly had a fruitful cruise and had secured many prizes which could be expected to yield well when sold in the prize courts. Mr Wynne listened in silence but clearly felt some relief that he might not be faced with the prospect of having to prise his daughter away from a Captain who had failed to achieve his objective and who had insufficient money to look after his daughter.

At last the party began to break up and Fremantle was very happy to escort the Wynnes back to Britannia with Captain Foley. After bidding them goodnight Foley invited him to his own quarters to take a brandy which Fremantle accepted.

Conversation between the two men was largely about service matters but Foley raised the issue of his passengers.

'You must know, my friend, that I have stated my position clearly to Miss Wynne and told her that I consider myself too old to engage with her. The look of relief on her face was touching and made me realise that she most certainly has an attachment only to you'.

'As you can imagine, this is the first time I have been in such a position', replied Fremantle. 'Indeed as I'm sure you know – everyone else seems to – I've been in the habit of enjoying a very wide range of female company, and the idea of settling down and being faithful to one alone is a little unexpected. But I certainly find I'm very much attracted to her, and the only reason for showing a certain coolness was the knowledge that I had not sufficient means to secure her future. All being well my recent cruise will have corrected that situation and I can now offer Mr Wynne greater assurances'.

'Have no fear on that account. Miss Wynne is a very determined young lady and I'm convinced she'll not allow her father to intervene where she has decided. In any case you have the Admiral on your side and I'm quite sure he's had a quiet word with Mr and Mrs Wynne'.

The two men's conversation continued into the night as the first brandy bottle was emptied and a second one broached, until six bells reminded Fremantle that he must return to his ship. Foley accompanied him to the ship's side and as he stepped down into the boat Foley said, 'By the way I am very jealous not only of your young lady but also of your man Luckett. He is not only a very competent seaman but he is a model of tact and wisdom in a very quiet and unassuming way; you are doubly fortunate'.

The walk ashore had to be postponed because the wind rose and the boat ride would have proved very wet, quite apart from the battering of the wind once ashore. But the day after that a party was able to go ashore. Ben watched as the Captain met and escorted the Wynne family in its entirety up the path from the landing. He could not avoid noting how the Captain and Miss Wynne strode out ahead of the others until they were clearly out of earshot and he wondered whether that had been carefully planned by her parents to allow the two lovers some time on their own.

When they all returned to the landing stage later in the day Ben saw his Captain walking with Mrs Wynne with whom he seemed to be getting along very well. He could not help wondering whether the conversation signalled the reaching of an agreement about Miss Wynne's future.

The Captain returned to Britannia with the family and took his leave of them there. At the gangway he said to Ben, 'Thank you Luckett. I hope it will not be long before I can get you back to your proper duties. Captain Foley tells me you've been making yourself very useful, and I can only tell you that where affairs of the heart are concerned Miss Wynne and I seem to be on the best of terms, and I feel that I've made good progress with her parents. As a result of the cruise my assets will show a substantial increase, and, by the way, yours will too since you are still carried on Inconstant's books. Thank you for your part in all of this'.

'Thank you Sir. I'm happy to hear that all may soon be resolved. I'll continue to look after the family as best I can until the right moment for me to return onboard Inconstant'. He saluted as Fremantle went down into his boat and was rapidly pulled away to Inconstant. By the morning there was no sign of her and she only returned the following day for long enough to report that she had fallen in with 37 Spanish ships and been chased by them all night before escaping.

It was early November when Mr Wynne received a letter from Admiral Jervis telling him that the whole fleet would shortly be quitting the Mediterranean under orders from England. He suggested that as Mr Wynne had made it clear that he had no great desire to return to England the best plan for him might be to land at Elba and take lodgings there. Within a few weeks the situation on the mainland should be clearer and he would then know whether he would be able to take his family safely through Austria and onwards to Germany. Sir John closed by writing how much he knew the officers of the fleet had enjoyed being entertained by his family and complimenting him upon the accomplishments of his daughters.

A few days later Britannia sailed into Porto Ferraio, Elba, and the Wynnes disembarked with all their belongings accompanied by the faithful Ben. They soon found lodgings which Mrs Wynne described as barely adequate and when they attempted to discover some form of social life on the island they found that there was none to speak of. They would be left to their own devices until....until something happened.

One day at the end of November after they had dined, Ben found Betsey lounging idly on the balcony and drew her attention to the ship anchoring off Porto Ferraio. He had recognised the ship she longed from the pennant she flew, as well as being able to judge from the way she was rigged, the number of her guns and her general appearance. Betsey went at once to her room to smarten herself and a few minutes later Captain Fremantle was standing before her again asking after her health and how her parents were faring.

'It's confoundedly boring here', replied Betsey, 'there's no one to make conversation with or to play music with and we resort to our books and our own company. I'm quite ready to go almost anywhere, but Papa is always ill and says he must go to Germany and our information suggests there's no way at present across Italy and into Austria. It was far more interesting being at sea. What news do you have, pray?'

'Naples has made a treaty with the French which should mean that they will not advance much beyond Rome. Sir John Acton is still the Chief Minister under the King, although it's Queen Maria Cristina who really pulls all the strings of government, and the British ambassador Sir William Hamilton wields great influence especially as Lady Hamilton is a very good friend of the Queen. It's a good place for British people to be at present'.

'I'm doubtful whether Papa would hear of it, but please tell him. I'd do almost anything rather than stay here. Might you be able to dine with us tomorrow?'

'I'm afraid I'm already committed for dinner but I could come to you for supper, and perhaps we could enjoy a little music as well as conversation. I wonder whether I might bring along two or three of my young gentlemen who have been particularly starved of polite company in recent months. It would do them good to get out'.

'I'm sure that will be in order. I'll tell Mama'. She paused, and went on, 'How long can we expect you to be in Porto Ferraio?'

'I hope to stay a few days here although if we hear of some good French prizes nearby, we'll have to go after them'.

Next evening Ben was waiting to greet the Captain and the three young gentlemen he had brought along to the Wynnes' lodgings.

'I'm not cut out for this courting business, Luckett. My patience is rather short. I want to get it all done one way or the other so that life can go on'.

'Perhaps, Sir, you should think of it as an appropriate investment which will potentially pay you back over the rest of your life'.

'You are too full of good sense, Luckett, as usual, damn it', retorted the Captain as he went into the house.

After supper the ladies provided some music, singing to the harpsichord played beautifully by Betsey. The young gentlemen joined in with the four sisters but though they were willing, none was as musically gifted as the girls. The Captain was finally persuaded by Betsey to sing to her accompaniment and despite his less than exceptional performance the accompanist clearly enjoyed every note.

As Ben served the party with refreshments he sensed that the light-hearted atmosphere where smiles, laughter and applause were plentiful would bode well for a happy outcome.

After a few days during which they had enjoyed Fremantle's company, and that of some of his officers on most afternoons and evenings, Inconstant sailed and the atmosphere in the household went flat again. Time hung heavily and the girls resorted to their books and their lessons. The few visitors who called seemed all to be elderly and distinctly dull. But then as Christmas Day neared things began to improve. First the girls got wind of a ball to be given by General de Burgh, but that only led to panic that they might not be invited and might find themselves, like Cinderella, left at home, whilst many others, even if there were no Prince Charming amongst them, enjoyed themselves.

Then on Christmas Eve the handsome, longed-for, dark-eyed man in a Captain's uniform arrived as they were eating breakfast. Inconstant had just anchored in the bay. Conversation quickly became excited, animated, full of laughter and joy. The ring of the doorbell heralded another caller and Captain Wyndham, a soldierly Captain, arrived with an invitation for the girls to the ball which would be given by the General on Christmas Day itself.

Ben was, once again, amazed at the speed with which the household seemed to switch from gloom and despondency to joy and happiness at the arrival of his Captain. Like a bucket of water poured over a wilting plant the restorative effect of his presence was instant and complete. Surely, he thought, there must be a permanent relationship in the offing, and it must be imminent.

Christmas Day arrived and after attending mass the girls began readying themselves for the ball. In due course they were waited upon by Commodore Nelson, with Captain Cockburn from his flagship Minerve, and Fremantle. The ball proved a magnificent affair attended by about three hundred people many in fantastic fancy dress, and several nationalities, French, Italian and English predominating. They danced until three in the morning before retiring to their beds so that it was mid morning on 26th December before they were ready to take on a new day.

Commodore Nelson and Captain Fremantle arrived to speak to Mr Wynne. They told him that Elba was to be evacuated of all British troops and all British ships had been ordered out of the Mediterranean. Their advice was that they would be much safer in Naples where the Ambassador would remain since the Kingdom of Naples remained an ally of Great Britain, although they had agreed a treaty with the French which would prevent there being any further hostilities. The Inconstant would be sailing from Porto Ferraio in the next day or two and the family should be onboard.

Ben overheard a conversation between Betsey and Eugenia. 'I'm not sure how much I want to go down to Naples', Eugenia was saying, 'we'll quickly lose touch with all the lovely naval people we've got to know. And I bet Naples is full of those awful French who'll do nothing but poke fun at us'.

'That's probably true', replied Betsey, 'but almost anything is better than staying here, especially after the army has left and gone home. I swing from joy to despair if ever I'll achieve happiness with the gallant Captain. I can't make him out; one minute he seems to be all charm and interest and the next he seems to be more interested in every other woman in the room except me. Then I think he is signalling to me to abandon any hopes I had of winning him'.

'But he does seem to have had several conversations quietly with Papa and Mama. And I've not heard Papa once say anything bad about him, which is quite different from when we were first in Britannia and all he could talk about was how charming and eligible was old Foley. If only Fremantle will recognise how happy you'll make him, I'm sure you'll yet be his wife'.

'How can you say such a thing. We're about to go to Naples, and he'll then come straight back here, remove the army and sail off to Gibraltar and we'll never see him again, because Papa will insist on returning to Germany. And I shall be abandoned to a life of misery with some dreadful German Count or other. It's a prospect of unmitigated misery'.

Two days later the lodgings had been packed up and Ben escorted the family with all their belongings once again to Inconstant. The weather was foul and they all got wet in the boat, but once onboard they were again settled reasonably comfortably into their quarters in time for dinner. Ben was delighted to be back at sea and quickly renewed his acquaintance with his shipmates of a few months previously.

They sailed on the following day but made poor progress towards Naples. Ben was back on the quarterdeck supervising the quartermaster when the Captain beckoned him aft.

'So what have you to report to me, Luckett?'

'Two young ladies are very unhappy at the prospect that they'll be dumped down in Naples and all their naval friends will be lost to them.

They predict having to return to Germany and being obliged to marry a couple of German Counts. If you've made up your mind Sir, I recommend taking bold action. From all I have observed they regard you already as part of the family, and you must notice how their mood changes as soon as you arrive in a room'.

'Well, I'm very much attracted to Miss Wynne, there can be no doubt. I don't think I've behaved very well towards her; I've been uncertain, and not exactly true to her. On the other hand I don't at all like the idea of parting for good. It's fortunate that she now has experience of life at sea because the only way we shall avoid a painful parting is for me to do a deal and for her to come away with us. Once we get to Naples I'll have to move quickly to put the last stitches in the canvas'.

'I'm glad to hear that, Sir. I've become very attached to the family myself and to Miss Betsey in particular. In my humble opinion she'll make a perfect wife for a successful naval man'.

'Thank you Luckett', and the Captain turned away allowing Ben to attend to his normal duties.

Late on 6th January, Inconstant anchored off Naples and on the 8th after the customs officials had done their duty the Wynnes landed and went to the Britannia Inn. This was, at the time, the home of Prince Augustus, a younger son of King George, whose scandalous behaviour had obliged the King to insist that he spent his life outside England. Many naval friends dined with them, and others whom they knew from earlier days in Florence and Venice called upon them, so that the next two days allowed little time to think much about the future. Then on Monday 10th January a letter from the Captain was delivered to Mr Wynne.

By the evening, when Fremantle called at the Inn he was welcomed by Mr Wynne who at once made it clear that he had no objection to the proposal contained in the letter and that he was happy to welcome him as his future son-in-law. The family were all delighted at the prospect of the marriage but felt much more gloomy when it was revealed that Betsey would go away immediately in Inconstant on whatever service they might be required to fulfil, arriving at some time in the future back in England.

Arrangements were rapidly made and Lady Hamilton offered her drawing room for the marriage ceremony which would be held on the Thursday. Suitable bridal gowns were acquired, and Prince Augustus was invited to give the bride away. Sir Gilbert Elliot, Sir William Hamilton and Mr Lambert stood as witnesses. After the ceremony bride and groom with the family and friends dined at the Embassy and then celebrated by visiting the opera. Late in the evening the newly married couple returned to find waiting for them a Catholic priest who had agreed to marry them again in the Catholic rite.

Ben of course took no official part in the ceremony but the First Lieutenant gave him permission to go ashore to observe the proceedings which he admitted later had given him great pleasure. The five month courtship which had begun at Leghorn had reached a dizzying climax despite all the doubts and setbacks, and Betsey had won the man of whom she had written at first sight, 'He pleases me more than any man I have yet seen'. What would the future hold for them?

Chapter 19

The days after the marriage were bittersweet, as Betsey's emotions swung from the ecstasy of knowing she was now fully attached to the man she loved, and the certainty that within a day or two she would be parted from her family who had nurtured and loved her, and from whom she had never before been parted. What she was quite sure of was that she was deeply in love with and much loved by her new husband, and it was this alone which enabled her to contemplate the parting, and the uncertain and still unfamiliar life on board a warship in wartime. Tears flowed, but so did smiles and even Fremantle, the hardened warrior, could recognise the strong ties of love and affection which bound Betsey's family together; this would be a perfect model for the family to which he and Betsey might aspire.

Inconstant sailed on the evening of Sunday 15th less than a week after the final agreement about the marriage. Fremantle had said he would have to act quickly and he had certainly done so. Ben would observe, and would focus on his job as Master's Mate, supporting the Master and the Captain as best he could. A happy and relaxed Captain would certainly lead to a happier and more efficient ship. Betsey was already well known to the officers, all of whom she had met, and now that she was living onboard she quickly got to know some of the sailors. Ben only had to tell her a man's name once and she would always use it when she saw him so that he felt known and appreciated by her.

A week later Inconstant was again at Elba and although orders seemed to have been given to abandon the occupation of the island Sir Gilbert and General de Burgh were against it, believing that it would weaken Britain's position irrevocably and damage relations with their allies by handing a strategic prize to the French.

For Ben there seemed to be plenty of activity and on the second day off Porto Ferraio he took a boat ashore to collect some guests to dine with Betsey onboard. As soon as they had arrived and been settled into the cabin the Captain asked to be taken across to Minerva where he was to dine.as guest of Commodore Nelson and Captain George Toury. The Commodore's dinner was a particularly alcoholic affair, but not nearly as toxic as the party which seemed to have been arranged by some of the seamen in Minerva. Ben was somewhat relieved that he was not involved in charge of the Captain's gig. The riotous behaviour of the sailors proved difficult to handle and the crew of the longboat were very severely tested in getting the drunken men back onboard Inconstant, where the First Lieutenant found it necessary to lock up the worst offenders so they could do no further damage. As Ben pulled the gig away from Minerva, the Captain said, with a touch of a slur in his voice and looking just a little unsteady, 'I have had a bottle too many, Luckett, and it's going to be a little difficult explaining to my wife'.

'By the time you've had some fresh air on the way you'll be fine, Sir. You have never let it affect you before so why should anything be different this time'.

The following morning Betsey asked Ben, 'What was all that noise about last night? Were there some sailors in trouble?'

'Yes Ma'am, indeed. Several of them had to be put in irons to stop them causing further damage. A party had been over to Minerva and seem to have been given a very large amount of grog. A fight started which caused a number of injuries and the Midshipman in charge of the longboat was insulted and abused on the return to Inconstant. They'll be up before the Captain this morning and he will be obliged to administer a severe punishment'.

'Oh dear. Why is it that sailors have a reputation for behaving like that? The Captain told me last night when he returned that he was tipsy, but he seemed quite fine to me and certainly not inclined to violence like you say of the sailors'.

Ben was obliged to turn out with all hands later that day after several sailors had been formally charged and sentenced to be flogged. The three worst offenders were to be sentenced by Court Martial which would take place the following day. Betsey remained in the cabin but could still hear the cries of the men as they received the prescribed number of lashes.

On the following day the three principal offenders were before a court martial and were sentenced to 150 lashes around the fleet. Each man was tied to a grating set up in the longboat and was rowed to each ship in turn where the necessary number of lashes was administered. By the end of the process every sailor in the fleet had seen what might become of them if they were inclined to commit a similar offence.

'It's a very barbaric system, do you not think?' said Betsey to the Captain after it was over.

'I take no pleasure in it at all, unlike some Captains who seem to think the only way to ensure a sailor's loyalty is to flog him. I'd far rather command a happy and contented ship where the sailors are treated with respect and feel valued when they exert themselves. If we're to be successful whether in defeating the King's enemies or securing a reasonable amount of prize money for everyone, we need to work together. I'd much prefer not to use the cat but sometimes it is the only language some sailors understand and if I did not use it, some would accuse me of weakness. No-one wants to serve under a weak and indecisive captain'.

Letters arrived from Naples on the following day and Betsey was immediately immersed in news from her family. But all was far from happy and she paced up and down the quarterdeck burdened with anxiety. That was where Ben saw her.

'You don't look very happy with whatever arrived in the mail, Ma'am, if I may say so'.

'No, Ben. You're right. Just as I thought everything in my life was perfect. Now I'm miserable. I have a letter from my mother accusing me of indifference, lack of gratitude. Because I did not cry at our parting Mama describes me as unloving and heartless, when I'm none of those things. How could she not know me better after all these years'.

The following day the whole fleet sailed. Most were returning to Gibraltar to rejoin the main fleet now blockading the Spanish in Cadiz, whilst Inconstant was ordered to remain near Elba ready to supervise the evacuation if it was to go ahead. In the meantime she too sailed to look for some prizes.

They did not have too long to wait as they came up with an American schooner called La Vittoria. Ben heard the master telling the First Lieutenant as he boarded that he was from the Barbary Coast and heading for Genoa carrying a cargo of grain. But when they looked at the papers it was clear that he was heading for Marseilles to sell the grain to the French; the cargo appeared to belong Jacob Bacri, the Algerian agent of a French company at Marseilles. In due course the prize crew was put aboard and the ship sent to Porto Ferraio to be sold, escorted by the frigate Blanche.

Over the following days they chased a few more potential prizes but were able to take nothing and after nearly two weeks they returned to Porto Ferraio.

'Luckett, Mrs Fremantle and I are going to take a house ashore for the next few weeks whilst the politicians work out what they want us to do. We shall be more comfortable. I should be grateful if you would come ashore with us, look after the place whilst we are there and make sure the local staff do what we require'.

'Aye, aye, Sir. I'll be happy to do that. Have you identified a property yet?'

'No but I understand Mrs Stephens has written a note to Mrs Fremantle suggesting a place which will suit us quite well. We'll take a look at it this afternoon and then move in tomorrow. Come with us today, please, so that you know where it is and can get it prepared for us'.

They set off from Porto Ferraio on foot in the direction described by Mrs Stephens up the hill above the town, and about fifteen minutes after they had left the last of the town houses behind, they saw a small house standing back a little from the roadside with a sign Casita de Ferraio. They walked up the path and found that the place was unlocked and while Ben went round to the back, Tom and Betsey knocked at the front door. There was no reply, so they pushed open the door and went inside. It was rustic with nothing more than matting on the floors and whitewash on the walls. There were tables and chairs aplenty and signs of lamps and candles having been recently alight.
Ben came in from the back. 'I've found the cook and the caretaker there, Sir', he said, 'They don't understand English but I was able to

indicate well enough who we are; I think, Ma'am, as you speak Italian it might be as well to go and see them'.

'But of course. I shall go through directly'. And Betsey disappeared into the kitchen to meet the staff. A few minutes later she was back.

'They'll expect us at about this time tomorrow. I've asked them to buy food for us to dine here and I've told them that you will be with us too, Luckett. Shall we take a look upstairs?'

The following morning Ben arrived with such luggage as they would require and some writing materials and books for them. He checked that all was ready before indicating to Paulo, the cook, that he would like to know where horses could be hired. Quite what the answer meant was not clear but Ben was certain that something would be fixed.

The married couple arrived at half past two in the afternoon, and a few minutes later a boy arrived with two reasonably good horses, which were stabled behind the house, and the boy made clear that he would stay to look after them. Ben supervised the serving of the dinner and then withdrew to allow Tom and Betsey the space they longed for.

Betsey referred to the house as Cottage Inconstant and it was not difficult to tell that she was delighted to be keeping house with her new husband for the first time. It made an enormous difference that she was able to speak to the locals and she got into the habit of discussing and ordering the meals which reflected the ingredients available in Porto Ferraio and the capability of the cook. After a few days they were brave enough to risk inviting some guests for dinner. General Horneck came with three army captains, Cousins, Woodhouse and Elliot, and two of Inconstant's officers, Lieutenants Hornsey and Barry. After dinner the naval officers made their excuses to return to the ship and Betsey withdrew, leaving Fremantle and the army guests to drink the port and settle the world's problems. Much later when the bottles were empty and they had all consumed too much, they invited Betsey to play the harpsichord to entertain them. Betsey was clearly embarrassed to feel the drunken General getting much too close to her, and resisting when she pushed him away. It was near midnight before the guests finally thought it was time to leave.

And so life took up a different pace as the lovers enjoyed each other's company, wrote letters, rode out occasionally, and seldom sought company in the evening. Ben found the days passing in a delightfully gentle way and his only regret was that he did not have Sally and his own family with him. The food was good and wholesome, and the weather, although it was February, was generally fair despite the occasional storm.

There was great excitement onboard and throughout the community in Porto Ferraio when the cutter, Fox, arrived with news of Admiral Jervis's victory over the Spanish off Cape St Vincent on 14th February. Betsey was also somewhat relieved that the Admiral's letter to Fremantle made it clear that he should remain at Elba for the time being whilst doing what he could to disrupt enemy trade around the coast of Italy. A couple of days later Inconstant weighed and set off to chase some prizes. The best they took was a small schooner which had $9,000 in cash onboard to buy corn in Sicily for the French. They heard about two Spanish frigates thought to be operating around Corsica and Sardinia, and all the officers became very excited about the prospect of taking them.

'How on earth do they think we, on our own, can capture two Spanish frigates. Surely they would out-gun us and we would end up the losers?' asked Betsey of her husband.

'We are a very determined lot, you know, and very confident of our ability. We've heard how Nelson captured two Spanish ships, both of which were larger than his', replied the Captain. 'So why would we not be able to do at least the same? We are better practised, more capable, more skilful than the Spanish, and of course braver. But success against two frigates would depend very much on circumstances, and retaining the initiative to windward'.

Two weeks later they had found no trace of the two ships and they returned to anchor off Porto Ferraio, but because the future was so uncertain they were unable to go and live ashore.

While they had been at sea the mail had arrived from Naples. After reading her letters Betsey said to Ben, 'Bad news today from Naples. It looks as though my sister is engaged to a German Count. She says she's madly in love with him but somehow the way she writes about it makes me think she isn't really so. Besides she writes that Papa will not allow it, and that makes her miserable. But I know the Count too; he is only 21, far too young for her. Perhaps he'll go away for a while and it'll all blow over'.

Ben also overheard a conversation at dinner between General de Burgh and the Captain regarding prizes. The General seemed to regard any prize which arrived in Porto Ferraio as belonging to him, a principle which the Captain absolutely refuted – prizes captured at sea were the property of the local naval commander, not a general. The argument resulted in a decision by both parties to avoid one another, although the general wrote endless letters on the subject and promised to write to Admiral Jervis despite all the naval people telling him he was in the wrong.

Early in April the weather turned very rough and a small frigate was seen entering the port with what looked like a prize.

'What ship is that?' Betsey asked Ben during the morning.

'It's Peterell, Ma'am, commanded by the young Lord Proby'.

'Oh yes, I remember meeting him. He's younger than me I think and I cannot imagine how he comes to be in command of a frigate; he seemed such a silly boy, I thought'.

'That may be so, Ma'am, but they say that this prize is a French privateer commanded by a crook from Naples who put up a strong resistance. They were at Castiglione loading bullocks and the French were not going to give up without a fight. I hear that the captain was wounded quite severely. So his Lordship must have some qualities of courage and leadership, despite your observation'.

Early in April letters arrived from England and from Admiral Jervis and with them came a direct order to withdraw the army from Elba and escort it to Gibraltar and then to rejoin the fleet off Cadiz. A flurry of activity followed as suitable vessels were found and chartered to carry the army and all the stores. The Captain was everywhere inspecting ships checking on storage facilities, ensuring seaworthiness and confirming that the masters understood the orders and would stay with the convoy.

Various passengers began to settle themselves aboard Inconstant and Ben, of course, was much involved in helping them adapt to life onboard. General Horneck was there, polite but boring, thought Betsey; and Major Hadden, smiling and laughing, for whom nothing seemed to present any difficulty; and grey haired old Major Duncan Campbell, entirely straightforward; Captain Montresor, a rather stiff and formal but very gentlemanly youngster; and Major Brindley, solemn and cheerless, but able to play the flute to Betsey's accompaniment on the harpsichord. Ten days after the orders had been received the convoy was ready and Fremantle gave the order to weigh anchor and set off for Gibraltar.

A few days out from Elba when all was going well, the cry 'Ship ahoy' led to a renewed flurry of activity as everyone prepared for the possibility that the sails might be hostile. As the distance closed the level of anxiety rose when three ships of the line were identified with three frigates. Telescopes were trained on the ships' mastheads to try to identify the pennants, and, with something of a sigh of relief, they were acknowledged to be British ships. As they closed it was clear that Rear Admiral Nelson, for he had been promoted after the Battle of Cape St Vincent, was approaching in Captain, accompanied by Colossus and Leander. The frigates Seahorse, Meleager and Caroline were also in company. With the addition of these six ships the convoy's escort was strong enough to fight off any threat from the enemy.

The admiral visited Inconstant for dinner one day and Ben was there to greet him at the gangway.

'How are you Luckett. Good to see you again. I guess you have been looking after our two lovebirds alright, eh?'

'Yes Sir. They seem to be flourishing as far as I can tell. But if I may Sir, congratulations on your great victory at St Vincent. Stories we hear tell of great exploits'.

'We put the Spanish into their proper place, and I daresay we'll do so again – and next time, I expect you to be somewhere close, rather than hiding away ashore in Elba'.

There was a bright twinkle in his eye as Nelson moved quickly on towards the Captain's cabin and several hours of discussion. There seemed to be something magnetic about the way in which Nelson was able to inspire his captains; he took time to get to know them and understand them. These long meetings and dinners, where much wine and port were consumed, were all part of the process whereby these leaders would know and trust each other so that in the heat of battle, despite being unable to communicate with each other, they needed to rely upon mutual support and understanding.

For the first two weeks the convoy seemed to keep quite well together, although progress was only as fast as the slowest amongst the transports. Then the weather changed and a fierce wind, rising to gale force, blew from the west. The sea rose and many of the passengers were seasick; meals became almost impossible. Ben went on one occasion to see how Betsey was coping and found her in her cabin sitting on the deck trying to read but obviously finding it very difficult with the motion and the lack of light. After two or three days of the blow there were only sixteen of the convoy of forty in sight, and the Admiral had taken his squadron off.

Just over five weeks after leaving Elba the convoy arrived at Gibraltar and approached the anchorage. Ben was at his post ready to let go the anchor at a signal from the quarterdeck. He could see Meleager closing up ahead and thought to himself that Inconstant was moving too fast. The anchor must go now to slow the ship down, but the signal did not come until too late. As the anchor hit the bottom and began to hold Inconstant struck Meleager, fortunately not too hard, but nonetheless Captain Fremantle was greatly embarrassed and annoyed that the Master had allowed it to happen. Ben had quickly ordered some sailors onto the bowsprit to check the damage and disentangle the ropes from Meleager. Fortunately everything could be put right within an hour or two.

Almost as soon as the anchor was down, boats came alongside and the passengers began to disembark. The Captain and Betsey were invited by Colonel Hill, whom Fremantle had met when living in London with his Coldstream Guards brother John, to move ashore and stay with him whilst they remained in port. The Captain spent most of his days onboard, dealing with naval matters.

'I am to move into Seahorse', he said one morning to Ben, 'and I'd like you to come with me. Apart from your obvious skill as a mariner you have been a great help to my wife and she would be much inconvenienced if you did not remain with us. I'm sorry that it'll delay your return home'.

'That's kind of you, Sir. I came out here to find you and do whatever I might to support you, so I'd be very happy to go with you. I miss my own wife and family and long to see how the children are grown but there's an important job to be done here. When do we move?'

'We'll go over tomorrow. Captain Oakes is so unwell he really must get home. Inconstant will sail directly taking the army people. Seahorse will be a challenge for us. The crew has not been used to discipline and order so we'll have to knock them into shape and she's in dockyard hands at the moment needing a fair amount of repair. But once that's been dealt with she should be as good as new. I doubt Mrs Fremantle is going to be very pleased about it as she's been expecting to go on to England'.

'Shall I make arrangements for her in Seahorse, Sir? She seems to have appreciated having her own cabin where she can stay out of the way, especially when you're entertaining. And she'll be requiring her harpsichord in the great cabin I suspect?'

'Yes, that's right. Please fix it all with the First Lieutenant. We'll stay at Colonel Hill's until Seahorse is ready but I'll be onboard every day to get to know the ship and people before we sail. We'll need to be very alert for signs of trouble. Have you heard about the mutinies at the Nore? It seems that a large body of sailors have expressed their discontent at their conditions of service'.

'There's been no talk about that on these messdecks as far as I know, but I'll keep an ear to the ground so I can warn you if any trouble is brewing'.

Two days later the Seahorse all the Fremantle's baggage had been moved and the harpsichord was set up. Meanwhile Inconstant sailed for home with a letter from Ben to Sally and his children. Ben began to get to know his new shipmates, and he found himself being much quizzed about their new captain and his wife. Everyone was anxious to know how things might change under a new captain and whether there would be more or less cat. Ben was happy to tell them that the Captain was a very determined sort of person who expected everyone around him to behave professionally. 'He doesn't like using the cat', Ben would say, 'but make no mistake, he's not afraid to do so when someone's let him down'.

On 25th June Betsey went aboard Seahorse which she said was much cooler than being ashore. A week later they weighed anchor and set sail to rejoin the fleet off Cadiz. On their first day at sea the Captain was anxious to exercise the crew at gunnery and all was made ready. It was a relief to find that the guns' crews were reasonably competent, although lacking recent practice; it appeared that Captain Oakes had not insisted on the daily gunnery exercises which enabled the British fleet to fire faster and more accurately than the enemy. They exercised too in the use of muskets and pikes. Although it would be the ships of the line which would take the brunt of any battle it would be a very unwise and slack frigate Captain who failed to prepare his own ship for action.

As soon as they joined the inshore squadron of the fleet on 1st July a message came from the Commander in Chief, now Admiral Lord St Vincent, aboard the Ville de Paris, for Betsey to go and dine. Her husband had been required by Admiral Nelson for some operational talks and so was unable to accompany her. She duly prepared herself and Ben escorted her across the short distance to the flagship. Onboard the Admiral greeted Betsey with the affection a father might have shown for his daughter.

'Well, well', began the Admiral, 'What a treat, my dear, to have the privilege of entertaining you onboard again. We had some most enjoyable times when you and your family were with us off Toulon last year. Now you must come and tell me all that you've been up to since then. Quite a lot to tell if I'm not much mistaken'. And he led Betsey off to the great cabin. Whilst Betsey was enjoying the Admiral's company Ben took time to explore the flagship and talk to some of the sailors. He had a sense of unrest although not to the extent of mutiny; most of the ship's company had been at sea for more than two years now and most of that time had been blockading first the French fleet in Toulon, and now the Spanish in Cadiz. Only the excitement of the battle off Cape St Vincent on St Valentine's Day had briefly alleviated the boredom. That was the overwhelming sentiment – boredom – living off boring food, every day scrubbing decks, exercising guns, repairing rotten ropes, no change of scene, no change of company.

Two evenings later there was some excitement amongst the inshore squadron which was commanded by Admiral Nelson. The Thunder, a bomb ketch, equipped with a 12.1/2 inch mortar and a 10 inch howitzer had arrived from Gibraltar, and she was anchored so that she could bombard Cadiz itself. In response the Spaniards had prepared a flotilla of small boats which set off to disrupt and end the bombardment. The British flotilla of boats, two from each ship of the inshore squadron led by Nelson himself, was there to meet them and a fierce, hand to hand fight ensued. Ben had started the evening by taking his Captain and some of the best sailors from Seahorse across to Thunder. The Captain had gone aboard to meet Nelson, who almost at once set off in his own launch, insisting that Captains Miller and Fremantle should accompany him. Ben immediately followed, shouting as loud as he could to the other British boats 'Follow the Admiral'. The men were armed with a fearsome assortment of weapons – pikes, cutlasses, pistols, sledgehammers, marlin spikes, and muskets – and as the two flotillas closed it was clearly going to be a hard fight. Ben encouraged his oarsmen to keep up with Nelson's boat and they met the Spaniards at almost the same instant. The fighting was furious and bloody but difficult since the boats of the opposing forces were moving up and down on the slight swell. At first the British thought that the Spaniards were yielding, but they were being enticed towards a stronger force. 'It was bloody and hard', said Ben afterwards, 'Cut, thrust, slash, fire, parry. No chance to re-load'. Ben could see the Admiral's boat ahead of him apparently alongside a Spanish launch and having a very tough time. He steered his boat straight alongside and joined the fight seeing out the corner of his eye Nelson and Fremantle in the thick of the fighting. Gradually the Spaniards gave in and those who could swim jumped into the water and struck out for land. Both sides began to count their dead and wounded, and in due course the British sailors took 121 prisoners, including the Spanish commander Don Miguel Tregoyen. Thirty of them proved to be fatally wounded.

It was around 5am when Ben and his boat's crew pulled wearily back to the Seahorse taking his Captain who had been cut and bruised about his face and shoulders, as well as the other men who had survived the fight. Betsey had not gone to bed and was distressed, but relieved that her husband had returned and began at once to tend and dress his wounds while the surgeons were kept busy looking after the other wounded. Over the following days it was clear that the attack had not achieved its objective of persuading the Spanish fleet to set sail and come to a full-scale battle. A fisherman came on board and told them that there were now virtually no women or children left in Cadiz, such had been the effect of the bombardment. He had heard of one mother and baby who had both been killed by a direct hit from the British. It was clear that the people of Cadiz were frightened, but not enough to force the Spanish navy to attempt to neutralise the waiting British fleet.

Chapter 20

After the incident off Cadiz Ben noticed that Betsey was a little nervous that her husband might get himself into another scrape and not come out of it quite so well.

'We can't just hang around here wishing our lives away. We must find something to do which will make a difference,' said the Captain to Ben as they cruised back and forth off Cadiz, waiting for something to happen. 'Admiral Nelson is advocating having a go at the Spaniards by intercepting the treasure galleon on its return from America this year, which should be quite soon. It always calls in at Tenerife, so we could try to intercept it there. It all depends on whether Earl St Vincent as we must now call him will authorise such an expedition'.

Nothing happened for some weeks beyond frequent meetings, when Captain Fremantle would visit Admiral Nelson in Theseus which was now his flagship, and the Admiral and other captains would visit Seahorse for dinner or just for talk. On 15th July an official order came. Nelson was to lead a small force of ships of the line and frigates, with some extra marines onboard, to sail to Tenerife with the particular object of cutting out the Spanish treasure galleon and taking any other prizes available.

The mood onboard changed markedly as the little fleet set off from the blockade heading south towards Tenerife. Plans were drawn up by Nelson and his captains which allowed an approach under cover of darkness in order to surprise the Spaniards and make the taking of the galleon an easier prospect. The masters of the ships calculated the course and speed required to arrive off Santa Cruz, the port and capital of Tenerife, as dawn broke. In the event the wind turned against them and the current proved stronger than expected and they were still well short of the target as dawn broke. The Spaniards were immediately alerted to the approach of a potentially hostile naval force and began to take defensive measures. The fleet approached the anchorage at Santa Cruz and saw at once that there were no full sized ships there; the galleon had either been and gone, or it had yet to arrive.

Disappointment onboard was palpable, as the ships hauled away from the island to consider the next move.

As Ben took his captain across to Theseus for a conference, the Captain said 'I can't believe Nelson will allow us to turn round and head back to Cadiz. Surely we can at least give the dons a bloody nose'.

The following day a new plan was ready to be put into action. Every ship would contribute a boatload or two of marines to make a landing force under the command of Captain Tom Troubridge, which would approach in darkness and take by surprise the fort which commanded the approach to Santa Cruz. The Captains estimated that there were very few full time soldiers on the island and that the militia would probably be an untrained rabble of farmers with pitchforks. Their assessment was reinforced by a German who came off from the island and sought protection from the British fleet.

During the night all the boats were loaded and cast off from their ships to pull the few miles to the target fort. But, once again, the adverse current had been underestimated and at dawn they still had a mile to run. As the boats approached they could see soldiers preparing to defend their fort. Guns were clearly seen pointing towards the boats. Captain Troubridge hesitated; should he carry on with the attack and hope that the boats approaching from different directions would mean that the defenders could not cover all of them. Some would get through. But the loss of life might be very considerable and it looked as though the Spaniards were, against expectation, quite well prepared. So they turned around and made their way back onboard.

There was no rejoicing at a great victory that day. The marines had been sitting in boats for hours through the cold dawn and into the heat of the day; the boats' crews had been pulling almost without a break for five or six hours. There was nothing to show for all that effort. Once again the captains conferred and another plan was hatched. A force would land a little further from the town on an easy beach which Troubridge had spotted. They would climb the hill, meeting no resistance from the garrison or militia, and would march relatively unopposed in overwhelming force into Santa Cruz.

Ben took charge of Seahorse's boat and the plan seemed to be going well as they ran ashore and the marines landed without mishap. They set off up the hill and only then realised that it was covered with small thorn bushes through which they must hack their way; added to that the surface consisted largely of broken slate-like rock which was slippery. Ben could see that progress upwards was slow; and it got slower as the sun rose in the July sky and the temperature approached 100 degrees. The sailors waiting with the boats on the beach wondered how far their colleagues would get. It was beginning to look like a shambles rather than a victorious army. By early afternoon marines were beginning to return to the boats in a state of exhaustion having run out of water and suffering from heat stroke. Gradually it became clear that this attempt had failed.

Captain Troubridge himself looked dejected and utterly exhausted as he reached the beach. His sergeant was collecting up a few stragglers. 'Set off back to your ships as soon as everyone is accounted for', ordered the Captain. Ben ordered his bowman to push off and backed out into deeper water before turning towards Seahorse.

'That was as close to hell as I have been,' said one marine, 'and when we reached the top of the hill there was a steep gully to get across and another hill to climb. We paused up there and we could see on the skyline a large force of militia forming up. So we would have had to take them on when they had all the advantage of the high ground. We would have been mincemeat'.

That evening there was another conference aboard Theseus. It was late when Ben brought his Captain back to Seahorse. 'Now we are going to do it properly', said the Captain. 'We will put all our forces ashore and drive a frontal attack on Santa Cruz itself. The Admiral will lead in the centre, Captain Miller and I will be on the right, and Troubridge on the left. The Spaniards will not know what has hit them'.

Later as they readied themselves for sleep, Betsey asked her husband 'What demands will you make of the Dons when they surrender to you?'

'We will get some sort of ransom from them, to make up for having missed the galleon'.

'That seems a poor return for a risky operation. But then, of course, I don't understand that sort of thing'.

'Nothing worthwhile was ever won without risk. We thrashed them in February so we shall do so again in July'.

Betsey was far from convinced, but realised that there was nothing she could do about it.

The following evening Nelson came aboard to dine in Seahorse with all the captains, before they set off to fulfil their latest plan. Claret flowed in profusion and Betsey could feel the enormous sense of optimism and excitement which electrified the cabin. They finished dinner and the captains prepared themselves for the action which was to come. At eleven o'clock they all boarded their boats and took station amongst the armada which made up the invasion force. Ben accompanied his Captain, armed with a cutlass and a pair of pistols, and they steered out to head the right wing of the fleet. It was a hard pull and the wind had risen considerably to create an uncomfortable lop which caused spray to drench those close to the bow. After three hours or more the beach could be seen ahead. But the surf was much higher than they had expected. It was going to be a real test of seamanship to get the boats ashore without broaching and tipping all the men into deep water. What was worse was that the largest troop-carrying boats had been towed and had very limited manoeuvrability. Ben was confident of landing the Captain successfully and he surfed onto the beach almost without hesitation. On the beach he was over the side almost as quickly as the Captain, who immediately began rallying the marines as some of them came ashore. He watched, horrified, as several boats broached tipping all the marines out. Encumbered with their weapons and ammunition even those who could swim found it difficult to save themselves. Many reached the beach exhausted, soaked, and without musket or sword. Captains Fremantle and Miller rallied as many men as they could find who still had weapons and energy, and started up the beach.

Meanwhile the Spaniards had mobilised their forces and opened fire on the beach. Grape shot from cannons began to take its toll of the men, and they had gone only a few yards when Captain Fremantle called to Ben, 'I am hit - my right arm - I can be of no use to anyone now'.

'I'm here, Sir. Let's get you back to the boat and see what we can do'. They turned and ran as fast as they could back down the beach to where Ben had left sailors in charge of the Captain's boat. There were already several other wounded men there, being tended by colleagues. Makeshift bandages were being applied to stop the flow of blood, and slings improvised to help support shattered limbs.

'How much are you bleeding, Sir?' asked Ben.

'It's a mess, but I don't think it's got the artery', replied the Captain.

'That's a relief. But we had best get you and these other men off as soon as we can'.

The Captain was clearly in great pain and he held the weight of his wounded arm in the other.

'Thank you, Luckett. Will you get the men into the boat first and I will follow. How many can you take?'

Ben was too busy to answer as he helped the other wounded men into the boat, ordering the seamen to hold it steady and to keep it afloat as it was gradually loaded. Finally he said to the Captain, 'Right, Sir, you now, please', and he helped the Captain over the gunwhale.

The sea was still running with plenty of surf and Ben would have trouble controlling the boat as it rose over the breaking waves. With a great heave the sailors holding the boat and Ben pushed as hard as they could and jumped in at the last possible minute. 'Give way together', ordered Ben to the men at the oars and the boat's bow bucked skywards as Ben seized the tiller and the rudder bit and held the direction steady. Then they were in calmer water, beyond the breakers and heading back to the ships. As they neared the fleet Ben recognised Zealous closest at hand and headed towards her. It was about 4 am.

Meanwhile Betsey had retired to bed onboard Seahorse as soon as the landing party had left. She had felt little apprehension about the outcome in view of the very positive attitude of Nelson and his captains as they set off. She woke at six with a start and an uncomfortable sense that all was not well. As soon as she could she went onto the upper deck to find out more. The Master was pacing anxiously on the quarterdeck.

'Good morning, Mr Johnson. Do you have any news?' asked Betsey.

'Nothing specific yet. We have seen a number of boats returning but none has come here, although I think that one there is heading this way'. They could see a boat pulling away from Zealous, heading for Seahorse. Betsey thought she could see a Captain's uniform and cocked hat in the stern.

The boat was soon alongside and Fremantle was being helped up the side, his right arm being held tightly in a sling. He was clearly in considerable pain and struggling to remain on his feet. Betsey helped her husband down to their quarters before asking him about his wound and the events of the night.

'It was a disaster', he said. 'Again we misjudged the weather and the current. And the surf was impossibly high. Many of the boats broached before they got to the beach; men were drowned, and those who survived were encumbered with soaked kit and useless powder. We didn't stand a chance. Besides, the Spaniards were far better prepared than we'd been led to believe. The information that German gave us was quite incorrect. I don't know what happened to Miller but I know that poor Captain Bowen is dead'.

'What about you?' asked Betsey, 'are you seriously hurt?'

'It seems that it's only a flesh wound, thank God. The surgeon in Zealous cleaned it up as best he could and has dressed it. I just have to hope it will all heal without infection. At least there seems no need to lose the arm at the moment. I have heard that Nelson took a ball and that his arm has gone. Has anything been heard of what is going on ashore?' Betsey was unable to tell him anything and continued to fuss around in an effort to make him as comfortable as possible.

Meanwhile Ben and the boat's crew had come onboard to dry out and get some food. Ben spoke to the Master.

'We will need to send the boat in again to bring off more wounded. And we may be able to see what's been achieved. Captain Miller managed to get a little further than we did as he was on our right, but he will have met fierce resistance and has probably made little progress'.

'Thank you Luckett. Well done to get our Captain off so quickly. Go and get some food and have a rest while I send someone else in with the boat.' And with that Ben went off below, wet and exhausted after the frustrating night's work.

Gradually during the day the situation became clearer. The Spaniards had been far better prepared than expected and the attack had indeed proved disastrous. Nelson had led the section towards the mole but as he stepped onto it the cannon at its landward end fired a round of grapeshot. One of the balls struck Nelson's right arm and he fell back into the boat into the arms of his stepson Midshipman Nesbitt. The young man had the presence of mind to apply a tourniquet immediately, to stop the flow of blood pumping from the artery, and within minutes the boat was heading back to the fleet. Although Seahorse was closest, Nelson ordered to be taken on to Theseus. 'I can give Mrs Fremantle no news of her husband', he said. Within minutes of arriving in Theseus Nelson's arm had been amputated and he was left to recover from the physical shock and pain as well as to contemplate the failure of his enterprise.

Later in the day all the remaining boats were sent inshore to wait off the mole for the British party to be re-embarked. The wounded came first and then a bedraggled body of men, with their arms and banners, doing their best to appear undefeated, although the truth was that their attempt to humiliate the Spaniards had seriously backfired.

The mood on the lower deck was morose. The sailors and marines all felt that they had been put through several days of extreme toil and hardship and had achieved absolutely nothing. There would be no prize money to show for it, no exciting stories to tell the people back home. But, at least in Seahorse, there had not been too many casualties with only two dead and fifteen wounded.

Nelson's bruised squadron headed northwards to re-join Admiral St Vincent and the main fleet. Betsey was encouraged when she received a scrap of paper tucked in with a copy of Nelson's official report of the events. It must have been one of the first things he had written with his left hand, a scrawl which said 'God bless you and Fremantle'. The report was masterly and drew attention to the valour of the British marines and sailors, and praised the humanity of the Spaniards and especially the Governor. Characteristically Nelson attributed no blame to Troubridge for the initial failure to take the fort, nor to Miller or Fremantle for promoting so strongly the plan for a frontal assault which had proved so utterly catastrophic. Praise was lavished upon the captains, officers and men for their 'daring intrepidity'.

The wind failed and for days as July turned into August they drifted, sails hanging limply from the yards. Captain Troubridge visited Seahorse and brought his surgeon from Zealous with him, believing that Fremantle's wound was not healing as it should. Mr Eshelby found that Seahorse's surgeon, Fleming, had not prescribed bark and port wine. At first this prescription seemed to offer some relief but after a few days the pain was as intense as ever. From time to time the wind got up a little and then the motion of the ship intensified the pain, and when it died the heat became oppressive and the slow progress frustrating.

More than two weeks passed before the Captain was again seen on the quarterdeck. Ben had the opportunity of a conversation with him.

'I'm not sure whether I ever thanked you properly, Luckett, for bringing me off after I was hit. I don't remember much about what happened'.

'We've all been concerned for your health, Sir, in recent days, and it's good to see you on your feet again. That surf off Santa Cruz was what really did for us. It was too difficult to control the launches with the marines as they approached the beach. If we'd had an easy landing on the beach I daresay we would have been victorious. But I only did what anyone would've done - I was lucky not to be hit myself, for I was only a few feet from you when you went down'.

'It's no good regretting the whole thing just now. Perhaps we just believed we were somehow magically invulnerable after the extraordinary victory in February. This has all shown that there is no magic, even in the name of Nelson; we're all humans, and make mistakes and misjudgements'.

'Please let me know if there's anything I can do to help your recovery and make life easier, while your wound heals'.

'Thank you Luckett. I can't possibly ask you to be more attentive than you are already. Mrs. Fremantle tells me you have always given her great encouragement. But for now I think I must go below again. The pain is returning and I'm not feeling altogether steady on my feet'. And so-saying the captain walked rather shakily off to his cabin.

The following day the main fleet was in sight and by afternoon some mail arrived and there was a continuous procession of visiting captains wanting to call upon the Captain and his wife and wish them well. All the activity seemed to aggravate the Captain's wound and on the day after, he remained in his cot unable to see anyone, even Earl St Vincent.

After four days with the fleet during which Betsey had renewed her acquaintance with many of the captains she had met previously, Admiral Nelson came onboard with Surgeon Eshelby and as many of the wounded from other ships as could be accommodated, and Seahorse set off again to the north, heading for Portsmouth.

The north-westerly wind required them to set a course well out into the Atlantic and although the breeze was fresh, driving into a moderate sea caused the ship to pitch and toss in a way which was very uncomfortable, not only for the two wounded officers in the great cabin but also for all the other wounded men lying below.

On the upper deck one morning Betsey took the opportunity for a conversation with Ben, to express her worries about her husband.

'Well Ma'am, if what the surgeon says is correct it's only a matter of time and the wound will heal completely'.

'Yes, but in the meantime he suffers so much pain. Surely he should be getting stronger by now and I see him being weaker - and more frustrated as a result'.

'These things take time. But you've other things to think about and prepare for now', added Ben thinking of the early signs that she was pregnant.

'Indeed I have much to look forward to. Apart from Captain Wells, I have not met any of my husband's family and I want to make a good impression from the start which would be so much easier if Captain Fremantle was well'.

'That's true enough. But I doubt you'll have any difficulty there. It was the other thing I was thinking about, which will have a profound impact on your life I'm sure'.

'What do you mean?' she paused. 'Are you suggesting…..No-one is supposed to know that I'm carrying his child'.

'That may be so, Ma'am. But it's very clear to anyone who sees you every morning'.

'I've felt queasy most mornings these last few weeks, but I try to keep it to myself as much as I can. If my reckoning is correct I can expect a new arrival in March'.

'So in the meantime there will be many preparations to make and the Captain, if he's unwell, will have to rely on you. No time to be sad and worried but rather happy and hopeful'.

Betsey smiled, knowing that, once again, Ben was right.

A few days later, on the afternoon of 1st September, Seahorse dropped anchor at Spithead. Despite the foul weather Nelson insisted on being taken ashore at once.

'Well, Luckett,' he said as the boat pulled away from the ship's side, 'That seems to close another chapter. And now I've no idea what life holds in store for me. Who on earth will ever employ a one-armed admiral who can only see through one eye, and who is frequently laid low with stomach cramps and malaria? I reckon you'll be back at sea before me'.

'I hope we can serve together again, Sir, some time, some place. But I must admit just now I'm filled with longing to see my children and my wife. I'm concerned about Captain and Mrs Fremantle too and I'd like to be able to serve them at least until they are settled somewhere'.

'You're fortunate indeed to have a family to return to. I long to see my wife, like you, but almost despair of ever knowing the joy of playing with a child of my own. Do you remember when we first went to visit Mr Herbert on Nevis and I managed to get lost playing games with young Josiah under the dining room table? Now that's the sort of worthwhile thing I could do even with only one arm. But first to London and the Admiralty to see if they'll let me back to sea'.

The boat came gently alongside the Sally Port and Ben saluted smartly as the Admiral stepped ashore and his servant Tom Allen followed carrying his bags. And before setting off up the street Nelson turned towards the boat and said, 'Thank you all, and good luck when you get ashore. There's a job for all of you when I get back to sea'.

He set off up the street as briskly as ever despite the fact that the stump of his arm must have been causing him pain. It was only six weeks.

'Let go for'ard. Let go aft', ordered Ben, and the boat pulled away and returned to Seahorse.

On the following day Captain and Mrs Fremantle went ashore into lodgings which had been found for them, and at their request Ben accompanied them. Visitors began to arrive to welcome them as a married couple, on English soil for the first time and Betsey did not have long to wait before she began to meet Fremantle's family. At first it was his brother William, to whom he was evidently very closely attached. They had much to discuss and talked late into the evening which left the Captain very weak. Amongst other things William needed to tell of his forthcoming marriage to a widow, Mrs Felton Harvey, who already had five children, but who was very rich. They needed to talk about plans as to where the Captain and his pregnant wife might live at least until the baby had arrived.

The excitement brought back the Captain's pain and fever and the medical men counselled that he must rest and see no-one for the time being. But his oldest brother John(Jack) arrived, with whom Betsey immediately formed a close bond. She called on Sir Peter and Lady Parker who had looked after Nelson like a son when he had been in the West Indies. And then Fremantle's mother arrived. Ben, standing in the background, noted with relief that the younger lady seemed to take an immediate liking to her mother-in-law and they seemed immediately able to laugh and joke together and generally enjoy each other's company.

Fremantle's family had clearly made a big effort to travel down to Portsmouth to greet their wounded hero, and meet his young wife. William made a second visit, and Mr Bishop and Mr Cathcart his brothers-in-law both arrived.

After three weeks the Captain said to Ben, one morning, 'I've had enough, Luckett, of all these visitors. I shall write today and ask to be relieved of my command so that I can recover quietly. We'll need to spend a few months in London, but as soon as we can, we'll find a place in the country where we can be together without this constant stream of people asking me how I am'.

'And might I ask, Sir, which particular bit of the country you had in mind?'

'I daresay somewhere not too far from Aston Abbots where I grew up. That would be quite convenient, don't you think'.

'If that were to come to pass, I should hope to be able to continue to serve you, with my wife and family, for they are now at Chackmore with her parents. I am hopeful that my prize money will be enough to get us a home of our own'.

'Let's not build too many castles in the air. For the time being Mr Eastman has found us a cottage on a farm at Purbrook a few miles north of here'.

The party moved into this secluded farmhouse as the guests of Mr and Mrs Sedley. Fewer visitors found them there and the Captain was gradually more often well than not, although he frequently complained of severe pain in his hand.

Ben found time hanging heavily with too little to keep him usefully occupied and he requested that he might be released so that he could travel to Buckinghamshire to see his family.

'We shall have to manage without you as I can see there is insufficient to keep you busy. I hope we shall only be here until the end of October and will then move to London. If all goes according to my present plan we shall be at Stowe for Christmas'.

So Ben left the Fremantle household. He had joined Inconstant 15 months earlier, and now he was leaving a happy and well-established couple still enjoying the months of discovery after marriage, expecting the arrival of a baby. How different, he reflected, was the navy he had been with through these recent months when compared with the navy on Norfolk Island, the one ever alert for the chance of a prize or of battering the French or Spanish enemy with gunfire, continually at sea, working the ship every day, cleaning, repairing, making and re-making.... the other struggling to provide food and equipment for a community of convicts to supply the parent colony with whatever they could. Both were focussed on survival, one in the face of the elements and the enemy, the other threatened always by starvation and the unknown at the other side of the globe.

He was proud to be part of King George's Navy, even though it was so big that it was incomprehensible. And yet those at the Admiralty in London who governed all its operations were apparently so few - a number of Captains, some politicians, and the civil servants to keep the records and communicate the decisions they made, all ensuring that matters were always dealt with in the correct priority.

He was glad to be going home.

Chapter 21

Ben's home-coming brought great joy, not only to his immediate family, but to the whole village of Chackmore. News of his arrival even reached Stowe House and Lady Buckingham herself expressed delight at his safe return. She had already heard from Captain Fremantle himself about his marriage and had written a letter of welcome to the new Mrs Fremantle, expressing the hope that both of them would visit Stowe and spend Christmas there to enable the Captain to recuperate and begin to take a full part in Buckinghamshire life. She sent Ben a message of welcome and asked Mr Sharp, the agent, to make sure that the villagers had everything necessary for a worthy celebration.

'It's not often', she declared to Mr Sharp, 'that a little land-locked village like Chackmore has the opportunity to celebrate the home-coming of a naval hero such as Luckett. Fremantle has spoken very highly of him and, indeed, how he owes his life to him'.

'That's good to hear, Ma'am. When I first met him I was impressed by his evidently steady character and what seemed to be a very balanced outlook on life. Would it be appropriate if I were to arrange some barrels of beer for them? And I can make sure that they have plenty of bunting at their disposal; if you recall, we used a great deal of it earlier in the year for your own parties'.
So very soon after Ben's arrival, the following Sunday had been declared party day in Chackmore. Her ladyship rode out to the village and greeted Ben, congratulating Sally too on the progress of the children, Thomas, aged 4, Sarah, 3 and James, 2; her carriage had been filled with all sorts of cakes, joints of meat and poultry from the Stowe House kitchens to ensure that no-one in Chackmore went hungry. It all contributed to the sense of excitement and joy.

By the time Christmas came round, routine had settled back to normal and Ben found himself wandering rather aimlessly around the Stowe gardens, lending a hand to the gardeners where he could. 'I must keep myself occupied somehow', he said to Sally, 'otherwise I'll just get under your feet and stop you getting on with looking after the children'. But it was the children who gave him greatest joy. James whom he had never met was suspicious at first of this strange man who had suddenly entered his young life. But Ben was a master at inventing toys for him and encouraging him by getting down on the floor and crawling behind him as his little legs scuttled uncertainly around the house. Thomas and Sarah were just able to remember him although Ben realised he must win their confidence again. He found a scrap of wooden plank, and with a few cuts of a saw had shaped a boat; a hazel twig, whittled, pointed and stuck into the boat formed a mast, and Thomas had a toy which at once connected him to his father's profession and gave him hours of imaginative play. Bits of old material became the waves, and scraps of twigs and some stones became the enemy. He found it more difficult to connect with Sarah whose inclination was clearly more towards her mother and the sort of tasks she did. Ben's triumph which finally won Sarah's heart was the little rocking cradle he made using sticks of various sizes cut from the hedgerows or picked up in the Stowe gardens.

Captain and Mrs Fremantle duly arrived for Christmas as guests of Lord and Lady Buckingham who pressed them to stay as long as necessary for Fremantle to recover fully from his wound. One day early in the New Year, the Captain asked Ben to accompany him on a tour around the neighbouring countryside; Mrs Fremantle, he said, would remain at home due to the cold weather and the fact that she was now well into the seventh month of her pregnancy. So they rode two horses provided by the Stowe stables, off towards Buckingham; through the town and out to Winslow.

'I want to go to Aston Abbots where I was brought up', he said, 'and see how that has changed. I have not been there for years. We'll stay at the Royal Oak and set off for home tomorrow'.

Fortunately the weather was kind and they reached the village during the afternoon. The Captain was fascinated to see how open farmland had now been enclosed with hedges, and the sheep seemed to be fenced in rather than being allowed to roam to find the best grass, supervised by a shepherd or a boy. They passed the Abbey which had been his home as a boy, rented by his father from the Earl of Chesterfield, and ventured up the driveway, and it was clear that the house was no longer occupied. They looked into the old church of St James the Great so that the Captain could remind himself where he and his brothers had all been baptised.

By the time they reached the Royal Oak the light was fading but the landlord and a roaring fire gave them a hearty welcome. Ben made sure that the horses were taken care of and fed, and then they were able to enjoy a glass of ale and a good dinner.

On the following day the weather was still fine and they set off as early as they could to the north. They went through the village of Cublington and the little hamlets of Dunton and Hoggeston and reached Swanbourne late in the morning. They passed the church and rode a little further along the lane past a farm and some cottages on their left. A larger house stood on their right, respectable but not grand, and as they reached the end of the village they found the Swan Inn.

When the landlord brought jug of small beer to refresh them and set it beside the fire, the Captain opened a conversation, asking about the village and who occupied the various farms and other houses. Not surprisingly the landlord was a fount of knowledge and was able to tell them about John Adams who owned Swanbourne House. His family had lived there for years and he had been granted considerable land as a result of the enclosure acts and had now moved a few miles away to Little Horwood. He no longer had much interest in Swanbourne House or the village itself. As the landlord warmed to the subject of Swanbourne village it was clear that he thought the place was going downhill. Not just Mr Adams leaving and taking no interest any more but old Deverell who had the farm down towards the church; 'He wants to finish as he's too old, he says, and has no family to take it on'.

Ben was bold enough to ask 'Would old Mr Deverell find some young hands helpful?'

'Why, I'm sure he would', replied the landlord, 'though, he's old now and I don't know what would happen if he were to die'.

'I just had a sudden thought that my wife's father is still fit and strong and although he is more of a gardener than farmer he might be someone who Mr Deverell would welcome. And if he has a house to rent it would be interesting for me and my family too'.

The Captain was listening to the conversation and was running through his mind the possibility of acquiring Swanbourne House from Mr Adams. And, he was thinking, if old Deverell dies in the next year or two, his farm might be for sale too.

The conversation was cut short as the Captain stood up and said they must get on; if they were to reach Stowe that evening they could delay no longer. But both men were lost in thought as they rode out towards Winslow and back to Buckingham, arriving at Stowe some while after dark. The Captain was tiring and his wounded arm had begun to hurt again so he was relieved to get back.

As winter set in hard in February the daily task of keeping warm, dry, and fed occupied most of the time. Nonetheless Ben was able to find opportunities to talk with Jack Grover about the possibility of moving to Swanbourne. Sally seemed to be delighted with the idea and gently encouraged her father and mother to contemplate moving, depending on whether there was a better house. When the weather began to improve in March, Ben announced that he was going to Swanbourne to see if he could make some sort of a deal with old Mr Deverell. Three days later he returned with the news that he had agreed that they would have the house opposite the farm which would suit them very well. Jack Grover would help Mr Deverell with the farm and, when he was not at sea Ben too would provide some extra manpower. They would move to Swanbourne as soon as they could.

While Ben was re-settling his own family at Swanbourne, using the money he had saved whilst in Norfolk Island and the prize money from his time in the Mediterranean, he received a letter from Captain Philip Gidley King. The Lieutenant Governor had returned home in a very poor state of health with his family in May 1797. Norfolk and Sydney had been sent home beforehand and were now settled in a school in Yorkshire aiming to enter the navy as midshipmen as soon as they were old enough. Phillip and Anna Maria were in good health and growing up well, but Utricia had died soon after they reached England; little Elizabeth who had been born at sea in February 1797 was doing well. After presenting his reports to the government in London, the family had moved to Launceston in Cornwall and, at the time of Mr King's letter to Ben, he had just received a commission from the Colonial Office appointing him Governor of New South Wales and instructing him to prepare for immediate departure to the colony. The letter concluded with an invitation to Ben to join him on his new adventure; 'Your service to Mrs King and myself on Norfolk Island was of such very great value that we would feel privileged if you would agree to serve us again and contribute your energy to us and this young colony for a few years.'

Ben was at once torn by between staying with his family and returning to sea. He could remain at home for the new baby which Sally was expecting in late September and to share in the upbringing of his children; or he could join the Kings and travel round the world serving a man for whom he had the greatest respect. If he chose the latter Sally might be on her own when the baby was born; but her family would be around her and she would very quickly make friends in Swanbourne. Being the Governor's right hand man would give Ben insights into the running of the colony which would be fascinating, and, perhaps, by relieving the Governor of some of his smaller anxieties and tasks he could help ensure success. Sally was flattered by the attention the Kings had shown Ben. Even though she knew that her husband had every right to decide for himself what to do, she welcomed the opportunity Ben gave her to talk about the options, and together they reached the decision for Ben to accept Mr King's offer. He would be the Governor's Coxswain, and on the outward voyage would also be Master's Mate. They concluded that this would be preferable to returning to the naval service and serving in one of the ships fighting the war against France.

On 3rd October 1798 while Ben was still at home Sally gave birth to a second daughter, Lucy, named after Ben's mother. Two weeks later, Ben received a letter from Governor King asking him to join the family at Deptford to embark in the Porpoise which would take them to Port Jackson. During the intervening months they had settled well into the lodge at Deverell's farm. They had found the little Swanbourne community of farm workers very welcoming, and Ben's departure was marked by many assurances that his family would be well cared for. He arrived in Deptford and found Porpoise in dock having an additional deck housing added for a botanical collection from Sir Joseph Banks which was to be carried out to New South Wales.

The ship appeared to be new and untested and Ben took the chance to walk around her and examine her construction, noting especially such things as the positioning and proportions of her masts, her keel and rudder.   When he met the Governor it was not long before they began talking about the ship.

'The Admiralty asked me to inspect her last year when she was under construction', said the Governor, 'and I was obliged to tell them that I believed the design to be flawed and the construction to be haphazard. In effect, this ship is unlikely to be seaworthy.   But they've taken no notice of me, and so we shall have to see what happens when we go to sea'. Ben could only agree with the Governor's judgement.

They had only a month or so to wait before the dockyard finished their work and Porpoise was cast off and began to drop down the Thames. From the first moment it was clear that the ship did not answer properly to the helm and despite Ben's long experience in other ships he found it impossible to hold a steady course. They put in to Sheerness and made some adjustments and sailed again for Portsmouth.   By the time they reached there, it was clear that this ship would never survive a six month voyage across the world without major repairs. So for the first half of 1799 Porpoise was in dockyard hands, always at the bottom of their priority list because ships destined to fight the French were far more urgently required.

Meanwhile Mr and Mrs King had made the heart-rending decision that only their youngest daughter Elizabeth would return to New South Wales with them. Phillip would live in a small school which would prepare him to enter the naval school as soon as he was old enough. Anna Maria would live with the King's old friends Mr and Mrs Samuel Enderby in London. Beyond the West country connection between their families Mr Enderby had inherited the successful whaling enterprise established in London and now increasingly interested in the Southern Ocean and the waters around New South Wales and New Zealand.

When the dockyard pronounced the end of the repairs, they had to delay sailing again because of the appearance of some French ships, apparently patrolling the south coast looking for English prey. Finally they sailed on 5th September 1799 with a fair south-easterly breeze which should have carried them comfortably down the English Channel and clear into the open sea. But even before they passed the Needles at the western end of the Isle of Wight it was clear that all was not well. Then the tiller cracked and split because of the weight of weather helm, and the rudder itself sprang apart. It was unsafe to venture any further and the master was obliged to hail a nearby fishing boat and ask for assistance to reach Weymouth.

Such a display of incompetence by the dockyard and shipwrights, despite all the warnings from the Governor, and the indifference or preoccupation of the Admiralty, was hugely frustrating. Weeks followed in the exchange of letters with the final acceptance by the Admiralty that Porpoise must be condemned and another vessel found. Almost immediately orders arrived transferring the Governor and his family to Speedy, an Enderby whaler, which was about to sail for Port Jackson with 50 female convicts and supplies for the colony.

They embarked in Speedy at Spithead and, within a few days of their arrival onboard, she sailed. They were on their way at last.

Part Four - Governor of New South Wales

Chapter 22

After an uneventful voyage Speedy, true to her name, arrived in Port Jackson in April 1800. What Ben saw when he first stepped ashore certainly showed that progress had been made, as the original settlement around Sydney Cove and the Tank Stream had now been completely cleared of trees and scrub and a neat row of cottages had been built. Government House was now a substantial building on the east side of the stream looking out towards the new barracks with its substantial Parade Ground.

The arrival of Speedy was greeted with much celebration. But that had nothing to do with the arrival of the new Governor; it was all about the demand for women to comfort the overwhelming majority of men. The supplies of food and goods brought by Speedy would also be very welcome; the colony could not yet be said to be self-sufficient, and there was always a shortage of simple manufactured tools and implements – spades and axes, saws and files, pots and pans – as well as basic clothing materials and little luxuries which could turn endless drudge into occasional delight.

But both the Governor and Ben were also struck at once by the amount of drunkenness. Ben learnt from one drunk that it was the army that was to blame.

'They put up the price of rum, and there's no competition. Spend a few shillings more than you have and within minutes an army officer will be charging you with debt on the one hand whilst giving you a solution on the other. "Give me a charge on your land," he will say, "and I'll lend you enough money to pay for your rum". And then a month later when you've run out of cash because the army hasn't paid you for the food you sold into the store, the weasel will be back, lending you more money against the land value. Then a month or two later when the debt is too high, he'll be back demanding that you sign over the land ownership, in return for which he'll give you employment on your land; but he doesn't pay you for more than an hour's work a week, so you get into debt again, and then there's no way out except to drive the pain away with more rum'.

Shortly after landing Mr King had presented a letter from the Duke of Portland to Governor Hunter, the content of which evidently informed the Governor that he was to retire with immediate effect and hand the responsibilities of the office of Governor to Mr King, a copy of whose commission was also provided. Governor Hunter made it quite clear that he had no intention of standing down, despite the Government's order to do so. This left the Kings in an impossible situation; they had expected to move into Government House at once, but they could not. They suffered the indignity of being billeted in a very inferior cottage, and they had no power to do anything until Governor Hunter chose to surrender his office.

'We'll use our time', he said to Ben, 'in making a full tour of the colony and assessing the state of affairs, and the strengths and the weaknesses. Then at least we can be prepared to get things done as soon as we have a chance'.

'I'll see what I can find out by befriending some of the non-commissioned officers, although I expect they're only interested in lining their own pockets and doing as little work as they can get away with; but there may be some who I got to know on Norfolk – I'm sure they are not all bad'.

Ben found Sergeant Tom Whittle who had been so pivotal when the Norfolk Island detachment had mutinied and invited him to come for a beer and a quiet chat.

'Well I never expected to see you out here again', said the sergeant. 'What was it that persuaded you?'

'Things are pretty hard at home with the war against Napoleon and the navy as usual very short of men and I reckoned that sooner or later I'd have to volunteer or be pressed. In the meantime Mr King wrote to me and asked if I'd like to accompany him. It was a hard decision as I have four children now, and I'd just got them moved into a new house. It seemed like abandoning them when they needed me. But you know

Sally. She's a very determined sort of girl and she calculated that she'd rather have me out here than in a fighting ship'. And he proceeded to recount something of his adventures in the Mediterranean finishing up with a description of the disastrous attempt on Santa Cruz. 'And what has been going on here in the five years since I left', Ben asked.

'You remember how Lieutenant Governor Grose was so much angered by Mr King? It was Grose that encouraged the officers to grab what they could, and fill their pockets. He it was who encouraged them to corner the market in whatever supplies arrived from England or India for sale, although some of them needed no encouragement. Lieutenant Macarthur seems to be the leader, who is clearly determined to make as much money as he can. And he minds not a jot who he damages in the process. So the officers cornered the market in rum, and then in cloth, and tea and coffee and everything you can think of which isn't provided by government. Governor Hunter made a half-hearted attempt to stop it, but when the officers spoke forcefully to him and told him they'd be unable to pay the wages of their employees if they couldn't sell the rum, he quickly caved in. Since then he's never tried to control them. The settlers all hate him because the officers have made life so difficult; there's no point in anyone working hard and making money because as soon as they do, Macarthur and his friends take it all off 'em. You've seen the drunkenness – the soldiers are almost exactly the same; they've too little to do and have no respect for their officers. It's as much as I can do to keep them from mutiny'.

'So what do you think can be done?' asked Ben, although he thought that the sergeant had just about given up on hope.

'Hunter has to go; he's just a waste of space now – weak, indecisive, and out of his depth. They say he's a very fine sea captain, and so he may be, but he's not done much good since he's been here. Now we need someone with strong principles who's prepared to stand up for the settlers and face down Lieutenant Macarthur and the officers – just like Mr King did when he stopped the mutiny on Norfolk. I reckon the first thing which'd attract a lot of praise from the settlers and almost everyone else would be to cut the price of rum'.

'But if you don't have any you can't control the price, can you?' asked Ben.

'The next time a ship comes in with rum to sell, Mr King should get on board and buy the whole cargo himself for government. He should then arrange for the Commissary to sell it at a small profit for the government, rather than the 500% the officers are taking, and the price would be lower for everyone. The big problem with that is that the drunkards might then go and buy more of it and get even more plastered so sales would have to be limited. It'll need a strong man to do that and I hope Mr King can and will'.

The conversation continued for several mugs of ale, and the two men clearly enjoyed each other's company. As they prepared to go to their own lodgings Ben said, 'I've found that all very interesting and I thank you for your confidence. I hope we can meet again before too long; but I think we should keep such meetings as private as we can. In public our relationship must be purely professional; privately we can exchange views and help stiffen Mr King's resolve'. The sergeant replied with a nod as he set off back to the barracks. Ben waited until he was well gone before returning to his own lodgings.

Mr King was very grateful when Ben reported this conversation and encouraged him to maintain a discreet contact with Whittle. 'But I've no authority to do anything before Governor Hunter stands down', he continued, 'we shall have to be patient, however frustrating that may be'.

The winter came and went and the air of lethargy pervading the colony seemed to be heavier than ever. Ben felt that there was no sense of purpose; many people longed to see the back of Governor Hunter, and expressed high hopes for what Governor King might achieve. Others would only support the new Governor if they were confident that they themselves would be more comfortable and wealthy. Meanwhile the friendship which had existed between Hunter and King turned to extreme animosity as the Governor-in-waiting informed his predecessor about the dreadful state the colony was in. It was quite clear that much work was needed to establish the colony on a proper footing so that it could be self-sufficient and become a net exporter of goods. Ben recalled the early days on Norfolk Island when Mr King, as Lieutenant Governor, had made it quite clear that enterprise would be amply rewarded; hard work would earn a good return and idlers would find life difficult and uncomfortable. How could it be right that the army officers had got into a position in which they were the only entrepreneurs. They paid a pittance for labour and goods, charged the earth for everything they sold, and went about bankrupting as many people as possible by calling in the collateral on loans. The army officers were the largest landowners, the greatest employers of labour, especially convicts who they were not required to pay, the wholesalers and retailers. It was true, he thought, that naval officers were accustomed to making money from taking prizes; but that was always as a result of action and was always aimed at damaging an enemy, adjudged by a court, and shared amongst the whole ship's company. This was different because the only beneficiaries were the army officers.

Ben had also come across a number of Irishmen who had arrived earlier in the year in a direct voyage from Dublin after being convicted of a variety of offences during the uprising in Ireland a few years earlier. Many of these convicts were well-educated and even titled gentlemen, who regarded themselves as political prisoners rather than common felons, and therefore they should not be required to undertake any manual labour. They should be fed, housed and exercised at government expense. And of course they should have complete freedom of expression to publish any calumny against the King and his government. How could that work, Ben wondered, when everyone else was trying to grow enough food not just to avoid starvation, but also to make the colony self-sufficient. It was difficult enough to provide food for the newly-arrived convicts many of whom were too weak to do anything.

Many of these Irishmen had begun plotting even before they arrived, to overthrow the army and the government and make their escape from New South Wales. Everything came to a head on Saturday 28th September when the Reverend Mr Marsden, the magistrate at Parramatta, was informed by his shepherd that the Irish were about to launch an attack which would involve taking and killing the soldiers and gentlemen whilst they were at church the following morning. They would then attack the barracks and capture or kill the remainder of the detachment at Parramatta; this would give them access to weapons which could be used to move on Sydney.

Mr Marsden immediately had the shepherd's informant, John Lewis, arrested, and whilst being questioned he began to reveal the other people involved in the plot. Overnight they were all arrested, and, instead of attending Divine Service on Sunday morning the officers were busily engaged in questioning and taking statements from those involved. Gradually the plot was revealed and more of the Irish in Sydney were arrested.

On 29th September 1800 with due pomp Governor Hunter departed from the colony and went onboard Buffalo, leaving behind him the unresolved crisis. The path down to the landing at Sydney Cove was lined with the men of the New South Wales Regiment, dressed in their smartest uniforms, and the people of the colony gathered to bid farewell to Governor Hunter. As the new Governor's Coxswain Ben was in charge of the barge in which he was to be taken to Buffalo, anchored a few cables away. On the landing stage the Governor made a short speech to those who could hear in which he thanked the population for their exertions during his period of office and wished them and the colony well under his successor. He shook hands with the new Governor, but without a smile, turned and stepped into the barge. 'Let go for'ard. Give way together', ordered Ben and the boat pulled away from the landing stage on its short trip to the Buffalo.

'I'm not sorry to be going', said Hunter to Ben in a rather distracted way, 'and I'm sad that relations between me and my successor have become so difficult in recent months. I hope he knows what he's doing and how tough it'll be to control the behaviour of so many different types of personality, not least the Irish. Every one of them has an agenda, and their only purpose is to improve their lot, get rich, do as little as possible, no matter the cost to anyone else. Mr King has high ideals like Captain Phillip, but they're not shared by many others, and they'll cause him much pain'. Ben could not find any words and, in any case, he was concentrating on the approach to Buffalo. The boat ran gently alongside as the crew tossed oars and the bowman caught hold of the ship. Governor Hunter stepped onto Buffalo, and disappeared quickly below.

Meanwhile, Governor King assumed the leadership of the colony and one of the first things he did was to order a Court of Inquiry to examine all the affidavits and evidence notes collected the day before at Parramatta and to recommend to him what should be done with the plotters. After a day's work in which they took more statements and heard more evidence, the board proposed 1000 lashes, or transportation for life for the ringleaders and two hundred lashes for the others. The Governor decided that it would be more humane to transport them all to Norfolk Island where they should remain for the rest of their lives.

During the afternoon of the following day Governor King called everyone who could be reached to Government House to hear the reading of his commission. He publicly declared 'My actions will be motivated by the commission graciously granted me by His Majesty and by the principles given to us in Holy Writ exemplified by our Lord Jesus Christ'. Tables had been laid out for everyone to celebrate with a glass of wine or rum and after everyone had a chance to take a glass a cry went up 'God Save the King'. Glasses were raised, and there followed a toast to 'The Governor', and another to 'New South Wales and all its people'. The good-natured crowd bustled and chatted, shoving each other this way and that as many people moved towards the new Governor and tried to shake his hand. His wife, Anna Josepha, was also meeting the crowd and both she and her husband seemed to be enjoying conversations with as many people as could get close enough.

Ben was mixing in the crowd and picking up the chat.

'At least we haven't got an army governor. That man Grose has a lot to answer for'.

'Yes, but will this one be tough enough to stand up to the army. Captain Macarthur won't want to give up all his benefits'.

'The army officers want to stay in charge of the economy. We'll never make a decent living unless we can buy what we need at reasonable prices, and that'll only happen if the Governor gets the army back to barracks and stops them trading'.

'How is it that Macarthur seems to be able to get all that land for nothing and then stock it with sheep? It's not fair on us either – he gets the labour of twelve convicts absolutely free'.

'Didn't Mr King have a good enough system going on Norfolk Island where even the convicts were given some land to work on their own account? I seem to recall someone saying that on Norfolk you could achieve anything you wanted provided you were prepared to work for it. Seems a good deal to me and far better than I ever had back home'.

'We'll have to give him the benefit of the doubt for now; but some people are going to give him a very hard time if he tries to stop the army's gravy'.

Over the next four weeks Buffalo with Governor Hunter still on board remained in the harbour. Letters passed to and fro as Hunter and his Commissary, Williamson, tried to finalise their accounts. It seemed that many people had bills which should have been redeemed by Williamson. Once he had left, the only way to receive value would be for Governor King to pay in the hope that he could recover cash from Hunter or Williamson through his agent, Mr Sykes, when they reached London. Governor King was concerned more for the finances of his people than for himself – he would take their risk.

It was the end of October before Buffalo finally weighed anchor and made for the open sea. She was going via Norfolk Island so that Hunter could report personally on the state of affairs on the island. It had begun to become apparent that the island was unlikely ever to be more than self-sustaining and would be unable to supply Port Jackson with any regular or significant supplies. The assertions of Captain Cook and Sir Joseph Banks that the island would supply masts, spars and sailcloth for a whole fleet had proved very wide of the mark, and, increasingly, Norfolk was being seen only as a place to send the most intransigent and troublesome convicts.

The latter part of the year saw the beginning of the enforcement of the new Governor's decrees about wine and spirits. The price in the retail market fell dramatically and the incidents of extreme drunkenness reduced. But the army was not happy. Captain Macarthur had been explosive when told that one of his retailers, John Harris, had failed to obey the rules and had accepted from two convicts their weekly ration of salt pork from the store in payment for rum. All his casks of spirits and wine had been broken open and poured away. Only the Captain knew that the casks actually belonged to him and they would not now be paid for.

'He was fuming when I saw him this morning', said Sergeant Whittle to Ben. 'He vowed vengeance on whoever had authorised the action'.

'He knows perfectly well it was the Governor; so surely that'd make it treason or mutiny or something; insubordination at the very least', replied Ben.

'Of course; but it'd be difficult to prove if it came to Court Martial. And you can be sure Macarthur would come along with something sharp up his sleeve to make sure he'd get away with it'.

Chapter 23

Early in the new year of 1801, a ship arrived from Norfolk Island and amongst its passengers was William Chapman who had been the storekeeper at Phillipburgh on Norfolk Island, and effectively Lieutenant Governor King's secretary. His first call was to Government House to renew his acquaintance with 'his family' as he had known them in Norfolk Island. There was much joy that day as the Governor and his wife welcomed him as a friend whom they could trust, and it was quickly determined that he would work as the Governor's secretary.

It had become very clear that the Governor needed a small group of people close to him whom he could trust absolutely. He had chosen as his ADC Lieutenant Neil McKellar and had formed a strong relationship with this young Scot who, happily for the Governor, was not formed in the same mould as his countryman John Macarthur. The Governor now had three people who were prepared to serve him with devotion and through whom he could expect to receive reports and information at an informal level. As Coxswain, Ben was clearly the junior of the three but his ability to connect with the settlers and the working people as well as the rank and file of the New South Wales Regiment was clearly a valuable source of news and opinion. His relationship with Sergeant Whittle had continued and the sergeant was now leader of the Governor's personal bodyguard.

Ben was busy visiting every ship which arrived in the harbour. He would invariably go onboard before the ship had reached the Sydney Cove anchorage and would welcome the Master on behalf of the Governor. There would be a letter handed to the Master from the Governor explaining that trade would be strictly controlled and that the Government reserved the right to purchase all the goods the Master might have for sale. Most particularly the sale of any wine or spirits by the Master to others in the colony was strictly forbidden.

'We have to wrest control of the market from the regiment', the Governor said to his team one day, 'and we can only do that by taking control on behalf of the Government. We can make a small profit for

Government of, let's say, 50%, and still sell to the people at a price far cheaper than they can buy at present'.

'Wont that mean the people who are already addicted to rum will just be able to drink more of it'? asked McKellar.

'Perhaps. But if we have control of the supply we can restrict the sales so that no-one is able to buy more than, say, a gallon at a time', replied the Governor.
'You could also make an order to prevent anyone from selling rum and wine without a Governor's licence, although that would encourage a black market. We know that several army officers have large quantities of rum stored which they will want to sell off even though they will not get the price they were hoping for'. This was Chapman's idea.

'It would be very difficult to know whether the officers were selling or not, but you might be able to ban the movement of wine and spirits in bulk around the colony', chipped in Ben.

'It is perfectly clear that the amount of alcohol which is washing around and being consumed is greatly damaging to the economy to the extent that there are many settlers now bankrupt, sick and incapable of work as a result of it, ' declared the Governor. 'Anything we can do to reduce it must be right, although nothing will be perfect. The officers and anyone else who has been engaged in this trade will suffer and they will hold it against me, arguing that it is unlawful and in restraint of trade. That we shall have to suffer. I have no option but to move in this direction. You could see that Governor Hunter started to take action but then gave way as soon as the officers complained'.

The necessary decrees were drawn up and issued, and the officers, as predicted, began a campaign aimed at undermining the Governor, claiming amongst other things that he was trying to damage the economy by preventing trade. None of them, of course, would admit to the level of profiteering from which they had benefited; none of them would accept they had actively participated in the reduction of the amount of land under cultivation by bankrupting many of the settlers, who were now unable to work. Accusations were frequently made against the Governor that he was creating unreasonable laws and restrictions, far beyond his authority as Governor.

'What no-one seems prepared to acknowledge', said William one day to Ben, 'is that before he left England, Captain King went frequently to London to meet with the Duke of Portland and Under Secretary King so that in conversation he could understand what was in their minds for the colony. The pity was that they never wrote it down so that, now he's Governor, Captain King appears to be operating entirely on his own initiative rather than in accordance with the wishes of his masters in the British Government'.

'So what you're saying really means the Governor was set up to fail – he's been given a task which is impossible. Either he incurs the wrath of the people he's governing, or he'll be slated by his masters for failing to govern as they expected'.

'Well, whatever happens, Macarthur's going to make life as difficult as he can, and will undoubtedly encourage anyone who has the slightest grievance to write at once to the Secretary of State to demand the Governor's removal. I guess the only thing we can do to help is to keep the Governor informed with as much information as we can. How much does Sergeant Whittle know?'

Over the following weeks the supplies of rum gradually dried up and some of the perpetual drunkards seemed to realise that life might be changing for them. Perhaps they could begin to return to respectability and earn a proper living without everything being spent on too much, very expensive, rum. They were all aware of the case of John Harris who broke the rules and forfeited his entire stock.

The Governor asked Ben to take a letter from his wife to Parramatta to Mrs Macarthur at Elizabeth Farm, there being no movements expected in the harbour. Ben took a horse and had a comfortable ride thinking as he went how lucky it was that he was familiar with riding as a result of his activities with Captain Nelson in Antigua back in the eighties. When he arrived at Elizabeth Farm he found Mrs Macarthur out in the fields with her men making sure that the tillage of the soil was as consistent as she wished it to be and that no part of the ground was ignored.

'Good morning, Ma'am', opened Ben as soon as he saw her and jumped down from the horse. 'I've a letter for you from Mrs King, and the

Governor asked me to bring it to you and to see how things are going here at Parramatta.'

'I think you must be Mr Luckett, aren't you?' replied Elizabeth Macarthur. 'Mrs King has often spoken about you and how helpful you were to her and her family when they were all in Norfolk Island. It's good to be able to put a face to the name'.

'Thank you Ma'am; I'm very pleased to be of service. But I'd very much like to hear how your farm is progressing. The produce of farms like yours is still obviously critical to avoid the colony falling back into starvation. How are your crops doing?' Elizabeth Macarthur was clearly delighted to have someone ask her about the farm and she proceeded to tell Ben all about it, the crops which had been sown, the timing, the type of soil, which crop did better where, and so on. And after showing him all the crops she took Ben to look at the sheep and cattle which also looked very well and happy.

A couple of hours later having walked around the farm Elizabeth said 'I dare say you'd be quite keen to have a drink before you set off back to Sydney', and she led Ben back towards the farmhouse. As they went inside John Macarthur appeared, not in the uniform Ben might have expected of an officer of the King's army, but in the clothes of a settler. Turning to his wife he said,

'And who have you picked up here, Mrs Macarthur? Some stray who wants to see how we do our farming so that he can steal our ideas?'

'No, certainly not', she replied. 'May I introduce Mr Luckett, the Governor's Coxswain who has come up here with a letter for me from Anna Josepha. I offered to show him how we are getting on with the farm. You know he was with the Governor on Norfolk Island a year or two back'.

'Well was he indeed. It would have been better for all of us if he had stayed there, Governor and all, and let us get on with our business. That man's out to ruin us, you know that? Almost every day we get another order from him as if it came from the King himself. Every one of them prevents us from going about our business. He's preventing us buying all the supplies of every vessel unless we undertake to sell at his price which gives us a paltry level of profit compared to what we have been making. And I've just learnt that he's banned the movement of spirits and wine without a license. I tell you, he's trying to bankrupt us'.

'We're doing quite well anyway', replied Elizabeth, 'and you must admit that you've benefitted hugely from the rum you've already bought. Perhaps now is the time to lie low for a while and allow matters to reach a new equilibrium'.

'Perhaps I'd better be moving on', interjected Ben, sensing that Macarthur was trying to pick a quarrel. 'Thank you very much Ma'am for the drink and for showing me around. You've a very nice farm here which looks much better cared for than any other I've seen'.

'Oh, very sweetly said' interrupted Macarthur, preventing his wife from responding. 'I can see you're one of the Governor's men. I suppose you encourage him to break us just because we're army and you're navy. Well, be off, we don't need any of the Governor's men hereabouts. And when you next see him you can tell him that I won't let him ruin my finances without one hell of a fight, and he's clearly thrown down a gauntlet. I'll break him just as I did his predecessor; eating out of my hand he was, at the end'.

'Good day, Sir; good day ma'am', said Ben firmly and turned to leave, pleased to be able to get away from such an obnoxious personality. As he rode back to Sydney he reflected on how the pleasant and charming Mrs Macarthur could ever have married such an ill-mannered, selfish, grasping individual who was clearly quite prepared to bring down the Governor simply in order to ensure his own pockets were well lined with cash. Ben had seen officers like that before who were always pushing the boundaries of their authority for their own benefit, thinking nothing of anyone else who might be affected by their actions. They would squeeze all they could from the law without actually committing a crime although many would say that they had committed a moral affront towards their neighbours. It was no wonder, thought Ben, that sparks would fly when two determined men clashed, one believing strongly that the tenets of the Christian faith and the authority of the sovereign trumped everything, whilst the other was determined that the only thing that really mattered was to make money by gaining power, without the slightest consideration for anyone who might be damaged or hurt in the process.

When the Governor asked Ben about his visit, he told honestly what he had observed, finishing, 'and I think, Sir, that Lieutenant Macarthur is determined to cause trouble for you'.

'Thank you Luckett. Yes, I know that; I knew it before we set off to come out here. But there's nothing I can do about it until he commits an offence for which I can court martial him; then I can get rid of him for a while. There are others too who resent any sort of authority, most notably the Irish, and they are certainly out to get me – they'd be after anyone in authority. You know when the rot set in? It was when Governor Phillip went home and that dreadful man Grose took over. He never believed in the idea of a colony and was more or less determined that it should fail, but only after he and some others had milked it of all the money and value they could. He it was who encouraged Macarthur in the first place. And then Macarthur broke Captain Hunter. And now it's my head on his chopping block'.

'If there's anything I can do to help, Sir, you know I'll do it', was all Ben could think of to say to the Governor's pained outpouring. He felt inside him that this was exactly why he had chosen a path of service rather than leadership; there might be rewards for leadership, but there were also costs and penalties which had to be recognised.

Chapter 24

As the months passed, some aspects of life in the colony improved. There was certainly less drunkenness and settlers seemed to have become a little less demoralised. Now there was at least a chance that if they produced a good crop they would be able to sell it profitably. And it was noticeable that when a ship arrived with goods from Europe they might be able to buy things at reasonable prices. Ben continued having regular discussions with Sergeant Whittle who told him how very unhappy the officers were that the Governor was now preventing them from making any money out of trading. All the officers had been given plots of land and were allowed two convicts to work for them on the land so they should have been able to make some money that way.

'They're just greedy', said the sergeant, 'and expect to get everything for nothing'.

'Well, for sure, that's not the way the Governor thinks', replied Ben. 'Always in Norfolk Island he made it very clear that anyone who was prepared to work hard and contribute to the economy would be reasonably rewarded. I remember him being absolutely furious when Colonel Grose ordered him not to buy surplus pork from those who had it; in fact he'd already committed to doing so because the latest information he'd received was that Port Jackson was starving and desperately needed food. As soon as a ship arrived from India carrying pork bought by the officers, Grose bought that rather than what had been grown on Norfolk Island'.

'Hardly surprising then that Governor King had little time for Grose. I'd rather have the King way of thinking. It's much fairer than making it easy for the officers and toffs to get rich on the backs of the workers'.

'Did you see the Governor's order the other day about stamping out monopolies?'

'Which do you mean?'

'The one when he drew attention to the war going on back home - you know the French are just itching to cross the channel – and said how the government is trying to send us all we need at a cheap rate, and "that must not and shall not be perverted to the improper purposes of monopoly and extortion". I remember those words very well'.

'I expect the officers see that as a direct attack on them, and I don't suppose they'll have been impressed. I hope he sticks to his principles. That's the only way this place is going to get going properly'.

It was in the middle of the winter of 1801 that the Governor sent for Ben one day and told him that he would like him to accompany Colonel Paterson north to Newcastle, sailing with Lieutenant Grant in the Lady Nelson.

'I've given them orders to explore the area more thoroughly and especially to look for some coal. It would be very helpful to the Colonel to have your assistance'.

Accordingly Ben reported to the Colonel, and on 11th June they boarded the little ship Lady Nelson and sailed out through the Heads and northwards along the coast. Two days later they anchored off the entrance to the Hunter River and on the next day the longboat was lowered to tow the Lady Nelson past Coal Island and into the shelter of the harbour. The tidal stream was very strong and the main anchor alone was not enough to hold the ship so they had to lay a second anchor and it was only on the Tuesday that they were able to tow the little ship round Pirate's Point into a better anchorage in Freshwater Bay out of the full force of the tides. The Colonel spent a day exploring the coastal strip to north and south and found that there were good seams of coal which could be very easily secured.

'Can we get the coal away by boat?' the Colonel asked Ben.

'I doubt it, Sir; that shore line is very exposed and there's a lot of surf. You might get a boat in without broaching but it would be very difficult launching a fully laden boat into the surf'.

'That's going to be quite a problem then. We shall have to carry it somewhere the ship can find some shelter'.

The colliers went to work with pick and shovel to extract as much of the coal as could be easily secured but the only form of transport was a wheelbarrow. Meanwhile the Colonel, accompanied by Ben, took one of the smaller boats and set off upstream. The river kept on dividing and they were amongst a maze of small channels and marshy swamp. Eventually they found a suitable place to step ashore to explore the river banks, and they walked up a small hill. It looked as though it would make excellent grazing for sheep and cattle and when they dug into the soil they found rich black silt which suggested that it might be excellent for growing cereals. They went on about fifteen miles inland walking up some gentle slopes, naming one of them Mount Ann and another Mount Elizabeth and found themselves in rich woodland with many very mature trees. The higher ground they thought would be entirely safe if there were ever a risk of flooding. But the river twisted and turned and often seemed to bring them back almost to the same point. The Colonel never rested from looking at every feature of the landscape, collecting samples of the plants, catching insects and any small animal which might come near. After about two weeks ashore walking and pulling the boat upstream Colonel Paterson decided he had learnt as much about the area as he could, and their provisions were running low. It was time to return to Port Jackson. By this time the little schooner, Francis, had been well loaded with coal and she too could return southwards with Lady Nelson. Ensign Barrallier had finished his survey of the entry to the Hunter river and Lieutenant Grant had completed the orders he had been given by Governor King.

When Lady Nelson arrived back in Port Jackson Ben noticed that there had been a new arrival. The Earl Cornwallis had arrived bringing some more soldiers for the New South Wales Regiment. Ben reported to the Governor at Government House shortly after Lady Nelson dropped anchor. The Governor looked rather distraught.

'Thank you, Sir, for allowing me to accompany Colonel Paterson and Lady Nelson. It's been a very interesting trip and I'm sure the colonel's report to you will be very valuable'.

'I'm glad you went with them', replied the Governor. 'But you and the colonel were away when Earl Cornwallis arrived, which was most unfortunate. We now have a dispute between the ship and the army about the possessions of an unfortunate Lieutenant who was lost overboard during the voyage'.

'But that ought to be simple enough', said Ben, 'It's tradition in both services that a dead man's possessions are auctioned for the benefit of the widow and family'.

'Would that this case had been so simple. It transpires that the First Lieutenant of Cornwallis, Lieutenant Marshall, took the possessions into custody and then decided to swap some with his own – a pair of pistols most notably – which were of lower value. The issue was considered by the magistrates who found Mr Marshall guilty and I issued a severe reprimand for conduct which gave reason for suspicion. That should have been the end of it'.

'It seems stupid and thoughtless, rather than evil', responded Ben.

'I agree, if only it'd stopped there'. The Governor paused and then continued 'A day or so later Marshall accosted Captain Macarthur and appears to have called him a rascal. Whereupon Macarthur goes into a full rage and gets Captain Abbott to challenge Marshall to a duel. Marshall appointed Mr Jefferies as his second, but Captain Abbott refused to speak to him – something about not being his social equal. Given that Abbott's father was no more than a cook and Mr Jefferies is a perfectly respectable ship's purser, it's hard to see what the problem was. It escalated to a point when Macarthur drew his sword and threatened to run Marshall through if he didn't back off. Fortunately some soldiers were nearby and managed to restrain Macarthur. These grown men seem to think they can behave like children in the playground and it's all for some overblown sense of honour'.

'You must've found that all deeply troubling, Sir', put in Ben, 'so what happened next'?

'At least I was able to prevent a duel and Lieutenant Marshall is to stand trial for assault on Captain Abbott. I think I should speak with Colonel Paterson now he's back. Would you please be kind enough to ask him to call as soon as he can'.

A few days later the court was convened, presided over by the Judge Advocate Richard Atkins. All the members of the court were army officers – Colonel Paterson and close friends of the allegedly aggrieved party, Captain Abbott. There was just one member who was not in the army and that was Lieutenant Grant, commander of Lady Nelson. Ben suggested to the Governor that it might be useful for him to go along and listen, and provide a briefing on the proceedings.

As Ben watched and listened he could not help hoping that he would never be placed in such an impossible situation. Various witnesses were questioned and it was clear that some members of the court were telling the prosecutor what to ask and that he in turn was whispering to the witness what the answers should be, most particularly when Lieutenant Marshall took the opportunity to cross examine a witness. Lieutenant Marshall defended himself robustly and expressed his astonishment at the effrontery of Captain Macarthur. It was clear, Ben thought, that having been denied the opportunity of a duel in the first place Marshall had tried to provoke one with Macarthur, who had, for some reason, refused to countenance such a thing and took to the law. It might have been much better if they could have sorted it out between them with pistols, and then let life move on. It was inevitable that Lieutenant Marshall would be convicted and he was sentenced to twelve months in prison and a £50 fine – a very harsh outcome for what should have been treated as a minor argument about very little. The Governor then ordered the court to re-convene to advise him to what extent it would be appropriate to exercise the royal prerogative of mercy. The court met but refused to consider such a thing because that would imply that the Governor was interfering with justice.

It was Sergeant Whittle who brought the next news.

'I overheard the officers talking between themselves and they seem to have entered into some sort of pact that none of them will have any dealings with the Governor. They'll all refuse to speak to him and Mrs King. They said the pact includes the Colonel but I don't see how that can be because Mrs Paterson and Mrs King are such good friends. But, you know', went on the Sergeant, 'I've a feeling that the whole thing is being stirred up by Captain Macarthur. Did you know that he'd asked the government to buy his land and stock, and it wasn't long ago that the Governor received a reply from London refusing the idea? I've a feeling that Macarthur has taken offence at that and is looking for every chance to undermine the Governor, to find fault with him, and get him removed'.

'But that's ridiculous', replied Ben, 'he's done so much for the settlers already, and the economy is far better than it was. And look at all the exploration going on – all that coal we have seen on the Hunter River could be a huge economic benefit'.

'You're right, but Macarthur isn't fussed about anyone else's good but his own. He's a strange way of going about it though, and clearly he doesn't mind who's implicated or distressed by his scheming'.

'We'll have to wait and see', said Ben as they went off about their respective business.

Rumours were always going around and the military seemed to be particularly full of them. To Ben it was quite extraordinary how almost every soldier appeared to know the details of the Colonel's letters to General Brownrigg at the War Office in London. Apparently some of these contained statements which were highly critical not only of the Judge Advocate but also of the Governor. The curious thing which also circulated with the rumours was the idea that Captain Macarthur was actually calling the shots while the Colonel, the commanding officer, was doing what he was told.

In early September, the Patersons dined at Government House and the general assumption after that was that relationships between the Governor and the army would improve. But Captain Macarthur once again had something to surprise everyone. He openly accused the Colonel of going back on his word to have nothing to do with the Governor. With that, and Macarthur publishing a private letter from Mrs Paterson to Mrs Macarthur, the Colonel felt that he had been pushed too far and called Macarthur to account by challenging him to a duel.

He chose Captain Mackellar, the Governor's ADC, as his second, whilst Macarthur chose Captain Abbott. The date was set but the weather proved too foul and it was agreed to postpone the meeting. When it did take place Ben looked on unobtrusively from a distance. He could see the seconds tossing for the first shot and then going back to the table where the pistols were laid and beginning to load them. He saw Macarthur muscling his way up to the table and grabbing his pistol from Abbott and proceeding to load it himself, a very considerable breach of the conventions of duelling. They paced out the distance of twelve paces. The Colonel turned to present his right arm to Macarthur and to narrow the target. Macarthur raised his weapon and fired. Paterson was hit in the shoulder. He tried to raise his arm to fire back but could not and the surgeon rushed over to bind up the arm and carry him off to remove the ball. Meanwhile Macarthur turned his back and began to walk off saying under his breath, but not very quietly, 'That serves him right'.

As soon as the Governor knew that the Colonel had been wounded he placed the two seconds under arrest, and then Captain Macarthur was placed under arrest too because if the Colonel died he would have to be charged with murder, and the seconds as accomplices.

'This is a ghastly business, Luckett', said the Governor. 'Now we're deprived of the use of four officers. Captain Mackellar particularly needs to get on with his role in charge of the public services - there's too much to be done to have him sitting around in his room with a guard outside. If we were closer to home we could get someone else to deal with it all, but out here we must do what we can to defuse the situation'.

'I heard that the Colonel seemed a little better today, Sir. Let's hope he survives so that at least we don't have a murder trial'.

'I'm glad to hear that. But there has to be a Court Martial in any case because duelling between officers is strictly forbidden by Army Regulations. I can't see how I can possibly convene a Court Martial here which has even the slightest degree of impartiality – all the officers are under the thumb of Captain Macarthur'. The Governor later instructed William Chapman, his secretary, to begin to prepare papers which could be sent to London to provide evidence to a court sitting in England. It would be problematic, for sure, as none of the witnesses would be present to be cross-examined. He would need four copies of everything, one to keep as a record and three to be addressed to the Secretary of State to be sent by different routes in order to ensure that at least one set reached its destination.

As spring turned to summer, the colonel began to recover although the ball had not been removed from his shoulder. Meanwhile the Governor had decided that Captain Macarthur must travel back to England to face a Court Martial. In due course he embarked in Hunter which sailed on 15th November. Two sets of King's despatches went in Hunter, one in the hold and the other in the possession of the master. Captain Mackellar, who was to be the prosecutor, carrying Macarthur's sword and another set of papers, embarked the following February aboard the American whaler Caroline. Nothing more was ever heard of Caroline, nor of Captain Mackellar. After some six months back in London John Macarthur resigned his commission, rendering a Court Martial no longer possible, and in due course the King was advised to make a rule that officers must always be brought to a court martial in the territory in which an alleged offence took place, so that witnesses could be called. No one seemed to recognise that in New South Wales the only officers who could comprise the Court were all friends and, it might be said, accomplices of the accused, making justice impossible. Macarthur was only able to return to New South Wales in the middle of 1805; so Governor King did achieve one of his purposes, to remove him and his pernicious influence from the territory, but at the same time he attracted some harsh and unreasonable criticism from the press and Government Ministers. Whilst in London Macarthur fought robustly to persuade English wool traders to accept New South Wales wool as of a superior quality which should be traded in London, and he won from the Government a concession for 10,000 acres of land in New South Wales with the services of thirty convicts to boost wool output and quality further.

Chapter 25

The departure of Captain Macarthur, thought the Governor, might relieve some of the pressure on him and it might follow that Colonel Paterson, as he recovered from his wound, would bring some better order to the officers. He knew that he must be able to count upon a reasonable number of loyal officers in order to ensure that the army would protect him and the government against the potential attacks by the Irish from within, and the French from the sea.

'These Irishmen are devilish clever, some of them', he said to Ben, 'it's not as if they'd all just come out of the bogs with pitchforks and no education. There are well-educated gentlemen amongst them who are determined to scheme and plot for the downfall of anything and everything British'.

'I'm keeping as close as I can to one or two Irishmen and I'll do my best to hear whatever buzzes are circulating', answered Ben.

'Thank you for that, Luckett. But in the meantime we must do all we can by way of exploration and commerce. There must be plenty of resources in this continent which we've not yet found. I want to send Lieutenant Murray in Lady Nelson down south again to explore the Bass Strait and look further into the entrance which Lieutenant Grant identified last year. Is Lady Nelson ready to sail?'

'I'm sure she could be made ready within a short time, Sir. She's a reasonably full crew and it'll only be a matter of loading enough victuals for her voyage'. Ben finished speaking but noticed that the Governor was clearly in great pain. 'Can I get you anything?' he asked instinctively.

'Give me your arm and help me into that chair. My foot's agony and my insides feel as if a pair of 96s are doing battle with broadsides'. Ben did as he was asked and helped the Governor into a position which seemed to give him a little relief.

'Please ask Mrs King to come to me', he asked, 'and go and warn Lieutenant Murray that I shall want Lady Nelson to sail as soon as she can be made ready'.

Ben acknowledged the order and left at once to find Mrs King, who on receiving the message hurried to her husband, looking much concerned. He found William Chapman and warned him that it might be worth drafting some orders for Lieutenant Murray to take Lady Nelson south to explore the south coast, north of the Bass Strait.

It was two whole weeks before Ben was sent for again by the Governor who even then looked washed out and tired.

The work of the colony continued, and the settlers worked at their land and generally seemed to be much happier now that they could get the occasional draught of rum at a reasonable price. Most of the articles which had been imported for sale had begun to fall in price as the Governor's restrictions on profit took effect. But whilst the settlers were generally happier, the officers, both civil and military, who were now deprived of their very lucrative trade, found it hard to be friendly with the Governor. None of them seemed able to recognise that their avarice might eventually prove more than the settlers were prepared to accept, and they would rebel. In the Governor's mind was the memory of the French revolution when the ruling class so dominated and oppressed the working class that a bloodbath ensued; this would not suit the Governor or his superiors in London.

Exploration had continued and Lieutenant Murray returned from his survey of the Bass Strait and Phillip Bay at the mouth of the Murray River. As the weather began to turn towards autumn, on 10th May 1802, a ship passed the Heads and Ben and his crew pulled out to meet it as it sailed gently towards Sydney. It proved to be the Investigator commanded by Captain Flinders. Ben was immediately fascinated by what he saw on the deck of the ship which was a hive of activity, not so much of sailors relieved to have reached port after a long voyage, but gentlemen fussing over plants and small animals. Ben had heard of Captain Flinders who had been in Port Jackson some years earlier, accompanying George Bass when he found the Bass Strait between South Australia and Van Diemen's Land.

'How was your voyage, sir?' asked Ben

'It's been most interesting and we now have extensive charts of what makes up the southern coastline of this great continent. We've explored some fine new harbours and identified one in particular which might be quite suitable for a new settlement. But the ship needs repair as we're taking around two inches an hour and the pumps are having to work all the time. How is Port Jackson and the new Governor?'

'Governor King will be very interested to know about your discoveries. He often talks about the possibility of establishing other settlements around the coast where the prospects seem good for people and agriculture. If I may, Sir, I will go ahead and inform him of your arrival. When you have anchored in Sydney Cove I've no doubt he'd wish you to call at your earliest convenience'.

Captain Flinders had indeed had a fruitful passage exploring the coastline from Cape Howe in the south west corner of Australia all the way eastwards to Port Phillip. The naturalist Robert Brown had spent many hours ashore collecting specimens, and every waking hour onboard drawing them all, classifying them and preserving them. All the officers had been engaged in surveying and they now needed to set all the measurements down in a single clear chart which could then be copied for wider use. There would be no time to relax.

Five weeks later Ben was again steering his boat out towards a new arrival, but this time his was one of several boats and the ship they were heading for looked as though it was in some difficulty. The worn looking vessel was wearing French colours and turned out to be the French survey ship Le Géographe whose Captain was Nicholas Baudin. Almost the entire crew was suffering from scurvy, painful and debilitating, and there were insufficient men able enough to work the ship up into the harbour. The sailors from the Investigator and Ben's small crew brought her to an anchorage in Sydney Cove. Some of the seamen were landed at once into the hospital and the Governor ordered supplies of fresh fruit and vegetables to be taken onboard to begin to reverse the awful effects of scurvy. The general ration of fresh meat at that moment had been cut because of a general shortage, so there was very little of that to contribute to the recovery of this sickly crew.

'Luckett, I should be grateful if you would try to find as much fruit and vegetables as you can to feed to this poor crew. They may be Frenchmen and they may be our enemies but we cannot see our fellow sailors suffer like this'.

'It's dreadful to see them so bad. And yet our British seamen are very seldom as seriously affected as these men. What do we do different?'

'It's all a matter of leadership. This Captain Baudin is a very fine scientist and his motivation is entirely for the advancement of science regardless of the human cost. Our view – my view – is that in any endeavour the health and morale of the men is critical. Happy men, happy ship, success. It's the same here on land; if the majority of the workers are properly looked after and are reasonably healthy, and can see their efforts pay off, then many of them, if not most, will work hard and reap plenty of personal benefit. Do you recall the way we used to reward the hard workers on Norfolk Island? It's more difficult here because there are so many more people'.

'And I guess it's not helped much when one class of people is hell bent on securing very much more than their fair share of the wealth'.

'I never thought for a moment that I'd find myself engaged in a life of politics. It's so much simpler in a ship where everyone knows the rules and that stepping outside them can be risky. Here it's more like being in a jungle where everything is changing from minute to minute and so many people don't seem to behave in what to me would be a rational manner. Selfish, grasping, scheming, dishonest; nothing is ever what it seems at first. But enough of all that; we're not going to resolve the problems of mankind in a few minutes so you'd best get off and sort out those supplies for the Frenchmen'.

Ben went first to Géographe to find out whether they had any money to pay for supplies and was relieved to find that they had. He then spent a whole day going from house to house buying a spare cabbage here, a few potatoes there until he had a reasonable quantity to take to the ship. The sailors were very grateful to be able to eat fresh food for the first time in many months and as time went by many of them began to recover and became friendly with the settlers. The Governor made it clear that the French scientists were to be welcomed and encouraged in all their investigation and research.

Long before the French ship was ready to move on, Investigator was being made ready for the next stage of its voyage. Ben was tempted to volunteer to go with them and help explore the whole of the coast of this new land Terra Australis, of which New South Wales formed a part. When he suggested it to the Governor he was told quite clearly and very gently that his presence was much more valuable in and around Government House.

'I need someone who understands the navy who I can talk to and trust. Please stay here. I know you originally wanted to limit your time to four or five years and I'll certainly respect that. But Flinders can't have you. I'll suggest to him that he recruits a few convicts to make up his numbers and, subject to their behaviour, they can have their freedom on the ship's return'.

This gesture was typical of the Governor; he had found a way of encouraging some of the convicts to earn their freedom through hard work and good behaviour. He had encouraged Commander Flinders in other ways too inspiring him as he set off to circumnavigate the continent and prepare a complete set of charts. The Investigator sailed on 21st July 1802.

A week earlier Ben heard a rumour that some of the settlers had become particularly friendly with the crew of the Géographe and had planned a little private enterprise. So on the evening of 16th July Ben and Sergeant Whittle chose to have a quiet chat at a point on Sydney Cove where they could see the movements around the ship. As dusk fell they saw William Kent's boat pull away and head for the shore. Ben and Tom Whittle were there to meet it.

'Evening friends. Had a good visit to the frenchies?' asked Whittle, innocently.

'What's it to you? We took over some supplies for them', replied the leader.

The other four were all faces Ben had seen before though he did not know them well.

'So would that pile of canvas you have in the boat be payment for the supplies, then?' asked Ben.

'Might be. But that's none o' your business'.

'No, of course not. We'll wish you all good evening then'. So saying Ben and Tom walked away in the direction of Government House.

'Do you fancy a little outing?' asked Ben when they were out of earshot.

'What did you have in mind?' replied Tom.

'Well, I reckon that canvas was not in exchange for anything, but was stolen, perhaps with the knowledge and help of some of the Géographe's crew. After all if it's good enough to have a value ashore it's certainly good enough to keep onboard to repair and replace sails. I think we might pop out to the ship and see if a transaction was authorised'.

'Isn't Captain Baudin dining at Government House this evening? If we went back there we could perhaps catch him before he leaves to return onboard'.

So the pair continued up the slope to Government House where they found Monsieur Baudin enjoying a glass of brandy with the Governor.

'Excuse us Sir', began Ben, 'but Sergeant Whittle and I have just watched a boat coming from the Géographe containing a pile of good canvas. I was about to go out there to check that it was an authorised deal but Sergeant Whittle told me we'd find you here'.

'Thank you Messieurs', replied Baudin. 'It is most likely that the canvas has been stolen; we need all that we have on board'.

'Will you please go and inform the Constable, Luckett', interjected the Governor, 'and ask him to detain the men you saw, and hold on to the canvas. In the morning Monsieur Baudin will confirm to us whether the transaction was authorised.   Then we'll know what needs to be done'.

Ben left at once to call the Constable and give him the Governor's order, while Monsieur Baudin left a few minutes later.   In the morning a message came from Monsieur Baudin that the canvas had been given to the men in the boat without authorisation and asking permission to arrange a court martial of the two crew members responsible.   He further reported that a quantity of gunpowder and ball had been stolen. The Constable arrested all five of the men from the boat and took them before the magistrate who sentenced them all to 100 lashes.   Under questioning it also transpired that one of them, Jacob Harrison, had already sold the powder and ball, although he would not admit who had bought it.   William Kent, the leader, had his boat confiscated, as well as the lashes; and Jacob Harrison was sent to work in the gaol gang for two weeks. In the hope of recovering the powder and shot the Governor issued a General Order requiring anyone who had bought any powder recently to inform the magistrate for fear of being branded a receiver of stolen goods.

Meanwhile there was work to be done to prepare for the establishment of a new settlement on Van Diemen's land.   It was essential in the eyes of the Governor to ensure that the French could not settle there, whatever Monsieur Baudin's declared policy, because that would effectively give them command of the Bass Strait and all British ships might then be faced with a much longer voyage to avoid the possibility of capture by the French.   So Lieutenant Robbins was sent off in the little Cumberland with orders to plant a British flag on King Island.

Land-based exploration was happening too and Ensign Barrallier whom Ben had met when travelling north to explore the Hunter River set off to try to cross the Blue Mountains to the west of Sydney where everyone hoped they would find a vast expanse of fertile grazing. He penetrated as far as 140 miles west of Parramatta but could get no further. He was deeply upset that after seven weeks he had failed to find a route through the mountains and concluded that they were impassable.

In November 1802 Monsieur Baudin and his men were preparing to sail. The Géographe had been joined by the Naturaliste and both ships were to depart together having been repaired and re-stocked, whilst most of both crews had recovered from their dreadful ill health. The Governor issued an order that a guard boat should be manned to patrol around the two ships during the hours of darkness until they sailed. Ben took the middle watch in the Governor's red cutter from ten in the evening until two in the morning. He did not have long to wait and soon spotted a number of small rowing boats being pulled quietly from the shore. He waited until they were approaching the Géographe before closing in on them and barring their way.

'No escape', declared Ben, 'and now you'll have to wait with me until 2 in the morning before we go ashore and I hand you over to the Constable. And just in case you're thinking of something desperate, the three muskets here are loaded and primed and all ready to fire and do you a power of no good'.

When he was relieved by the next boat Ben took the cutter and the escapees back to the quayside and they were marched off to find the Constable. By the following morning forty men had been taken trying to escape in the French ships, and delivered to the magistrate where they were duly sentenced. Ben had reported to the Governor early in the morning.

'I took fifteen and I'm sure the other guard boats picked up some others. It seems that they caused little upset onboard and the French would have handed them over even if we'd not been there'.

'I suppose we shouldn't be surprised that people wish to escape. But I've always tried to make it clear that the easiest way to achieve early release is to work hard, be productive and do some good in this place to earn it. It's time I put out another general order to try to explain that even if these men had got home they would have been sought out by the local sheriff; we have been writing about all escapees to the places where they were originally convicted so that authorities there can be on the lookout for them. I think I will be lenient this time and make it clear that in future, attempts to escape will be severely punished. Would you please ask the Magistrates to let me know their decisions and I'll ask Mr Chapman to draft an order for me'.

Two days later on 22nd November Géographe and Naturaliste set sail for Europe. They had no convicts onboard but Surgeon James Thompson took passage home and carried the Governor's despatches. During their stay the Frenchmen had travelled extensively around the British settlement and had become very friendly with the Governor to whom they regularly spoke about what they had observed. Monsieur Baudin always sought to reassure the Governor that the French had no intention whatever to attempt to settle any part of the continent, and it was only several years later that the official report to the government in France revealed that Baudin's motivation had been as much to spy out the state of the British colony and its prospects as to advance scientific knowledge.

As the months went by Ben's friendship with Tom Whittle continued and they enjoyed many hours chat. Both men were fiercely loyal to the Governor and would frequently debate what made so many people in the colony determined to undermine him and make life generally more difficult. But the Irish were a different matter entirely, and that problem was not going to go away. With almost every ship arriving from England came more Irish.

'The problem for us is this', said the Sergeant one day, 'there are now so many Irish that if they were all to work together we in the army would have great difficulty controlling the situation. Besides there are a few unhappy and bored officers who've been getting far too familiar with some of the Irishmen. The Governor has done his best to keep them spread around the different settlements but they all seem to work closely together and have a network of communication'.

'The talk is often about pipes; not something you smoke, but a document containing scurrilous disinformation or comment about the government. They seem invariably seditious and some of the comments I've seen about the Governor are extreme'.

'I don't think there's much anyone can do about them. If the Governor were to ban them the people would only find some other way of spreading lies and falsehoods. I reckon the most we can do is to keep listening and hope that we can inform him if anything looks particularly dramatic or awful. I reckon that Father Dixon is at the heart if it all; you can bet that his flock use the confessional to talk secrets'.

'I can't help thinking that if we could have a few good harvests things would look up. Then more of the settlers would be able to sell surplus to the Government and buy a few more luxuries. And if the Governor's measures to restrict profiteering work properly the luxuries will become much more affordable'.

In January of 1803 Ben was on the waterfront watching a brig being hauled down so that her copper could be repaired. This was Venus, George Bass's vessel, in which he had recently returned from a trip to Tahiti where he had bought a large consignment of pork and salted it for the stores in Port Jackson. Ben caught sight of Mr Bass carefully watching the work.

'Good morning, Sir, I hope the shipwrights will not find anything amiss when they can see the ship's bottom', said Ben.

'I believe not. She's a lovely vessel, as strong as anything and I'd be happy to take her anywhere. But her sheathing has worn after so many miles and I am anxious it should be in perfect order before we set off again', replied Bass.

'I might have supposed you had discovered enough by now – after all the Bass Strait bears your name and you probably know more about New Zealand than anyone else'.

'Well, that's true. But the trouble is that one doesn't get paid for discoveries and I need to earn some decent money. I've just had authorisation from the Governor to go off in search of pork and beef, and if all goes well to bring back some cattle and alpaca from South America, specifically from Chile'.

'I'm tempted to ask to come with you but I know the Governor would prefer me to stay. He let me go with Colonel Paterson up to Newcastle but that was only for a few weeks. I suggested going with Mr Flinders but he wouldn't hear of it'.

'And I think my voyage is rather less certain than his. One thing we'll try to do is to recover the Norfolk which was driven ashore in Tahiti and send her back here with another cargo of salt pork'.

Ben took his leave of Mr Bass.   As subsequent events proved it was just as well that he did not go aboard Venus for after she left Port Jackson a few weeks later she was not heard of again.

Chapter 26

For the Governor the start of 1803 was marred by another violent attack of gout which left him unable to move from Government House for about four weeks. And it was during this time that the New South Wales Regiment under Major Johnstone seemed to do their best to make life even more difficult for him. Sergeant Whittle and Ben frequently discussed matters.

'I know', said Tom Whittle, 'that some of the officers have been having a great laugh at the Governor's expense, writing scurrilous poems to poke fun at him. What's made it so much worse is that they then publish the material outside the barracks which can do nothing but inflame everyone who has anything like a grievance with the Governor'.

'Yes, if that were the army in England poking fun at King George there would be Court Martials for treason, wouldn't there?' put in Ben.

'Probably so. I don't agree with everything the Governor has done but I can see that at least the settlers and the ex-convicts are happier now. They know that they can make a reasonable living and even enjoy the occasional tot or two without having to take a loan from one of my officers'.

The Governor ordered three Courts Martial but Major Johnstone refused to designate officers to sit on them. For a few weeks there was a stalemate with letters passing to and fro. Finally the Courts were held and sentences passed which the Governor refused to ratify without guidance from England.

'These courts are a joke', said Tom Whittle one day, 'How can you expect one officer to give an impartial verdict on one of his closest friends. But I heard that the Governor has decreed that officers are subject to civil law when it comes to the beating of convicts. That's definitely a good thing'.

In March 1803 Ben went out to greet a vessel arriving in the harbour to find that it was HMS Glatton, a frigate, commanded by Captain James

Colnett, modified for carrying convicts and supplies. When Ben stepped aboard he introduced himself to the officer on the gangway who gave his name as Lieutenant Bowen.

'You wouldn't be the son of Captain Richard Bowen, would you?' asked Ben at once casting his mind back to the Seahorse and Tenerife.

'No. My father was Captain John who was Master of Howe's flagship at the Glorious First of June. The Richard Bowen you speak of would have been my uncle who was sadly killed at Tenerife in 97'.

'Ah, yes, Sir. I was there too, Coxswain to Captain Fremantle of the Seahorse. Mrs Fremantle who was with us was very attached to Captain Bowen and was greatly affected by your uncle's death. But her mind was quickly taken up with nursing her wounded husband and Admiral Nelson who wasn't in the best of humour after losing his arm'.

'And so what brought you out here then?'

'Well, I had served Governor King before on Norfolk Island, and when he was standing by to come back as Governor, I was paid off from Seahorse and had a few months ashore with my family. Just when I was getting bored with country life the Governor asked me if I'd like to accompany him for a year or two. I've done three years and I reckon I'll head home next year and see what Captain Fremantle is doing'.

'I'm thinking of staying out here rather longer. I like the idea of exploring a new country and beginning to turn it into a civilised place to live happily and reasonably without all the hassle of having to fight the French and the Spanish all the time'.

The meeting had set Ben thinking about his own family and whether he should seek the Governor's permission to return home. Another six months, he thought, and he would start looking for a ship.

Within a few weeks Lieutenant Bowen was commissioned by the Governor as acting Lieutenant Governor of Norfolk Island, but then, a few days later, his orders changed to take a small force with settlers and supplies to create a new settlement on the Derwent River in Van Diemen's Land, which later became the town of Hobart in Tasmania.

In the meantime Captain Flinders was limping along the south coast in Investigator. He reached Port Jackson on 9th June 1803 having completed the first circumnavigation of the continent then still known as Terra Australis. The Investigator was in serious danger of falling to pieces and the pumps had to be worked constantly. The crew was not in much better condition since they had been at sea for eleven months without any chance to stock up with proper fruit and vegetables and most men including Flinders himself were suffering from scurvy.

When he came to anchor Flinders struggled to walk up to Government House because his feet had been badly affected by scurvy. Ben provided a suitable hand cart on which he could ride and it enabled the two to engage in conversation.

'You must be pleased to have sailed the whole way around this great continent,' suggested Ben.

'I suppose I must be', said Flinders, 'but I'm unhappy that so many men are seriously sick and the ship is falling apart. We made some good surveys of the East Coast and the whole of the Gulf of Carpentaria, but then things got really difficult'.

'Did you find any inhabitants up there in the North?' asked Ben.

'Oh yes. They live in small communities some of which were quite friendly, while others were definitely hostile and saw us as a threat to their way of life. Poor Ben Morgan was taken ill and died ashore there quite suddenly and then close by the same place Whitewood was speared several times despite trying hard to convince the natives that he was friendly. He suffered badly but did survive'.

'Were you able to get any supplies and fresh food from Timor or any other Dutch Islands? They seem mostly to be quite friendly now, although I suppose one is never quite sure whether Britain and Holland are at war again'.

'In fact the Governor at Kopang was very friendly. But it's not a very easy place as the water though fresh looked as though it may have been contaminated with something. But we were desperate to fill some casks; I think it may have been that which caused an outbreak of dysentery a little later, which we did not need. And besides that, the Dutch had very little fresh fruit and vegetables to satisfy their own needs so we couldn't buy enough'.

Captain Flinders was looking distressed but went on. 'I had to make the decision not to delay as we came south. The men were all too weak and I feared for the survival of the ship. We came south as fast as we could and were much relieved when we were able to head East again on what is now a more familiar sea. At least we could check out some of our previous observations there. I hope the Governor will not be too disappointed'.

'I'm sure that will not be a problem, Sir. He's had a lot to be thinking about recently with the army still giving him plenty of grief, and the Irish stirring up feelings against him. And his gout's been pretty bad too'.

'Thank you Luckett for bringing me up here. I hope I'll soon recover enough to get down to the serious work of drawing up fair copies of all the surveys and make some charts which will be of value to future mariners. Those reefs and islands up in the north east inside the Barrier Reef are very dangerous and we were lucky to escape being torn apart like Captain Cook's Endeavour. I'm thankful that we made it back here'.

Governor and Mrs King welcomed Captain Flinders warmly and before he could begin to tell the Governor about his voyage they insisted on him settling down for a good meal and a night ashore, despite protestations that he must look after his men.

'Don't worry about them for now. You all need a good rest and I'll ask Luckett to make sure that supplies are delivered at once so that they can all begin to recover. There may be some who need to get to the hospital and Luckett will see to that as well'.

Over the next few weeks most of the crew of Investigator began to recover from their ordeal although three of them died. The ship was inspected by the Sydney carpenters who found that it was too rotten to be worth repairing. There were some places where you could poke a cane through the timbers. The little ship was only six years old and had clearly been built with poor quality timber and many instances of shoddy workmanship. The general opinion was that it had been very fortunate that there had been no storm to battle through along the south coast of Australia, for that might well have been fatal for them all. As his strength returned Flinders himself continued to work on his charts whilst at the same time de-commissioning Investigator and re-deploying the crew. The Governor had agreed that Flinders should take passage in Porpoise back to England, taking as many from Investigator as wished to go, so that he could then persuade the government to find another better vessel to complete the survey work.

Porpoise was to sail in company with the East Indiaman Bridgwater and the merchant ship Cato both of which were heading for Timor. Flinders would navigate the new and shorter route he had discovered around Cape York. The three ships were ready to sail on 10th August and, once again Flinders bade farewell to Mrs King, and the Governor accompanied him out to the Heads.

'We will be expecting you back in the next two years', said the Governor. 'You have a job to finish for the benefit of all of us and future generations'.

'I hope that on my next visit I shall be able to introduce you to my wife', replied Flinders. 'I am ever hopeful and, as you know, she is closer to my heart even than my passion to complete this work. We shall be back'.

As Luckett steered the boat back to Sydney, the Governor said 'There goes a great man who will be remembered for many years. I hope we shall see him again but I'll not be surprised if his love for his wife and the popular acclaim he'll receive in London detains him'.

The following week, Ben was at the wharf to greet Francis which was returning from Norfolk Island. The little vessel carried despatches from the Lieutenant Governor and some pigs to be sold in Sydney, but the most important passenger was Nathaniel Lucas. The Governor had particularly asked Lucas to come to Sydney so that he could assume the role of Master Carpenter and instil some discipline and good practices into the various tradesmen. Lucas was delighted to find Ben waiting for him and they were quickly in conversation. He politely asked at once about Sally and the children.

'I've had no news for some months now but when I last heard they were all well. They're living in a village called Swanbourne not far from Buckingham where Sally's father is working for one of the local farmers; I must admit to being just a little homesick – it's nearly five years since I was at home. How about Olivia and your family?'

'We've been getting along pretty nicely since you left Norfolk although I've had a few run-ins recently with the Lieutenant Governor. Mr King always seemed to appreciate hearing opinions honestly and openly even if he was sometimes inclined to disagree. I expect you know that he wrote and asked me to come here to sort out the carpenters, and finish the watermill. I've left Olivia behind for the moment with Ann who's 14 and the smaller children – seven of them now. She's due to be confined again in December and we thought it best if she stayed there until a little later. William and Nathaniel have come with me though'. And Nat Lucas introduced his two older sons who were 11 and 10.

'They look a couple of fine lads, ready to learn their father's trade, I daresay'.

'Indeed and the first job the Governor has is this watermill. I gather it was started a few years ago but has never been finished'.

'Yes I know plenty about that. But right now let me take you to your lodgings and show you around – it's not at all like it was the last time you were here in 88. Fifteen years has made a lot of difference'.

As they walked up from the wharf the two men chattered warmly, exchanging news and views as they had been accustomed to do on Norfolk Island. After settling him in Ben suggested that he should call on the Governor who would surely be very pleased to know he had arrived safely.

Ben was delighted to have his old friend close at hand again and the trio, made up with Tom Whittle, the other Norfolk Island old-stager, spent many evenings together whenever they could. It was some five weeks later when Ben was going to meet his friends that he saw two very dishevelled-looking ruffians walking up the hill from the landing stage. As they came nearer Ben approached them.

'Good day gentlemen. Can I be of any assistance?' asked Ben.

'You certainly can, Luckett. You will find it hard to believe, I know, but it is Captain Flinders upon whom you look'.

'Good gracious, Sir, I see it now. Forgive me for not recognising you at once. You seem to have faced some new mishap. The Governor is at dinner with his family just now but I'm sure he would wish to see you at once. Let's go on in'.

Ben led Captain Flinders and Lieutenant Park into Government House. He knocked on the dining room door and opened it for the two officers. The look of utter amazement in the eyes of the Governor spoke at once of his astonishment at seeing this spectre before him, who had departed for England only five weeks before. Mrs King started in astonishment and dropped her knife and fork on to her plate with a clatter.

'Are we seeing a ghost, my dear?' she addressed her husband.

'No Madam', replied Flinders, 'I'm afraid we're as real as we ever were, but appear before you after spending two weeks in an open boat. You remember Lieutenant Park, of course'.

'Yes, yes, of course. But come, draw up some chairs. Luckett, please ask cook to bring in some food for the gentlemen whilst they tell us more. So, Flinders, what's all this about; no repeat of Captain Bligh's experience in the Bounty I trust'.

'No, Sir, happily nothing like that', replied Flinders drawing up a chair, whilst Lieutenant Park pulled one up alongside Mrs King. 'We've left the Porpoise and 78 men on a reef. The ship is dismasted, high and dry. The Cato is also a wreck and will go nowhere. Bridgwater sailed on and we were not a little distressed that she appeared to ignore all our signals and lights. It shows how perilous those reefs are and how quickly you can pass from no bottom at eighty fathoms to being torn apart by coral. Lieutenant Fowler did all he could to haul his wind at the last minute but she'd not make her stays and struck the reef. We came away on the following day in the cutter with all our charts and navigational records, but leaving Fowler and the others there. They have food and water from the ships and will build a couple of boats from the timbers in case we cannot get back to them'. He paused.

The Governor was deeply affected, as was Mrs King. Pulling himself together he replied.

'We must at once send a vessel to rescue those brave men. Let's just think how best we can do that'. He paused. He called for Ben, and when he appeared, continued, 'Luckett, how quickly can the schooner Francis be ready for sea?'

'She should be well stocked with water and supplies, Sir, so should be able to leave within 24 hours'.

'Good. So she can go to the reef and rescue as many as want to return here to Sydney. Then the Rolla is about to leave for China and India, I believe. I could ask her master to stand by to take as many men as would be interested in going in her and eventually finding their way back to England. But that route is likely to be long and we ought to do something with you Flinders to get you back quicker. What about the Cumberland, Luckett?'

'She's very small, Sir, for a passage back to England. She's less than thirty tons and I don't know how she'd fare in a heavy storm'.

Flinders chipped in, 'Well I'd rather get going in something than sit around in the hope that another vessel will turn up. I'll take the risk if you will allow me to take the vessel'.

'Where is she now?'

'She's up the Hawkesbury, Sir. And I don't know when she's due back', offered Ben.

'Try to find out, please. If necessary we'll have to send a boat after her'.

'Speed is important', said Flinders, 'My men are very vulnerable out there on that reef and they may try to get away in home made boats if we're not back there soon'.

'I'll go down to Francis and Rolla and alert them to the situation first', said Ben, 'and then try to find out when Cumberland is expected back'.

Two days later there was still no sign of Cumberland and Flinders decided he must go and find her. He set off in his cutter, which had been named Hope, to get them back. After rapid re-stocking in Sydney, Cumberland was ready to sail with Francis and Rolla on 21st September. Yet again Flinders was being seen off by the Governor and Mrs King but, as fate decreed, this really was for the last time. Although he did survive the voyage and arrive in England it was only after being held captive on Mauritius – then the Ile de France – by the French governor for seven long years; what a poor dividend for the welcome, kindness and trust shown by the British Governor in Sydney to the French explorers and spies under Monsieur Baudin.

Chapter 27

By the beginning of 1804 the Governor felt in a stronger position than at any time. Much had been achieved in the three years of his command of the colony. He had brought to an end the exploitation of settlers and convicts by the army, he had provided an environment in which agriculture had improved significantly. The colony was now able to feed itself and he had succeeded in reducing sharply its cost to the Government in London which had been one of the most important objectives he had been given before he left London. Lord Hobart in London had written him a very complimentary letter approving warmly his success. But a number of tensions remained.

The army officers clearly did not like the Governor, a matter which was frequently a topic of conversation between Tom Whittle and Ben.

'You can't really be surprised that he's not their favourite', suggested Tom.

'No, but they still have quite a comfortable life, and they can make some money. After all they all have grants of land and some labour provided free. What the Governor dislikes is when one class of people starts to exploit another, which your bosses certainly used to be able to do'.

'And then they resent the fact that the Governor is a naval officer and the navy is the senior service'.

'Well we all know that', laughed Ben, 'that shouldn't be a reason for picking a quarrel. There was that business about the Courts Martial early on last year. What did the officers think they were doing publishing all those cartoons? In my book it was straightforward insubordination – publishing insults about your senior officer is something that in the navy would see you flogged around the fleet. And then, as acting Commanding officer, Major Johnston was about as awkward as he could be, far from supporting the Governor. The letters were flying back and forth between them – I delivered some of them myself. And I know the Governor was exasperated that the Major was unable to see the wider perspective and let the unimportant issues drop.

It'd be like going into battle in a ship and arguing about how the gun captain held the lighted match rather than concentrating attention on how quickly the guncrew could spunge out and re-load, or how accurately they pointed the gun'.

'I agree that it was totally unacceptable for the officers to start poking fun at the Governor behind his back; they deserved to be disciplined for that. But then naval people can be awkward too. Look at all that about Captain Colnett of Glatton. He was trying to wind the Governor up. For whatever reason he'd been looking after that convict girl Mary; we can all suspect what the relationship was although Colnett tried to dress it all up as altruism in a worthy cause. He wanted to take her home in the Glatton and enjoy her company and was terribly upset when the Governor said that she must spend at least a twelvemonth here before she could be emancipated'.

'I didn't much take to Captain Colnett. He tried to pull rank over the Governor because he's higher up the list of Captains, quite without recognising that the Governor's authority stems not from his naval rank but from his commission as Governor and Commander-in-Chief. It was ridiculous for him to expect the Governor to give even conditional emancipation to a convict without her serving any part of her term. It would be like the Governor over-turning the sentence of a judge back in England on nothing more than a whim'.

'It wasn't only the Governor he didn't take to', said Tom, 'That business of my boy being given a thrashing by that Lieutenant Stewart. He'd been invited onboard by one of the sailors he'd met and had no idea he had to have a license. The Lieutenant started abusing him, so young Tom gave him a bit of lip back. "Mutiny" says the Lieutenant. Silly man he should have been big enough to laugh it off instead of lashing out at Tom'.

'He was very small-minded. But then it wasn't very helpful when you were heard declaring you'd like to give the lieutenant a sound thrashing – however justified that may have been. It's one thing saying it to me, but wasn't it a little rash to shout it out on the parade ground where the whole world could hear?'

'Yes, I'll give you that. But I just got so furious I had to let it out somehow. And yes, I do regret that bit of it. If I'd been an officer I'd have called on Lieutenant Stewart and challenged him to a duel. Probably just as well I couldn't, because I'd have killed him and then been up for murder. By the way, have Colonel Paterson and the Governor got on better terms again? The Colonel was all of a dither over the Macarthur affair and I think he always found it difficult to steer between the Governor who he likes and respects, and his junior officers who want him to stand up against the Governor. He wants to run with the hare and hunt with the hounds and get the best of both worlds'.

'Don't we all want that at least to some extent?' asked Ben. And so their conversations continued in a friendly way, both recognising the value in the other and enjoying the fact that they could well disagree about things but could do so without falling out with each other.

Unrest continued to bubble away under the surface whilst outwardly everything seemed to be progressing reasonably well. There had been a serious flood on the Hawkesbury River which had washed away some of the crop, but not so severe as to threaten starvation. Various commercial enterprises were being set up and there was now a fair supply of non-essential items in the shops which people had established. The supply of liquor was quite sufficient and the prices were all at a level which would not immediately bankrupt the buyers. The underlying problem seemed to stem from the Irish convicts who had been transported after the 1798 riots in Ireland. Many of these had been the ringleaders of that uprising and saw themselves as political prisoners entitled to a life of ease at government expense. They thought it their duty to criticise the Governor locally and in letters to influential friends in London.

'I can't be giving them any privileges beyond anyone else', the Governor commented to Ben, 'somehow they just have to recognise that we're all under pressure to try to create a new country here, and life can be tough and difficult. But anyone who works hard and remains within the law can do very well. By the way, how are the Lucases getting on? It is remarkable how quickly Lucas seems to have been able to complete the watermill – just like Norfolk. And he seems to be into every building project too. How much land does he have?'

'I think he already has a couple of hundred acres here and I daresay they are amongst the best cared for in the colony. He's supervising the building of a much larger boat now. You know he personally selected all the timber which is being taken home in the Calcutta?'

'I'm glad to hear it. I'll go and inspect its progress as soon as I have the time. The current task is all about getting the despatches ready for the Calcutta's departure at the beginning of March'.

During the latter days of February the Governor was heavily engaged through the heat of the day writing reports for Lord Hobart, the Secretary of State for the Colonies. He must give a clear impression that life was proceeding well and that all the inhabitants were well-behaved. He must report that the costs of the colony to the Government were falling rapidly as self-sufficiency came closer. New South Wales would need many manufactured items to be sent out regularly, but gradually it would become possible for the inhabitants to pay for everything they might need, rather than receiving things free as government support. The Governor knew very well that there were some articulate characters in the colony, Irish convicts such as Sir Harry Hayes, who were determined to stir up ill will against him at every possible opportunity and so he must provide all the objective evidence he could to counter such criticism and avoid it taking hold in London.

The despatches had all been completed, dated 1st March, and Ben had delivered a large box addressed to Lord Hobart to Captain Woodriff aboard Calcutta which would sail within the week. But then on Sunday 4th March just as Ben was getting ready for bed there was a great commotion outside Government House. A lathered horse had arrived and the rider was looking anxious. Ben realised at once that this was not a simple emergency and as he pulled his clothes back on he scooped up a brace of pistols, some ammunition and a cutlass, grabbed his hat and set off at a run to Government House.

In the hallway he found the messenger with the Governor.

'Ah Luckett, a rebel group of escaped convicts and others is at the edge of Parramatta. I shall ride there at once. A note to Colonel Paterson please; "Take command of the Sydney area, and prepare to defend against a substantial force; send a company to reinforce Captain Abbott at Parramatta; I'll ask Captain Woodriff to provide you with assistance of his seamen and marines. Bring in all the men in the Sydney area so they are under your control – that will prevent any of them from aligning with the rebels'".

Ben left at once with the note and ran across to Colonel Paterson's house where he roused the Colonel. Once sure that the message had been received, he returned to Government House where two horses had been prepared. The Governor leapt onto his favourite, Ben took the other and they set off at a gallop for Parramatta. A little over half an hour's hard riding saw them coming into the little settlement there. They went immediately to the barracks to find Captain Abbott. All the local inhabitants had already been warned, and the Loyal Association, the militia, had been called up and was being armed. Some of the settlers from outlying farms had been brought into Parramatta for their better safety. Meanwhile the rebels seemed to be holding back as there had been no actual clashes in the darkness.

'A company is marching at once from Sydney, which I presume will be commanded by Major Johnston. You concentrate your efforts on securing Parramatta and the safety of everyone here, and Johnston can go after the rebels, when he arrives', said the Governor addressing Captain Abbott. 'I shall make my headquarters in Government House; come Luckett'.

They rode the short distance to Government House in Parramatta and the governor immediately settled down at the desk.

'I shall proclaim Martial Law in the area between here and Castle Hill including Hawkesbury, Prospect, and Vinegar Hill. I shall need your help Luckett to produce some copies'. So the proclamation of Martial Law was made, and Ben took copies back to the barracks to be posted in the most prominent places, informing everyone he met. He spoke to the Captain to make sure that a system of passes was in place and that he had established a password to distinguish between inhabitants and rebels. The proclamation made it clear that anyone out after sunset without a pass would be fired upon.

Just as the sun was rising at about five thirty Major Johnston and his company marched in from Sydney. They had made good time and were tired and dusty. At the barracks they were given some refreshment.

'You'll need to get over to Government House', Captain Abbott said to the Major. 'The Governor's waiting for you there and will give you further orders'.

'Directly', replied the Major, 'Will you look after my men and make sure they're all ready to go on to whatever the Governor wishes?' And the Major jumped onto his horse and rode off.

'Well done Major', was the Governor's greeting, 'I'm very pleased to see you, and so quickly. I've had some reports of the rebels waiting outside the town, but now it's getting light I daresay they may choose to advance. I'd like you to anticipate that and march out to meet them so that you have the initiative. They're an unruly rabble by all accounts and they'll be intimidated by a smart body of disciplined men. If they withdraw, follow them and do your best to bring them to a stand. Invite them to surrender but if they don't after due warning, fire upon them and pursue them until they do. Martial Law is in force; those who fail to obey you may be shot. Oh, and take Father Dixon with you. They may find it somewhat persuasive if he's seen to be at your side'.

'Thank you sir. I have but one trooper on horseback. I should like to take a few of the inhabitants who have horses so that I can use them to keep you informed'.

'Why not take Luckett here? He may be a sailor, but he rides well and is a good man to have close by'.

'Aye, aye, Sir', responded Ben – and he looked the part with a pair of pistols tucked in his belt and a cutlass slung over his shoulder.

Ben's horse had by that time had a rest and a feed, and he followed the Major as he returned to the barracks to collect his men. Before 7 am they set off again with the Major at the head of an orderly column. He deployed Captain Davies with a detachment to take the road towards Castle Hill to sweep up any rebels who might have made off in that direction, and to be able to cut off any who tried to retreat to Castle Hill.

The Major could see signs of activity ahead. So he sent a Corporal and a few men out to the left on a flanking operation, but it did not seem that any of the rebels was preparing to make a stand. Then as they began to go up Vinegar Hill towards Hawkesbury their way was blocked by about 200 rebels. Ben could see that some were armed with muskets, but he wondered how good they would be at loading and firing them especially when they were facing a regular fire from trained soldiers.

The Major and his trooper had ridden on ahead and coming up within pistol shot they dismounted and continued to walk forward until about fifteen paces from the rebels.

'Who will come and talk with me?' shouted the Major.

'We will talk if you come among us', was the response.

'I am here within pistol shot, send your leaders to talk'.

After some minutes of discussion amongst the rebels, two men ventured forward. They were Philip Cunningham and William Johnston who had evidently been behind the uprising.

Major Johnston again invited them to surrender or face the full force of military action from which none should expect to escape. Cunningham's reply was unequivocal; 'I will never surrender', and then at the top of his voice 'Death or liberty'. At that moment, as quick as lightening, the Major caught hold of Cunningham and held his pistol, cocked, at his head; following his lead and almost as quickly the trooper did the same with William Johnston.

'Quick march', ordered the Major as he forced Cunningham, barely recovering from his surprise, back into the body of the soldiers who were by now ranged in line and ready to fire. As soon as they were within the lines, the Major nodded to Quartermaster Laycock who gave the order to fire. The soldiers had fired three or four volleys whilst the rebels managed to get off a few shots, all of which went wild of their mark. Several rebels had fallen, others had been hit and the remainder turned and began to flee.

'After them, men', ordered the Major, 'take prisoners and only kill if you are threatened'. One or two of the settlers tended the wounded.

'Luckett, will you please go back to the Governor and report to him that the rebels are in flight and we have taken the two ring-leaders, Cunningham and Johnston. Tell him that I will report again when we have swept up the rest, but that I do not think we shall have much trouble now'.

'Aye, aye, Sir', Ben responded, as he turned his horse and galloped back to Parramatta. When he reported to the Governor he could see the look of relief in his eyes, tinged with a sense of frustration.

'Why, oh why do they do it? Cunningham and Johnston will have to be executed and perhaps a few others, and we shall have to administer other punishments. They have achieved absolutely nothing except to prove that government forces can respond quickly and effectively in the face of such threats'.

He sighed and went on, 'I'll stay here for the night, and as long as everything stays quiet I'll return to Sydney tomorrow. Would you please ride to Sydney now and give Colonel Paterson news of the current situation, and then call at Government House and tell Mrs King that I'm in good heart and will return to her tomorrow'.

Ben took his leave of the Governor and after calling at the barracks to inform Captain Abbott, he rode off towards Sydney at a leisurely pace.

Back in Sydney all was quiet. The soldiers were manning outposts on all the roads into the capital whilst on the barrack square the male inhabitants who had been brought in were being drilled, and instructed in the use of a musket. The seamen and marines from the Calcutta were standing by to go wherever they might be needed. All was calm. The Colonel was very happy to receive Ben's report and to know the rebellion had been effectively and decisively quashed. Captain Woodriff was invited to take his men back onboard the Calcutta, and when the drills and instruction had been completed the Colonel allowed the inhabitants generally to return home and get on with their lives. He maintained the soldiers' outposts on the Parramatta road, and set a guard on Government House and the wharf, just in case a few stragglers chose to make mischief.

Ben found Mrs King and Mrs Paterson together at Government House with the children, and gave them the news.

'Well that's a blessed relief', declared Mrs King. 'And is the Governor feeling a little less worried now?'

'Yes Ma'am. He asked me to tell you that he's well, and he certainly looked that way when I left him. Tell Mrs King I am smiling, he told me'.

There had been rebellions before, although none had seemed to be quite as determined as this one. The leader, Cunningham, had been executed immediately under the terms of martial law. A further ten leaders were tried three days later, found guilty and sentenced to death; only two of them were reprieved. About thirty more rebels suffered corporal punishment and were sent to the gaol gang. It was now clear that as long as the army remained trained and ready they could deal with any threat posed to them from inside the colony. What had not been proved was whether the colony could defend itself from an external attack from the French, the Dutch or the Americans.

The searing temperatures of summer began to moderate and the prospect of winter loomed. A plan was beginning to develop to reduce the number of people sent to Norfolk Island; it would never be the predominant supplier of timber and flax for the British navy in eastern waters as Captain Cook and Joseph Banks had envisaged, and it was too remote and difficult of access to make it a realistic supplier of wheat and pork to the main colony. The conclusion was to encourage as many of the settlers as possible to exchange their land on Norfolk Island for plots four times the size in the much larger Van Diemen's Land. Colonel Collins was now establishing the settlement at Hobart on the Derwent River started by Lieutenant Bowen, and Colonel Paterson would shortly establish another settlement at Port Dalrymple. Captain Flinders had sailed round the continent and was now on his way to London with his charts. He was expected, eventually, to return to complete some more surveys. Mr Brown and Mr Bauer the naturalists, were continuing to make discoveries of new species as they gradually pushed back the frontiers of the early settlements. Ben began increasingly to think of home and his growing family. And then there was the growing threat to England from Napoleon, which had emerged again despite the brief period of peace after the Treaty of Amiens kin 1802; the navy was growing once again and the older ships were being refitted. There was, as always, a great and growing shortage of seamen to man the wooden walls and Ben wondered whether he should really be back home defending his family against the possibility of invasion.

In July the whaler Albion returned to Sydney under the command of the well-respected Eber Bunker. Ben had first heard of Captain Bunker when he sailed with Captain Raven in Britannia to New Zealand, for the two men were firm friends. On previous visits to Port Jackson, Ben had regularly had the opportunity to talk with the Captain who often tried to persuade Ben to sail with him on one of his whaling trips. In 1803 he had taken Lieutenant Bowen and the first settlers to Hobart on the river Derwent in Van Diemen's Land before going off to hunt for whales and seals. Now it was time for him to return to London with a good cargo of whale oil and about 13,000 seal skins.

'Well Luckett', said the Captain as they walked together up towards Government House, 'I'm ready for returning to England. Can I persuade you to come back with me?'

'It's no secret that I have been thinking of returning. I said to the Governor originally that I would give him five years but then wanted to return to my family. And the five years is up. Would you allow me to work my passage with you?'

'That would be fine – and you will help us repeat our record-breaking run – it was three months and fifteen days when we came out. We'll be going to Norfolk Island for a few days and then down to the Southern Ocean and to Cape Horn. We'll be risking falling upon a Frenchman on our way up the Channel but I think that's a risk worth taking. If you'll come with us you can show my boys how to fire the guns. We've only got ten of them and we're not well practiced. You can be the Gunner'.

'I shall have to ask the Governor but I believe he will agree'. They parted with a handshake on the steps of Government House and Ben began to feel that the process of getting home had at last begun.

Over dinner that day the Governor was sitting with his habitual glass of claret when Mrs King spoke up.

'You are looking very thoughtful, my dear', she said. 'What's on your mind now?'

'Luckett spoke to me earlier and asked if I would agree to him taking a passage in Albion. He has been with us for five years and he is anxious about his young family'.

'Well you would not be surprised about that, would you?' said Anna Josepha, 'you miss your two little ones as well, I know; and so do I. But at least we have the consolation of having Elizabeth and Mary here with us – and we have each other'.

'Yes, yes. You are right of course. And Luckett has been a very great help and relief to me when everyone else seemed to be against me. I have been so sorely tried, as you well know, by being isolated and vilified by everyone, even those who seemed to share the same ideals and values. Of course I made one very big mistake at the beginning'.

'What was that, my dear?'

'In the rush to get everything prepared for sea and to get our affairs in order I failed to make sure that the Duke of Portland gave me specific and written instructions regarding the dismantling of the trading monopolies and cartels. So no one has ever believed that I have only acted in accordance with the orders I received verbally in all those meetings at the Ministry. Even good Colonel Paterson has questioned my authority from time to time. And now I feel my health is getting so much worse. That gout, or whatever it is, is never far away and I fear the pain it brings and the way it weakens my resolve in everything. I have asked Lord Hobart to seek the King's permission for me to return home and we can only be patient for the reply. In the meantime I have agreed to give Luckett permission to leave.

'It seems like a change of the guard,' replied Mrs King. 'William has left us and I doubt much whether we will see him again. The Colonel and Mrs Paterson are away to Van Diemen's Land. Mr Flinders now seems to be detained in Mauritius by the French and we must doubt how long it will be before they release him. That makes me sick when I think of all the care we lavished on Monsieur Baudin when he was here, despite suspecting that he was making observations about this place which would certainly be reported back to his government.

'God alone knows and He alone will judge,' the Governor continued, 'but I am confident I have done all that any man could, to implement the orders of the government and to create here a colony which can look after itself. When you consider what happened in the early days of America's development, after the Pilgrim Fathers settled there, it soon became a very tough, dangerous and lawless place. We have plenty of problems here but everyone knows that there is a rule of law and that those who work hard will be rewarded, whilst those who exploit others may be found out and brought to justice'. The Governor was reflecting on the seventeen years in which he had been involved in this enterprise.

'No-one – not even Governor Phillip – realised what a massive project was being undertaken', he went on, 'and there was remarkably little detailed planning, and no recognition that the uncertain communication line, nine months long, would create so many difficulties. Do you remember Colonel Grose and Major Ross making it so clear that they had absolutely no belief in the future of New South Wales and that the only possible benefit would be for them to milk it for their own personal gain. If they didn't, they said, someone else would, and in any case the place would be abandoned within a few years. Seventeen years on and I see it in a much better light; within a few years this land will be able to survive well without significant government support. It will continue to need a judiciary provided from England and it will be some years before it is ready for a Parliament'. The Governor was in full flow and his wife needed to say nothing to encourage him further but she did manage to intervene.

'It would be very agreeable if the government at home would give you more recognition for all you have achieved – only four years ago this was a lawless place, filled with drunkards and dominated by lazy, greedy money-grabbers, where the honest hard-working man would find himself unable to make a decent living.' Mrs King was warming to her theme; 'That's gone; that's been your legacy and you can be proud of it. I know – you know – you've made some mistakes; what man wouldn't have done. But you – you've lived by your principles, you've refused all the temptations to create and build up wealth for yourself. Look at the Macarthurs; Mrs Macarthur seems always a little embarrassed that through her husband's actions she's become very wealthy, and not without causing you the greatest pain and anguish. Even dear Mr Marsden, a man of the cloth, has created wealth for himself whilst developing and breeding the best sheep for these lands. And you – you've carried all the responsibility and have been vilified and blamed for every wrong, and you've never taken anything for yourself or your family. Where would the sheep be now unless you'd taken the initiative in the Cape and insisted on buying that flock from Mrs Gordon? I know you had to lean hard on Captains Waterhouse and Kent to buy some of them and ship them back here. And who's won the credit – Macarthur and Marsden – not you'. Anna Josepha was highly animated on behalf of her husband. She could not change him from the deeply committed Christian he was, concerned only in doing what was right in the sight of God, believing in the fundamental goodness of every soul, and trusting that in the final judgement he could hold his head high. His descendants would have an outstanding example to follow and would be proud of all he had achieved against the most horrendous odds, but they would not have great financial assets handed down to them, and the harsh voices of his critics would continue to be heard above the gentle persuasiveness of long-term reality.

Ben spent his final few days in Sydney bidding farewell to all the friends he had made and the people he admired. Rev Marsden at Parramatta was one who, as well as being a man of God, had worked very hard to improve the strain of the sheep within the colony. He and Mrs Macarthur who had been left to run Elizabeth Farm nearby when her husband was sent back to England, had produced wonderful fleeces which had been sent off for inspection and valuation. They were hopeful that the government would support new initiatives to develop Australian wool into a major export on which the growth of the colony could be built.

Nat and Olivia Lucas and their children were very important to Ben. Their eldest daughter, Ann, was now just fifteen and turning into a very pretty and capable young woman. Twelve year old William was already following his father everywhere and learning all his many skills. Having learnt that his father had died Nat had decided to remain in the young colony where his position would be much more advantageous than if he were to take his family back to England. After all the success he had achieved on Norfolk Island he was wondering whether they might all do better by going down to Van Diemen's Land. But for the time being he had built the new watermill which would have been operating well if there had been enough water, as well as some new windmills.

Tom Whittle was his other close friend whose life was now completely committed to the new country. Little did they know at that time that Tom would play an important, though small, part in the eventual arrest of Governor Bligh, but that was still several years into the future, and he was determined to do as well as he could for his young family.

The Albion sailed from Port Jackson on 21st August 1804. The Governor, Mrs King and Elizabeth and Mary had been to see him off and wish him well as he left the wharf for the last time. As Albion set sail towards the Heads he tried to fix in his mind the whole of the scene he was leaving behind. They passed the Heads and gradually the land fell away behind them sinking slowly and gently out of sight below the horizon.

Ten days later they came to Norfolk and Ben was anxious to step ashore and see how it was now. The watermill was still working and many of the buildings seemed much the same as when he had left the island ten years earlier. He walked up to Queenborough and called on Richard Morgan and his wife who were considering the future with the offer of four acres in Van Diemen's Land for every one they had here; he was still the gentle quiet giant that Ben remembered and they enjoyed reminiscing together about those days. 'When I think back to when Mr King was here', said Richard, 'it seems like a different world. We had problems aplenty but the atmosphere he engendered was good and kind. We ate well, we worked hard, we had some fun. It has never been the same since then, and it's that which will drive us out. This has really become little more than a prison for the most awkward and difficult of the convicts'.

The Albion only stopped three days and then sailed again for the Southern Ocean and Cape Horn. Definitely the end of an era for me, thought Ben.

Part Five - Trafalgar

Chapter 28

The river Thames and London were all of a bustle when Albion came to a mooring on Sunday 3rd March 1805. She had been across the southern ocean and around Cape Horn. She had called at Capetown and joined a convoy of East Indiamen sailing northwards to London and, without coming across any French ships which might have caused her a problem, she sailed peacefully up the Thames. Ben was not alone in the sense of excitement he felt as they passed the familiar sights. At the Nore he remembered his first experience of the Royal Navy when he was taken from the little Norfolk coasting vessel he had grown up with and went aboard Nelson's frigate Boreas. How times had changed and life had moved on.

It was late on the Sunday evening when they moored the ship close to the Greenland Dock where the whale oil would be landed. Captain Bunker and Ben agreed that it would be prudent to wait until the morning before setting off with the despatches for Westminster and the package for Mr Sykes, the Governor's agent in Arundel Street.

'I'll take a boat up to Westminster on the tide and deliver the boxes to the Colonial Office first and they should pass on anything for the Admiralty and other departments. I'll call on the Enderby family to give my respects to Miss Maria and then Mr Sykes at Arundel Street. And when I have seen him I shall make off for Buckinghamshire unless you need me back here'.

'No, no. You go on. You have a way to travel to find your family; mine are here in London. I hope we'll meet again, maybe in New South Wales where I expect to be living with the whole family within a couple of years. Thank you for your help on the voyage and goodbye, for now'. The handshake was warm and their eyes met, each knowing and respecting the other.

It only took a matter of moments once at Westminster to hand over the box of despatches for the Secretary of State, Lord Hobart. Ben then set off along Whitehall to call on Mr Enderby. As he came up to the Admiralty a number of officers seemed to be leaving and entering the building resplendent in their full uniform as they arrived to receive orders, plead for a command or deliver their various reports. His surprise was complete when he saw the familiar face of Captain Fremantle emerge from the main entrance. A meeting was not at all what Ben had planned but when fate intervenes in such a manner it would be foolish to turn the other way. So Ben approached the Captain.

'Good Day Captain,' said Ben, saluting and looking him in the eye, and then fearing that the Captain might have forgotten him during the past five years he added, 'Ben Luckett at your service, Sir'.

'Why, Luckett, how extraordinarily good to see you. This is a fine chance meeting indeed. Do I find you in good health?'

'You do, Sir, and very happy to have arrived at Greenhithe yesterday from New South Wales. I have some parcels to deliver and then plan to make my way home to Swanbourne'.

'Well what a very fine coincidence. Let me tell you I have just been talking to Lord Garlies who is now a Lord of the Admiralty about a new appointment and he has told me I am at the top of the list for a First Rate as soon as the opportunity arises. You must have heard about the situation the country is in, and the Admiralty is very much engaged with the defence of the Channel and the defeat of Napoleon's fleets. If that command comes along how do you feel about joining me?'

'It's very kind of you to ask, Sir, but after more than five years away I need a little time at Swanbourne to see my Sally and the family – I owe them that'.

'Yes, of course, of course. I feel the same as you and place great value on the time I can spend with my family. I really regret the separation and feel very lonely away at sea – not at all like the old bachelor days. In any case I doubt it will be less than a month or two before anything crops up. But before you go down to Swanbourne could you please call at Cork Street and visit Mrs Fremantle. I know she'd be very pleased to see you again and I'm not sure how soon she'll be going back to the country. If you were to come at five I'm sure you would find us in with the children. Then there will be an early morning coach up Watling Street, and you will be home tomorrow just the same'.

Ben was torn between his desire to get home and the feeling that complying with the Captain's wish might serve him well in the future. And in any case he had developed a great affection for Mrs Fremantle since before their marriage.

'That would be a pleasure, Sir. I'd be very happy to meet your children if they are there as well as Mrs Fremantle, of course'.

'Splendid. Till five this evening then'. Ben saluted, the Captain acknowledged, and they went their separate ways.

The Enderby family's home was close to St Benet's Church and Paul's Wharf where the family had their business. Ben was greeted as a friend by Mr Enderby who at once wanted to know all about the Governor and Mrs King. Little Maria who had been only six years old when she had been left behind by her tearful parents was now 12 and Ben could not recognise the baby he had known on Norfolk Island when she was born. But there was a pleasing family resemblance, and Ben was able to undermine normal convention and give her the kiss he had been asked to pass to her from the Governor and Mrs King.

'How are matters in New South Wales?' asked Mr Enderby, 'I have worried much about Mr King's health and from what he told me before he left he was handed a poisoned chalice'.

'I've had an enormous privilege working under a man with such high principles', said Ben. 'He was absolutely determined to fulfil every task set by the politicians in London before he left, but in practice he found it even more difficult than he had anticipated. As soon as he put the necessary measures in place he became fearfully unpopular and attracted vicious criticism from everyone except the free settlers and the ex-convicts. You may have heard about Captain Macarthur who, above all, placed the Governor in a quite impossible situation'. He paused and changed the direction of the conversation. 'But your business out there seems to flourish and the whalers are very important for the growing economy as well as for the additional transport they provide'.

'Indeed; and I am very happy about that. But I know Mr King has always been driven by a powerful desire to fulfil his orders and do whatever he perceived as best for his fellow men. And he did it all in the name of God to whom he believes he, and the rest of us too, will answer in eternity'.

Ben told Mr Enderby as much as he could about the state of the colony, most of which was very favourable. After more than an hour Ben set off to walk the short distance to Arundel Street, where he found Mr James Sykes. The office was a busy place with several clerks copying letters and documents and making accounts and records. Fortunately Sykes was in and was pleased to see Ben, who handed him the packet of letters and bills from the Governor. Sykes called over one of his clerks and in a few moments had in his hands the accounts for Ben's own affairs.

'I know of no claims on me which will be outstanding', said Ben, 'but perhaps you had better keep a balance of, say, £10, and there should be some more pay due. As I returned in the Albion there should be some small amount to come from its owners, Champions, as Captain Bunker kindly took me on as Master's Mate and Gunner for the return voyage'.

All was soon settled and Ben had cash in his pocket and was ready to set off for his appointment at Cork Street.

Rather than going straight up to the front door of the house he went down to the servants' entrance. There he was greeted by a kitchen maid who ran off to find the butler, and within a few minutes Ben was being led upstairs where he found the Captain and Mrs Fremantle and their four children, Thomas 7, Charles 5, Henry 3 and the baby Emily. He could not have hoped to see a happier family scene with laughter and smiles for all. Things quietened immediately as Ben was ushered into the room. Betsey rose at once and greeted Ben with a warm handshake.

'What a wonderful surprise to have you call, Luckett. How have you been going along these last years. As you can see we've kept busy; I think you may have met Thomas before you left but I am sure he doesn't remember you'. And addressing Thomas she added, 'Mr Luckett's home is next to ours at Swanbourne – he is James's father'. James was about the same age as Thomas and they had formed a regular friendship and a taste for adventures about the village. Ben was encouraged to talk of the places he had been to and what he had seen and done, and the children were delighted when he described a kangaroo and demonstrated how it leapt around. He, in turn, asked about the Captain's exploits since he had been away.

'Nothing as exciting as you', replied the Captain. 'It took a long time for my arm to recover and I was only fit to return to sea in 1800. They gave me the Ganges, and we started off with the Channel Fleet under St Vincent, and later we were transferred to the fleet going to the Baltic under Sir Hyde Parker. Admiral Nelson was there as his second. You probably heard about the Battle of Copenhagen when Sir Hyde ordered Nelson to lay off, and Nelson chose not to see the signal and led us into battle. It was a vicious and hard fought slog, but we prevailed and it was declared a great victory. We spent a few more months in the Baltic with Nelson after Sir Hyde had been recalled and saw Karlskroner in Sweden and Revel in Russia. Then we went to Ireland and once again down to the Channel fleet. Ganges paid off at the end of October so I had last Christmas at home'.

The children were taken off to bed and Ben knew it was time for him to leave the Fremantles for their evening activities. As he left Fremantle said to him, 'Think about my suggestion and come with me if you possibly can; I'll be happy to take your boy as well and he can study with the young gentlemen'.

It was late on 5th March when Ben walked into the village of Swanbourne. How much had changed. As he passed Swanbourne House he noticed how it looked so much better cared for than he remembered when he had first seen it with the Captain in '98. His arrival at the cottage could not have been for him a happier moment. Sally greeted him with an embrace which warmed his heart and he was thrilled to see his children. Thomas was now just 12 years old and beginning to look like a strong and bright boy. Sarah, James and Elizabeth were all so much larger than when he last saw them. The younger two were suspicious of the strange man who had suddenly entered their lives but they soon realised that he was more than just friendly and they were happy to play games with him and chase him round the village.

It was not long before news of Ben's return reached every cottage in Swanbourne and he was questioned closely about his travels and happy to talk about the strange new country on the other side of the world. The impression he always tried to leave with people was that it was a tough life out there and not for the faint-hearted, but if you looked for adventure and opportunity it was there for the taking and you could build up land and wealth. He often referred to the Lucas family and Richard Morgan as examples of men who had left England as convicts but were now respected and valued members of the community with wealth and standing.

Ben was very happy to renew his acquaintance with Farmer Deverell who, in his turn, was happy at the thought that Ben might now be on hand to help on the land. Ben said nothing to him about the possibility that he might go again to sea quite soon, and made it clear that he would be very interested in becoming more deeply involved.

After the thrill of their reunion Ben and Sally began to settle quickly into a routine and it seemed that he had hardly been away. The children quickly got used to him being around and would regularly ask him to make or mend something for them. One of the things he much enjoyed was making little boats out of sticks and larger pieces of wood and racing them in the stream, or blowing them across the pond, or even a puddle. The two of them talked about the future and Ben of course told her of the chance meeting with the Captain in London, and his offer.

'If it comes up, I must go,' said Ben. 'I know how dangerous things are with Boney sitting on the other side of the channel just waiting for the chance to invade. And if ever that happened we would all be in serious trouble'.

'I know, my love, and you are quite right although I can't say I like the idea of you going off in a great warship towards the enemy. So many things might happen which would leave me without you, and I can't bear the thought of it'.

'You prick my heart when you say that. I know that all the time I was away I was thinking and dreaming of you and the children and regretting being on the other side of the world. But we can't just sit at home when our King requires us to go out and fight. It'd be better by far to defeat Boney's fleet so that he can't bring his army across the channel. If everyone thought they must stay away because there might be danger then we'd not deserve our freedom from Boney's tyranny. Did I tell you that the Captain said he'd like to take Thomas as well, whether I go or not. He's the right age and could get a better education at sea than ashore. If he can get rated Midshipman and then pass for Lieutenant he will be on a path to success – much better than being in Buckinghamshire as a farmer's boy'.

'That grieves me too, except that I know you're right. I've had him close to me all his life and he's been a great comfort especially with you on the other side of the world. You'll speak to him of course and warn him to be prepared'.

It was barely light on the morning of 8th May when there was a fierce knocking on the door of the cottage, and Ben tumbled out of bed to see what was up. It was a messenger who had ridden overnight from London with a letter from the Captain. Ben thanked him and quickly broke the seal and unfolded the paper.

'I have the Neptune which comes into Plymouth in a few days,' he read. 'I shall go at once to Portsmouth to collect my things and then on to Plymouth as quickly as I can. Will you please to come to Plymouth and join the Neptune. Please bring Master Luckett with you. Make ready for anything as we shall have a great task. Do not trouble to reply to this as you will reach Plymouth quicker than the mail'.

'There's no reply, thank you', said Ben to the messenger, 'but you'd be welcome to stay for some breakfast if you'd like some'. Sally had followed Ben downstairs and nodded as she turned to liven up the fire and heat some water.

'Is it what I fear, my love?' Sally asked.

'Indeed it is. He invites us to go at once to Plymouth to board the Neptune – that is one of the biggest and best ships in the navy. We shall have to leave at once. I'll go and rouse the children'.

Later that day the cottage was filled with tears as Ben and Thomas bade farewell and many of the people in the village came by to wish them luck. Buckingham was their first stop where they hoped to pick up a coach going southwards towards Bath. Ben was thoughtful as they strode out, his oldest son at his side. He was sad, for sure, but proud that Thomas was with him, keen and eager for adventure, and grateful that the Captain of one of the navy's largest ships had invited him, even insisted, that they should join him.

Three days later they arrived in Plymouth and went straight down to Plymouth Hoe to ask where the Neptune was. With several other ships she was anchored in Cawsand Bay a short boat ride away and, rather than hang around ashore, Ben decided that it was time to introduce Thomas to the Royal Navy. They had talked about it all the way from home, Ben trying to re-assure a young boy that he would be well able to cope with life onboard.

'Besides,' said Ben, 'you've met the Captain and can be sure that he will be fair and reasonable in all his judgements. He expects all his men to do what they're told, at once and without question, and as long as you do that all will be well'.

'It's not him that I'm worried about', said Thomas, 'but all the other people who think that the only way they can get people to work is by beating them. That's not right is it, father?'

'There are rogues like that and you have to be careful not to get on the wrong side of them. It never pays to make enemies however difficult that may seem at times'. And so the conversation went on as Ben educated his son into the life he was about to embark upon.

When they arrived onboard Ben informed the quartermaster that he and Thomas had arrived on the orders of Captain Fremantle and they quickly found themselves ushered towards the Captain's quarters. Thomas's eyes were darting around trying to take in all the activity, with men rushing to and fro carrying bales and barrels to be stowed down in the hold, whilst others worked at sails or ropes. Carpenters were carrying out repairs, painters were over the side painting, caulkers patched up seams between the deck planks. The Royal Marine sentry stood outside the Captain's quarters.

'Can I leave our bags under your care while we see the Captain, please', asked Ben of the sentry.

'Carry on', replied the sentry, 'The Captain said he was expecting you around now'. They knocked and entered to find the Captain at his desk with his secretary, to whom he was giving instructions. In a moment he turned towards the newcomers.

'Ah, Luckett and son. How pleased I am to see you both. It's been extraordinarily difficult to find any young people from Buckinghamshire to come with me'.

'Well, Sir, I can only think of one better place to be and that you know already', replied Ben knowing that the Captain would realise at once that he was referring to being at home with his wife and the rest of his family.

'Yes, yes. But just now we have a job to do and that has to be our priority. Now I've secured one other Bucks man for the gunroom and that is Midshipman William Badcock whose home is at Missenden Abbey. I'll ask him to keep a special eye out for Thomas.

'Thomas, I have rated you Captain's servant and you will mess in the gunroom and attend all the lessons provided by the schoolmaster. Midshipman Badcock will instruct you in your other duties especially your role when we prepare for action'.

'Thank you Sir', was the only reply from Thomas, looking the Captain in the eye with an intriguing mixture of shyness and confidence.

'And for you Luckett I would like you as my Coxswain and Quartermaster. Both of you will need to visit the tailor and get fitted out with some suitable clothes. Oh and I think and hope, Luckett, that my Gig has been delivered from Portsmouth. Will you check it out please and get it properly stowed'.

'Aye,aye, Sir', from Ben. 'We'd best get out o'your way as I'm sure there are plenty of things for you to think about'.

'It's good to have you on board. We sail tomorrow to join the Channel fleet off Ushant'.

Ben and Thomas left the great cabin, picked up their bags from the sentry's care and set off to find their quarters.   Ben was thrilled that Captain Fremantle was taking Thomas as one of his servants, a great privilege and, if Thomas could manage the school work, it should prove to be the first step on the path to being an officer in his Majesty's Navy, and who knew where that might lead. For now practical considerations had to be foremost – the dream must wait.

The following day, 16th May, the Neptune weighed anchor and set a SSW course to rejoin the fleet under Admiral Gardner.   The Captain was at once concerned to evaluate how well the officers and men of his new command worked together and how proficient they were at the various things they would have to be prepared for. He had immediately formed a favourable impression of the ship as a sailing machine; she was not fast but she was steady and the topmen had proved themselves to his satisfaction when they were hit by a gale a week after arriving on station. Every day during the afternoon they exercised at the great guns, with competitions to find which crew could reload quickest and which gun could be directed most accurately at a target. Thomas began to learn his way around and to get to know the seven other young men whom the Captain had selected to take with him. There was such a lot to take in, and this massive three-deck ship was like a rabbit warren in which there always seemed to be something hidden around the next corner. Not only did he need to find out all the basic practical things like how and where to wash, how and where to sling a hammock, but he also had to understand who the various key people were, the role they played and where they fitted into the hierarchy. At first when he looked on the upper deck everything seemed a complete mystery – different sizes of rope in every direction, and each one with its name and specific purpose; gradually he learnt.   He did not see much of his father who always seemed too busy about other things and, in any case, he did not want to earn a reputation for having his father sort out any problem he might have.

As had been the case in the Mediterranean eight years earlier the Captains would visit each other regularly which meant Ben was often in the gig with his Captain. Off Toulon visits happened almost every day, but here on the eastern fringe of the Atlantic it was often too choppy to make a visit a pleasant experience.

'How long do you suppose we shall be here?' asked Ben of the Captain one day.

'I've no idea – it could be weeks, it could be months. It depends very much on what the French decide to do. I saw in a newspaper that Bonaparte has been in Italy getting himself crowned as King over there, which suggests that he is not too anxious to invade England', replied the Captain.

'Will he really do that, do you think?'

'Well, he has an army camped at Boulogne, with a massive fleet of small boats to carry them across the channel. But in order to shift a large enough army across he needs to command the sea. As long as we stay in command we can defend the country against any French attack. We are here to keep the French ships in Brest and to prevent any others from getting in there – the danger is that if the wind blows strongly and consistently from the East we shall have difficulty staying in position and the French ships will be able to get out. I expect you know that we have a squadron under Rear Admiral Sterling blockading a few French ships in Rochefort and another under Vice Admiral Calder looking after Ferrol. And then there is Nelson somewhere, although it seems that no one knows where at the moment'.

'I hope you don't mind my asking all these questions, but I find it really interesting to know a little about why we are here and what is going on. Do the French have any ships actually at sea?'

'I'll tell you when I get bored with answering questions, but to tell the truth I enjoy talking about it because it helps me think about all the tactical issues we face. And to answer your last question we believe that Admiral Villeneuve is at sea with a fleet of between 15 and 20 of the line. He escaped the Toulon blockade some weeks ago when Nelson was blown off in a storm and it is generally thought that he went to the West Indies. But he may be choosing his moment to come back and drive us out of the Channel'.

'I heard that Boney likes to command his ships as if they were armies and I can't see how that could ever work. If armies want to move they can move, more or less, where they like. Ships can only go where the wind will allow'.

'All our strategic thinking is done at the Admiralty by Lord Barham, Captain Gambier and Lord Garlies. Sharp as a knife is old Lord Barham despite being 80; his despatches seem to be clear, and concise and allow the local Captain or Admiral a degree of discretion according to local conditions and knowledge. I think we have probably become quite good at that over the last twenty years or so'.

On 12th July there was a flurry of activity. First, Caesar, 80 guns, with Sir Richard Strachan in command arrived from the south, and a new set of orders emerged from Admiral Cornwallis, who had resumed the command from Admiral Gardner, establishing an inshore squadron of five ships. This would allow the remainder to patrol further out to sea ready to catch any Frenchmen trying to get up the Channel. But no sooner had that been done than another brig arrived from Portsmouth with orders from Lord Barham.

On the way back from a visit to the flagship Captain Fremantle said to Ben, 'We now know that Villeneuve is bringing a fleet back from the West Indies. We are not clear where he is heading, so we are going to stand off to the West and spread a line of search to intercept them. Our gamble is that Villeneuve will not stay so far to the north that he can creep around our line of defence close to Ireland; but we are also risking the possibility that Admiral Ganteaume in Brest gets out and goes up channel. Let's hope Lord Barham has made the right judgement'.

So Cornwallis and his ships dropped away from Brest to the SW leaving a line of frigates to watch the French. They sailed in strict order and practised manoeuvres for battle. Every ship was exercising the crews at the guns every day and all was made ready in anticipation of an approaching battle. But there was no sign of Villeneuve or any other French ship, and on 20th July the fleet returned towards Brest to confirm that Ganteaume was still there. On 22nd July Neptune was ordered to return to Plymouth for the ship's company to be paid. It was more than a week later that news arrived that Sir Robert Calder had been in action on that day against Villeneuve's fleet. It had not been the decisive defeat of the French which everyone hoped for although it had succeeded in persuading Villeneuve to run for shelter in Vigo. Reports were also filtering out that the activity of the French army at Boulogne had reached fever pitch with the arrival of Bonaparte himself. There were reports of around 100,000 French troops beginning to embark. But the reports also suggested that there was chaos because no-one had ever tried such a massive project as to embark so large an army in thousands of small vessels. The logistics of moving thousands of people with their equipment and horses was proving to be an insuperable challenge.

Neptune was in Plymouth for ten days re-stocking with food and water, receiving pay and carrying out some repairs. Some cloth had been delivered to the Captain from which he had the tailor make up suits for his servants, so Thomas began to look as smart as the other young gentlemen. He continued to study with the schoolmaster and was being encouraged to read more widely than had been possible at Swanbourne; he relished the tuition in mathematics and was looking forward to the time he would be able to begin to understand about navigation. He was being taught how muskets and pistols worked including the intricacies of the various types of striking mechanisms and how to use a sword both to defend himself and to attack. He could lift one of the sailor's cutlasses but would need to grow larger and stronger before he could do anything useful with it. There was much to learn and he was clearly enjoying the challenge.

Neptune sailed form Plymouth on 2nd August and rejoined Cornwallis's fleet off Ushant to continue the blockade of Brest and the defence of the English Channel. Admiral Calder in his action on 22nd July had given the French a bloody nose but had not wiped the fleet out as Lord Barham had hoped. Nonetheless Villeneuve had been prevented from linking up with the squadron at Ferrol and had suffered greater casualties and more damage than Calder. Now there were murmurs of dissatisfaction that Calder had let the navy down by not pressing home his advantage in the action and sunk or captured more of the French. But no-one seemed to be entirely clear about what had happened because during much of the action the ships were hidden from each other by fog, so that broadsides were being fired blind in a general direction, rather than at an identifiable target. When the fog lifted and darkness fell the English ships were mostly down to leeward of the French, who had the advantage but showed no sign of wanting to fight. Gradually the two fleets had diverged and the French headed to Vigo. Debate would continue for many years on whether Calder had shown an unwillingness to fight or not; but most importantly he succeeded in keeping Villeneuve out of the English Channel. A strategic victory, but a tactical draw perhaps.

The routine of blockade continued, and the French and their Spanish allies remained in their various harbours, Brest, Rochefort, Ferrol and Vigo. On 15th August Nelson arrived with his squadron which had come originally from blockading Villeneuve in Toulon, and had been east to Egypt and west to the West Indies, chasing after Villeneuve. He had come within a few days of catching him – not close enough – and after making contact with Collingwood whose squadron was responsible for covering Cadiz and the Strait of Gibraltar, and confirming that Villeneuve had not returned to the Mediterranean, he headed north to reinforce the massive English fleet under Cornwallis. As soon as Captain Fremantle knew that Nelson had arrived in company, he sent Lieutenant Proby across with a sheaf of recent newspapers. Proby spent less than two minutes with Nelson and reported to his captain that the Admiral looked sick and tired.

When the Captain saw Ben at the wheel he moved over towards him. 'Well Luckett how does it feel to be at the helm of one of the largest ships in one of the most powerful fleets that has ever been? Bit of a contrast to your island in the tropics'.

'Indeed it is Sir. But just like in 96 off Toulon, we spend an awful lot of time doing very little but sailing back and forth. You know, no doubt, that the lower deck is abuzz with the fact that Lord Nelson has joined us. It's extraordinary how everyone somehow feels different when he's around – more animated, a sort of "Well, if Nelson's here everything will be fine". How does he do that?'

'He has that effect on all of us for some quite inexplicable reason. But Lieutenant Proby reported that he looks very tired and unwell. So we must hope that he can quickly recover his strength enough to come back here to inspire us to achieve a great victory and beat these Frenchmen once and for all. Whilst they stay in their harbours, we can't get at them'.

It was no surprise that Cornwallis ordered Nelson to return to Portsmouth in the Victory to re-supply and repair the ship after their epic chase through the Mediterranean and twice across the Atlantic, but also to give Nelson the chance to recover his health and strength. On 16th August Nelson left to the north.

Chapter 29

Neither Ben nor Captain Fremantle knew that towards the end of August a fascinating strategic game was being played as Lord Barham and Admiral Cornwallis attempted to forecast the movements of the French fleet at its various locations. The main debate was whether the massive concentration off Ushant under Cornwallis could continue to be justified in view of the knowledge that Villeneuve was now in Ferrol and might have been joined by the French squadron under Commodore Allemand, which had escaped from Rochefort. If Villeneuve were to come north from Ferrol, with Allemand, and attempt to force his way into the Channel, Cornwallis would need every ship available to match the numbers, especially if Admiral Ganteaume were able to break out of Brest. On the other hand if Cornwallis's fleet remained of a size to match the French, Villeneuve would be able to escape from Ferrol and either head for the Mediterranean where he outnumbered Collingwood's squadron, or attack the homecoming convoys which were due at any time from the Cape or the West Indies.

The calculations were made. Barham and Cornwallis reached the same conclusion at about the same moment. Eighteen sail of the line, including Neptune, were detached under Vice Admiral Calder to join Collingwood. This fleet would counter the threat of Villeneuve entering the Mediterranean, where he might upset the diplomatic attempts being made by a European coalition to counter Napoleon. Calder's fleet sailed close enough to the Spanish coast to confirm that Villeneuve had left Ferrol. Various frigates appeared and gave intelligence to Calder about Villeneuve's movements; Calder hesitated briefly but pressed on towards Cadiz. There they found Collingwood watching the port in which the combined French and Spanish fleet was now berthed. The waiting game began again.

'I don't know what it is', the Captain confided one day to Ben, 'but the Admiral doesn't seem to be at all interested in meeting with his captains. And that means I've not felt able to invite any of them over here to dine with me. It's lonely sometimes being stuck in the cabin and hearing some of the frivolities going on elsewhere'. He did not expect Ben to answer and, in any case, it would have been difficult to make anything

311

more than a very bland comment. Being the captain of one of these great ships could indeed be very lonely.

'I wish Lord Nelson would come; the mood would change at once and you'd be very busy in the gig', he continued.

'I doubt there's a man onboard who doesn't think the same. It's strange for me thinking back to my early days in the navy and sailing with Captain Nelson as he was then in the Boreas. He taught me more than a thing or two and he won huge admiration for standing up for his men. We all knew that he'd support us unless we did something obviously dishonest or disloyal – he just seemed to be that sort of person'.

'We can but hope that we'll see him back here before too long'.

Ben certainly hoped that something would happen before too long because the Captain seemed to be increasingly irritated by his First Lieutenant. The Captain had some fixed ideas about how he wished things to happen, which worked perfectly well when the First Lieutenant agreed. But he too had his own way of doing things and could not see the point of change just to satisfy the Captain's particular whim. Ben hoped that tensions would rise no further for when a First Lieutenant is at odds with his Captain the whole ship will know it and will not work as well as it should.

The Captain and Ben were on the quarterdeck on the evening of 27th September when they noted the arrival from the north of the frigate Euryalus. It was not long before the news spread around the fleet that very soon Admiral Nelson would arrive in the Victory. There were to be no gun salutes or fuss made on this account because Nelson had made it clear that he wished to give the French as little reason as possible for not coming out of Cadiz and fighting. Sure enough on the 28th the Victory arrived with four other ships and, at once, the whole fleet was buzzing.

Within a day of the Victory's arrival the captain was invited to dine with Nelson and Ben was delighted to see the look of pleasure on his face as he steered the gig towards the Victory. As it was a fine day without much wind almost every ship of the line was stationary with men over the side re-painting the ships in the black and yellow colouring that Nelson had chosen for the Victory. Frigates and brigs were close at hand transferring casks of water to the larger ships and bringing out supplies from Gibraltar and Tetuan. That day eleven bullocks had been hoisted aboard the Neptune – they were not very good looking beasts but they would provide everyone with some fresh meat as a change from the regular diet of salt pork.

It was about nine o'clock in the evening when the Captain was ready to return to the Neptune and he was very clearly in a good mood.

'I'm sorry to have kept you for so long Luckett, but I have to say I have just passed a very entertaining hour. The company in Victory have just put on a play, which was quite hilarious. The young sailor who played the leading female role was particularly clever and made everyone laugh till they cried'.

'And was his lordship well amused too?' asked Ben. It was important that the Admiral should appear to be relaxed, for the mood would spread throughout the fleet.

'Oh yes; very much so,' replied the Captain, 'and he was in great good form during the time I had with him over dinner. He's been meeting with all the captains who have not served with him before so that they know and understand each other. And besides that we were able to reminisce about 98 when we were last in these parts and trying to get at the Spaniards in Cadiz'.

'That seems a long time since, Sir. But we certainly were led into some mad scrapes by his Lordship's enthusiasm and courage. I take it we'll not see quite the same from him this time'.

'His courage has not dwindled in the slightest, and despite everything he's still energetic and forward-looking. The great difference just now is that he wants Admiral Villeneuve to believe that he's taken the fleet away to the West, and that he'll therefore be encouraged to come out of Cadiz and sneak back into the Mediterranean. But we have a line of frigates between here and Cadiz so every movement can be watched. As soon as they hoist their topmast yards we shall know about it. The Admiral has even devised a system of night signals just in case they try to break out at night'.

'Has he given us a new order of battle or order of sailing yet?'

'Yes. They are the same. The fleet is split into two divisions with Victory at the head of one and Royal Sovereign, which has just arrived, to be Admiral Collingwood's flagship at the head of the other. Neptune is third astern of Victory, after Temeraire'.

'So we should get a fairly early slice of action when the time comes,' concluded Ben as they returned alongside.

Back on board, the gig's crew was able to report that their Captain was in great good spirits, and much more cheerful than before Nelson had arrived, and in no time everyone on board knew about it and was excited at the prospect that they might soon be able to do what they were all there for – beating the French and Spanish fleets by sinking their ships.

But the days passed with regular exercising of the gun crews, and the marines were drawn up to practise their musketry. Sailors were given practice at handling a boarding pike and a cutlass. Cartridges were prepared ready for the armament, and shot was placed close to each gun. And life went on; scrubbing and cleaning, mending ropes, stitching sails, caulking the decks and providing for the daily needs of about 800 men.

During the first week of October the Captain was further delighted by the arrival of Lieutenant Green who had been with him in the Ganges and who had been appointed Third Lieutenant, and signal lieutenant, after his predecessor had pleaded illness and asked to be sent home. But there was no sign of Midshipman Badcock until the middle of the month. After a visit to Buckinghamshire he had arrived back at Portsmouth at the end of September to find a brig or cutter sailing with despatches for Admiral Nelson off Cadiz. Within a couple of days he had got away but the cutter first had to call on Admiral Cornwallis off Ushant and deliver material for him and his fleet. When it reached the normal rendezvous point there was only a frigate stationed there. A brief call on the captain yielded information that the Admiral had withdrawn to the west two days earlier in order to search for a French squadron which had recently taken nine prizes out of two returning convoys – one coming from the Cape and the other from the West Indies. So the cutter set off to the west to chase after them; the commander gave himself a week to find the fleet. If there was no sign of them he must press on to Cadiz because some of the despatches for the commander-in-chief there might well be time sensitive.

'We chased away to the west, close hauled in a south-westerly and saw no ships for two days; then we bore away to the north for a day when we spotted what looked like a lone frigate on an easterly course. For a time we thought it might belong to the French squadron but to our relief we soon saw the union flag at the masthead and we came to alongside. From this frigate we learned that Cornwallis and his fleet were further to the north and west and that the frigate had only parted company from them that morning. We caught them the following day and the commander went at once to call on the Admiral who, having received despatches and mail for his ships, ordered him to proceed with all speed to Cadiz where he would surely find Nelson.' William Badcock was full of the exploit.

'How long have you been sailing since you left Admiral Cornwallis?' asked Thomas.

'We've been over three days sailing close-hauled at a cracking pace without any let-up. It took some amazing seamanship by the commander and his crew to keep the boat going that fast for so long; it was exciting, I can tell you. Not good for getting a lot of sleep or food though'.

'I'm glad you're back,' said Thomas, 'I have missed you. How is my family? Did you see them?'

'Oh yes, I certainly did. The whole of Swanbourne was anxious to hear news of the Captain, and you and your father. Everyone there seems very well and they have had a better harvest than they expected. But all around you hear people worrying about the possibility of a French invasion, and they think that we in the navy are the only people who can prevent it'.

'So you won't be surprised to hear that we've been practising every day at gunnery and sword drill and musketry. I'm getting quite handy with a cutlass'.

Early on Saturday 19ᵗʰ October a signal was spotted from the frigates watching Cadiz. 'Enemy have their topsail yards hoisted'. Thomas who was on deck at the time was sent below to inform the Captain. His face lit up.

'Ah, at last. That means they are putting to sea and we shall have a chance of getting at them. Tell the officer of the watch to continue as at present but to watch the Victory very carefully for the Admiral's signal'.

Not long afterwards the Victory signalled the order to prepare for action, and then followed the order for 'General chase south east', in order to ensure that the route from Cadiz to the Straits of Gibraltar was cut off and there was the best possible chance of bringing the French and Spanish fleet to battle.

However, as the day wore on it became clear from the continual flow of signalled reports from the watching frigates that the enemy fleet had not all left harbour, and those which had were remaining very close by or even anchored. For the whole day the enemy seemed to remain uncertain about getting to sea, and there was no possibility of action. Elaborate precautions were put in place to maintain contact through the night to ensure that the fleet did not become separated or allow the enemy to escape and at daybreak on 20ᵗʰ it soon became clear that Villeneuve's ships were still mostly in Cadiz. By 10 that morning all but one of the ships were clear of the harbour. Tension was building. All the intelligence suggested to Nelson that Villeneuve would be making for the Mediterranean but on leaving Cadiz he made a course to the west. Was there a possibility that he might turn and head north to the Channel challenging Cornwallis's fleet? Nelson believed that he would turn to the south east as soon as the wind allowed and he now turned the British fleet to the north west. Sure enough, during the afternoon the French and Spanish fleet was seen by the British frigates to be turning to the south west as close as they could get to the now westerly wind. In practice the allied fleet was not making better than due south, and the British were effectively blocking their path. But now that Nelson knew Villeneuve was heading for the Straits he must turn south again to be sure that he blocked their entry. On the Sunday evening, steering south east again, Nelson concentrated his ships into a formation for fighting as soon as day broke.

At dawn the Captain found Ben ready to take his turn at the wheel.

'Good morning Luckett. A fine sight we have before us this morning with all those Frenchmen to leeward'.

'True enough Sir, but at the pace we are sailing it will take us all day to catch them and bring them to battle. We have just had signal seventy two, form line of battle in two columns so we are heading to fall in line astern of Temeraire and Victory'. Captain Fremantle looked for the Master and moved away from the wheel to assess the ships' relative speeds and talk with him about the set of the sails and whether some should be set or furled.

'Another signal from the Victory, Sir,' called the signal lieutenant, 'Steer course east-north-east'.

'Very well. Master, that will point directly towards Cadiz will it not?'

'Aye, Sir. I believe the Admiral is wanting to be sure that the enemy can't escape back to Cadiz'.

Following closely was the signal 'Prepare for action' at which the Neptune became a flurry of activity. Everything which was not essential for battle was packed up and sent below into the hold. All the bulkheads dividing individual officers' cabins and their furniture were removed, packed up and sent below. No one could fail to share the sense of anticipation and excitement which pervaded the great ship.

They held that course until 6.40 when another signal came from Victory to steer two points to starboard, due East. Victory and her column was now steering towards the rear part of the enemy line, whilst Admiral Collingwood, leading the leeward column to starboard was heading towards the van.

There was activity aloft as the sails which barely filled with the light wind were being tended by the topmen, one of whose tasks in preparing for battle was to secure chains around the yards so that if rigging was shot away during the battle the massive spars would not come crashing down to the deck.

'Ask the Bosun to report to me when he has completed all preparations for battle', ordered the Captain to a midshipman standing close by.

'Mr Harrison', said the Captain addressing the First Lieutenant, 'How are all your preparations going?'

'Almost complete, Sir. All the officers' furniture and kit is below and they are just striking down the last of the mess tables. The galley stove has been dowsed. The gun decks are clear and the crews making their final preparations. You can have confidence, Sir, that everyone knows what he must do. Now we just have to prove that we can prevail over whatever enemy comes in our sights'.

'You may have heard Lord Nelson's instruction that no captain can go far wrong if he lays his ship alongside an enemy; that's what I shall be aiming to do. And if it is our fortune to lay alongside the Santissima Trinidad we shall need all the skill and bravery of the men to make our guns count the double of theirs'.

'I understand that his Lordship expects us to break the enemy line. I presume we shall have the chance of firing down the length of their ships and that as we pass ahead or astern so each gun will fire as it bears, double shotted'.

'Once through the line we will put the helm up and try to go alongside; a few broadsides, then grapple and board'. They had discussed all this before but it was good to have a chance to rehearse it all again.

'If you'll excuse me, I will go and make sure all the lieutenants are briefed and know what they must do. Many of the marines will be manning guns until we are ready for them to form up and prepare to board – I'll speak to the Captain of Marines so that he is clear about your intentions'.

'Thank you Mr Harrison'.

And then the wait, bearing slowly down towards the enemy, two or three knots, ten miles to close. The Captain left the poop and walked below to see for himself that all was well. He stopped at many of the guns for a word or two with the men to uplift them and encourage them. Stripped to the waist with bandanas around their heads and over their ears to deaden some of the noise they looked a fearsome bunch of men. As he passed each section he called for the attention of the men and said: 'Well, men, we have reached the point of trial, the moment we have all longed for and exercised for. Every one of you has an important part to play and every one of you must know that the happiness and security of our dear ones at home depends upon the outcome. Happy are those who are bold and courageous. And if you should survive the battle to come, and enjoy the victory which will be ours, how sweet will that be for us all. But those who fall may do so covered with glory and honour, remembered by a grateful country. May the brave live gloriously and those who die be long lamented'. From their looks the men were determined and confident; they knew what they must do, they had practised well and welcomed the opportunity to prove that they were the best to be found in any ship.

Gradually the British fleet was forming into two lines led by Victory and Royal Sovereign. Then one by one the French and Spanish were seen to be turning, reversing their course away from Gibraltar and towards Cadiz. Were they running back to their port, or were they seeking to come more quickly to battle. The three massive ships leading Nelson's column were Victory, Temeraire and Neptune, and their Captains were all piling on the maximum amount of sail they could muster. Studding sails extended every yardarm and the Captains urged them forward into battle. Temeraire and Neptune were closing the gap astern of Victory, suffering as she was from many months at sea and the growth of barnacles and weed below the waterline. They could see the Admiral on his poop deck pacing to and fro, anxiously looking towards the enemy and then back to his own force. It was shortly before 10 that he took up a speaking trumpet, and his words were heard clearly in Neptune.

'Remain astern of me Neptune. Mine will be the first strike'.

Captain Fremantle acknowledged the order and said to the Master.

'I am reluctant, but have no choice, it goes against the grain to order you to shorten sail as we go into battle, but we must remain astern of Victory at least until the action begins'.

William Badcock, standing not far away, muttered almost under his breath, 'The old Neptune has never sailed as well as this; it seems such a shame to hold her back'.

Gently Neptune dropped astern of Victory and Temeraire as little by little the enemy fleet drew closer. Shortly before midday the signal lieutenant began to read a long signal which was flying in the Victory; England expects that every man will do his duty. The words spread rapidly from the poop down to the maindeck and below to the gundecks and a cheer arose which filled the whole ship; everyone knew that his part in what was to come would have an impact on the result.

Silence returned and the waiting continued. All were apprehensive, hearts thumping amidst the shiver of excitement and the surge of adrenaline. A few minutes before midday; 'Signal from the flagship, Sir. Close action'.
And then the first rumble of gunfire was heard from the Allied fleet opening fire as the Royal Sovereign leading the starboard line came within range. Ten long minutes later Royal Sovereign opened fire and from the quarterdeck of Neptune they could see her challenging the massive Spanish three-decker Santa Ana.

Then Victory came under fire, although still at about 1000 yards. Things would be getting hotter. By twenty past twelve Victory was in range of the allied ships and was taking a massive amount of punishment. Round shot crashed through her sails and tore at her rigging. The foremast came down and the upper deck crew frantically cut at the remaining ropes so that it was cleared overboard and out of the way. She had managed a broadside at the French , but ten or so of them, including the 130 gun Santissima Trinidad and the French flagship Bucentaure were firing at her whilst Temeraire and Neptune had yet to be able to turn, and allow their broadsides to bear. The closing speed was so slow; the agony long. By 12.30 Victory was abreast of Bucentaure and steered for the gap between her and the Redoutable.

Meanwhile Neptune came in range of the enemy. The Captain ordered everyone on the gun decks to lie down and any shot which was on target did relatively little damage. Ben at the wheel saw men lying flat on the deck at each gun, and the marines too in their scarlet tunics, whilst the Captain and officers continued to strut around as if nothing was happening. Fortunately the rate of firing from the Bucentaure was not high and shots were spasmodic and irregular. Seeing the Victory being entangled with Redoutable the Captain ordered Ben at the wheel to steer to starboard so that the Neptune would pass between Victory and Bucentaure thus protecting Victory from the possibility of being boarded from the French flagship. Then as Neptune came level with Bucentaure he ordered the helm to larboard, judging perfectly the turn and the speed of the ship to pass close across the stern. As the stern of the great French flagship came into their sights the Lieutenants ordered their guns to be loaded with double shot and each one in turn loosed a devastating fire which sent cannon balls skittering at 600 miles an hour along the length of the enemy's decks.

As they passed the stern of Bucentaure the Captain again ordered Ben to put the helm over to larboard to pour more broadsides into the stricken Bucentaure and to begin work on Santisima Trinidad approaching the larboard beam.

'We need to stay on the Spaniard's quarter', said the Captain to the Master, 'so that we can rake her without taking her broadside. And Neptune's full broadside now targeted Santisima Trinidad upon whose other side both Britannia and Conqueror had contributed. Before long the mizzen mast and the massive mainmast came down leaving the great ship wallowing helplessly as Neptune and Conqueror, now joined from the north by Africa, poured their broadsides into her and created further havoc and mayhem. Her foremast was last to go, falling aft along the deck and a great cheer arose in the Neptune. Then it was that a flag was spotted being draped over the quarter aboard the Santisima Trinidad.

'She is signalling us with a union flag', cried Lieutenant Green, 'they want to surrender'.

'Cease firing', ordered the Captain and the message was taken at once to the Lieutenants in charge of the gundecks. It was now about 2.15pm.

'Where now?' asked the Master.

'Look ahead', replied the Captain, 'those French ships in the van are turning and Leviathan is going towards them. We go there. Can you set some more sail?' Neptune sailed north to engage, having formed into an impromptu line of battle astern of Leviathan and Britannia with Conqueror and Africa on the port bow to windward. A French and a Spanish ship bore down upon the line, seeking battle, whilst three others seemed to turn away from the fight towards Cadiz. The first, the French Intrépide, exchanged broadsides as Neptune passed and then locked horns with Africa. Leviathan had turned fully to come alongside and tackle San Agustin. Neptune engaged with five more ships to windward.

Soon after 4.30 the signal came to cease firing, and haul to the wind on the larboard tack. Then there was a huge explosion as the French ship Achille exploded a little way to the south. Thomas happened to be passing the gangway as a boat came alongside and an officer in the boat called up "From Admiral Collingwood aboard the Euryalus. We have achieved a great victory but Admiral Nelson is dead". Young as he was, Thomas immediately understood the significance of this news; everyone in Neptune, in the fleet, in the country, would feel the loss, as of a friend. He ran as fast as he could to find the Captain and passed the message on. Captain Fremantle's face changed from its normal eager determination; it softened; the corners of his mouth turned down, his eyes relaxed and you could see at once that he was close to tears.

In words which Thomas heard, though they were said to no-one in particular, the Captain said 'I have lost a true friend; the navy has lost an Admiral of outstanding courage, wisdom and sensitivity; the country has lost a great leader whose memory will continue for ever'.

The news spread like wildfire through the ship and everyone onboard knew within minutes that their revered Admiral was dead. They all felt as if they had lost a personal friend even though only a very few had even seen him, let alone spoken with him. Somehow he had succeeded in reaching them all through the stories which had been told down the years of his courage and his professionalism, of his sensitivity and compassion, of the care he took to ensure that every man had a fair deal. Meanwhile the officers all knew that he expected much of them but that, provided they gave their total commitment to him and the objectives he had set, that they could be sure of his full backing if something unexpected confounded their success.   There should have been a sense of elation after so resounding a victory over the combined French and Spanish, especially as in Neptune casualties had been extraordinarily light despite having been in the thick of the battle – only ten of their shipmates had died and thirty-seven had been wounded.   But they were so exhausted after many hours spent in anticipation and five hours of intense and violent activity, that the loss of their figurehead was the over-riding sentiment.

Every man, young and old, would remember this day for the rest of his life.   Individual stories of heroism would be told, but it would be the death of that small and weak-looking man with but one eye and one arm, who had once described himself as a burden upon his country who would be remembered by everyone and for all time.

Chapter 30

During the course of the afternoon and evening, the swell from the Atlantic had built up and now tumbled and rolled the wounded ships in a way which set blood and bodies sliding across the decks. The rising swell warned the Captains and the Masters that a gale would soon be upon them. They must work fast to repair as much of their rigging as they could in order to ensure that the ships with masts could sail and stay clear of the threatening rocks of Cape Trafalgar a mere twenty miles away to the east. And they must decide which of the wounded ships could be fitted with jury rigs to keep them safe, which could be taken in tow and which must be left to their fate. And then on top of those concerns they must remain on their guard against the French and Spanish ships which had escaped to Cadiz and might threaten to re-open the battle.

Captain Fremantle, like every other Captain and many of the officers and men, was also very anxious to establish his claim to the Santisima Trinidad as a prize. For the act of surrender – displaying the Union Jack – had been made to the Neptune alone. The possibility of prize money was a powerful motivator to secure the enemy ships and get them safely to harbour. He called Lieutenant Green to lead the prize crew of forty men who would begin to clear things up and prepare for a tow.

'Take Luckett with you in the gig and he can escort the senior officers back here'. Ben gathered together the crew and checked that the boat was still intact and tied to the stern. Fortunately it looked undamaged and he was able to bring it around to the larboard side under the gangway. The crew went aboard and began to prepare the boat to take the lieutenant to the massive Spanish ship. Oars and boathook must be unlashed and readied and the tiller mounted. In minutes all was ready and Ben and Lieutenant Green climbed down. The swell was huge by now and the wind rising as they pulled quickly away from the Neptune, but it did not take long to reach the side of the Santisima Trinidad. They hooked on and the Lieutenant jumped onto the ladder followed closely by Ben, and started climbing up the massive ship's side. Soon they had disappeared inside and found themselves on the lower gundeck. The sight that met their eyes was truly horrific and sickening. The deck was awash with blood and there were remains of bodies all over the place. Hardly a single canon remained on its carriage. There were a few men still on their feet looking totally bewildered and lost.

They asked to see the Captain or the Admiral. They were taken up to what had been the Admiral's quarters and there found the Admiral recovering from a severe blow on the head received from some part of the ship's foremast as it fell along the length of the ship. The Commodore and the Captain, both of whom had been wounded, were with him and all three recognised that they had no realistic option but formal surrender, and there they presented the lieutenant with their swords.

The Lieutenant responded by saying; 'I thank you Admiral and am sorry you should have suffered to this extent. Captain Fremantle of Neptune invites you to join him with your Captain and we will arrange for your ship to be taken in tow in order to hold you to windward and away from the Cape and get her to safety. In the meantime I trust we may count on your men to do as much as they can to stop the shot holes and reduce the water inflow. We will bring further medical assistance if we can'.

The lieutenant escorted the Spanish officers to the gangway and they descended into the boat.

'Take the gentlemen onboard, Luckett. I will remain here with the prize crew and we will try to get things patched up and ready for a tow'. And Ben slipped quickly down to the boat and ordered the crew to cast off. The rising wind was beginning to blow the tops off the vast swell; the men were tired out after their exertions through the day but they knew that survival demanded that they work together to return safely to Neptune.

The Captain greeted the Spanish officers with courtesy and respect and invited them aft to his quarters, notwithstanding they were still in a fighting state without furniture or privacy.

'The Prince will take your ship in tow', said the Captain, 'as she is less damaged than we are'.

Meanwhile it took Neptune until midnight to have sufficient of the rigging repaired to be able to make sail. All that time the wind was rising and had backed to the south west. At 4am on 22nd Neptune was able to take another of the wrecked allied ships in tow but no-one thought to take notice which ship it was, for every prize saved would mean a payout in due course. The damaged fleets were, very slowly, making a little headway to distance themselves from the fearsome rocks of Trafalgar.

Sailors were working like automatons, dog-tired and exhausted, mentally and physically. Then, later that morning, a signal was received that some Allied ships were coming out of Cadiz. It was known that as many as ten had escaped there the night before. Admiral Collingwood must prepare as many ships as he could to meet a threat and the towing ships were told to cast loose their tows and form a line to prepare for battle. All the time the weather was deteriorating.

It was too rough to leave the lower gunports open and it would be extremely difficult to maintain any effective fire. Some enemy ships were seen but it seemed that they were not really seeking battle. Two succeeded in getting lines aboard their stricken comrades who had been set loose by the victors. Meanwhile the Admiral ordered his fleet to ride out the gale as best they could. The Neptune went straight for the Santisima Trinidad.

A tow was passed and secured and Neptune began to take the strain sailing as close to the wind as she could. All through the next night they struggled in the storm as the howling gale tore sails to shreds. Sailors were exhausted and slept wherever they could find a corner – many of the hammocks had been wrecked during the battle and others were soaking wet. The wind rose to the most horrendous gale and for more than twenty four hours everyone worked hard to survive.

It was probably on 24th October – it was easy to lose track of time – that a signal was shown in Euryalus, where Admiral Collingwood had moved, ordering all ships to abandon their tows and scuttle the captured ships. He had assessed that the danger to the British ships was too great and the captured ships must be sacrificed.

'First Lieutenant, get the boats out again and take off our prize crew, and then the ship's own crew. We will continue to bring them off as long as we can, both wounded and fit. Send Mr Badcock with a carpenter to do what is necessary to sink the ship'.

Young Thomas heard the Captain's orders and immediately sought out William and told him.

'Can I come with you?' asked Thomas.

'It'll be hard', replied William, 'but you can come if the Captain will let you'. Thomas ran back to the Captain and asked if he might go.

'It will not be a pretty sight and you will have to look sharp getting on and off the ship, and you will not have a comfortable ride on the boat'.

'Thank you, Sir, I'll go'.

Thomas joined William in a boat as it rose and fell violently on the steep swell. They pushed off and made across the cable's length which separated the two ships, rising up the steep waves, trembling on the top and crashing down the other side in a welter of foam and spray. By the time they arrived alongside the Santisima Trinidad they were all soaked through.

More heroic activity followed as the boats began to bring off the wounded. The risks were huge as the massive ship rolled heavily on every swell and the boats had to be held alongside without crashing into the ship or being capsized.

William and Thomas made their way into the heart of the massive ship where there were still dead bodies and parts lying untended. Gun barrels crashed across the deck as the swell rolled the helpless vessel from side to side. People were moving up and down the main companionways carrying the wounded, who could be moved, up and aft. They could be lowered through the stern windows into the Neptune's boats below. But they must move quickly and complete the work as soon as possible for fear that the weather might well deteriorate further and place the boats' crews in even greater peril.

At one point a father and son were climbing down into Ben's boat. The father came first and the bowman indicated that the boat was full and could not take any more without placing them all at greater risk. At this, the son, refusing to be parted from his father jumped into the water and struck out for the boat, catching hold of the gunwhale. The crew did their best to beat him away, some reaching for cutlasses, prepared to cut the boys fingers off to force him to let go.

'Stop, stop,' cried Ben, thinking of how it might have been had it been Thomas in the water, 'We are not such devils as to part father and son at a moment like this. Let him aboard and let us all get to safety. Pull him aboard now'.

And Ben's command was powerful enough for the crew to realise that such humanity was exactly what they would hope for themselves if they were in a similar position. The boat rose on the waves, and water sprayed over them all, before digging deep into the next trough, but they arrived safely. The wounded were taken below to the orlop to join the Neptune's own wounded being tended by the ship's surgeons and as much care was administered there as they could have hoped for in their own ship.

During this frenetic activity Thomas came across a pug dog puppy and quickly devised a sling from some pieces of rope, to enable him to be lowered down into a boat. William found himself in the ship's chapel and noticed a beautiful statue of a Madonna and he thought that this was something which should be saved from the doomed ship. A rope around her middle and she was lowered as carefully as possible into one of the boats.

William and Thomas went to find the carpenter who was looking for a place where he might cut a hole in the ship's side below the waterline. Explosives might have provided a solution but the magazine had been locked and no-one seemed to know where the key might be. But as the wounded were taken up the carpenter was making headway and water was beginning to fill the hold. He came up through the orlop onto the lower gundeck where William and Thomas were opening all the gunports so that when the ship settled lower in the water the sea would rush in on each roll of the swell and speed the process of sinking.

'How long left do we have?' William asked the carpenter.

'It's time for us to leave now', came the reply, 'I can't tell. It all depends on how violently she rolls. And I don't want to find myself left behind'. The small group of British sailors went aft to the cabin with an extra length of rope, secured it and slid down into a waiting boat. There seemed to be no crew members remaining although they all knew that many of the more seriously wounded and dying men remained helpless in the orlop. They could only hope that the end for them would come quickly and relatively painlessly.

The last boat pulled away leaving the great ship to her fate and from Neptune they watched in horror as the once stately Santisima Trinidad slipped under the waves, smothering the cries of anguish of those left onboard, and taking them to a watery grave.

Meanwhile Redoutable, from which the fatal shot at Nelson had been fired, had sunk by the stern after about 100 wounded and 30 fit men had been rescued by Swiftsure; the following morning nearly a hundred more were spotted clinging to rafts despite the appalling conditions, and boats were launched again to take them to safety. Other French and Spanish ships foundered too. Even some which had succeeded to get back towards Cadiz had run aground and broken up.

Despite the odds some ships, by a miracle, survived like the British Bellisle whose jury rig had just managed to hold it in position long enough for the frigate Naiad to secure a new tow as the wind began to abate. These two were the first ships to arrive in Gibraltar, met with a cheer, but also consternation that the triumphantly victorious fleet should have been so severely shattered.

On 26th October, the wind dropped enough for everyone to think about the next steps. That day Neptune was ordered to take Victory in tow and take her to Gibraltar. The Spaniards from Santisima Trinidad had been moved elsewhere, and Neptune was now playing host to the French Commander-in-chief Admiral Villeneuve. Slowly life was beginning to return to a more normal routine.

Thomas Luckett had survived although he was not quite sure how. The battle and the week which followed had merged into some sort of a blur through which it was hard to distinguish any specific events. He talked to William Badcock on the way down to Gibraltar.

'I think my mind has gone numb', said Thomas. 'I know we went through a bloody battle. The noise and the smoke below decks was terrifying – I shudder to think what it must have been like up top'.

'Terrifying up there too, I can tell you. The Captain's order for everyone to lie down as we approached must have saved us from lots more injuries', replied William. 'But I can remember that all the officers refused to lie down and continued pacing the deck as if they were going about their daily exercise. I felt scared stiff but knew that I must not show it. Perhaps we were all just determined to show that dying gloriously is far more noble than cowering below the bulkhead'.

'I suppose in battle there is so much activity and noise and everyone is very busy doing as much as they can to beat the enemy that you forget you are frightened. The storm was far worse because you can't get away from it and you know that if the ship goes down that is the end. I think that was why I really wanted to go with you to the Santisima – to give myself something definite to do'.

'Difficult to put into words and I doubt that anyone who has not had those awful experiences can ever understand what it is really like. But, you know, it is extraordinary that so few ships were actually lost, and it was only the ones which had lost their masts, effectively rendering them powerless'.

'What happens now? Does this mean that the war against France and Spain is over?'

'Not at all. Napoleon is still a winner of battles on land. I suspect what it will have done is given the French and Spaniards very good reason to remain in harbour and not get in the way of our ships and trade and convoys. For us in Neptune, we'll have to wait and see. We're less severely damaged than many and I guess the more damaged ones will have priority for going home. We'll still need a fleet out here to protect the convoys going into and through the Mediterranean. But perhaps more important still is that Napoleon can't now plan to invade England – he could never make it across the Channel without command of the seas. We have that. That means that our families back home are safe. That's what really makes it all worthwhile'.

On 28th October Neptune towed Victory into Gibraltar and as they dropped anchor in Rosia Bay all the ships around let out a massive cheer from the yard arms – a welcome to the victorious, despite the pervading gloom over the death of the revered Lord Nelson and of so many other brave souls.

Subsequent days saw the continuation of the repairs to Neptune, as other vessels came in to the port to repair their damaged rigging, patching and replacing sails and making good the emergency measures they had taken to fill shot damage to the hulls. Many of the sick and wounded were put ashore into the Gibraltar hospital where they could be more comfortable. The ships which were going home set off as soon as they could. Victory herself with the body of Lord Nelson sealed in a cask of brandy sailed on 3rd November without being fully rigged; her voyage took five weeks and she arrived at St Helen's off Portsmouth on 4th December.

Meanwhile Ben found himself ferrying the Captain to and fro and escorting him to visit various old friends and acquaintances in Gibraltar.

'It's not like it was when we were last here in 97', he said to Ben.

'Well, you were just married then, Sir, and Mrs Fremantle was with you', he replied.

'And General O'Hara as Governor was much more hospitable and welcoming than the Duke of Kent. But I suppose being a son of King George makes a difference. Now tell me, how is your boy bearing up? He looks well enough and I was pleased that he volunteered to go across to Santisima Trinidad with Mr Badcock, but you never can be sure what young men are really feeling after the dreadful experiences we've just come through'.

'Thank you for asking, Sir. Like everyone else he was obviously very frightened by the action and the horror and brutality of it. But he told me that he was even more frightened by the gale and the incredible power of the wind and waves, tossing the ship about like a cork. Having been through that and survived he'll be more confident in future gales. I keep on telling him that the seas were far bigger in the Southern Ocean between the Cape and Australia – and it was cold there, too. Have you heard yet, Sir, what plans the Admiral has for Neptune?'

'We will not be going home for the time being', replied the Captain, 'and I think we will be sailing with some others to watch Cadiz for a while.'

Neptune left Gibraltar at the end of November and joined the blockading squadron off Cadiz. Captain Fremantle was the senior captain of the ships present so he was in command of them all. One of the frigates he had was Seahorse and he and Ben were delighted to be able to go onboard and see their former home being well cared for. There was little activity in Cadiz and the nearest they came to any excitement was to intercept a brig laden with brandy. A prize crew was put onboard to take her down to Gibraltar but the Captain was not hopeful of much more than £100 prize money in total.

Just before Christmas news was received that Bonaparte had been killed, a possibility which filled the Captain with joy. But without further confirmation he was reluctant to believe it was more than a rumour. If it were true, then peace would surely follow and they could all look forward to going home; if false, they must remain at sea. Another strong gale blew up just before Christmas and the squadron ran before it into the Mediterranean. By Christmas Day they were further north having joined Admiral Collingwood off Cartagena to take a look at the Spanish ships there, and then gently back to Cadiz.

Midshipman Badcock was promoted to Lieutenant early in January and transferred to Melpomene as third Lieutenant. Thomas was sad to see him go as he had become a good friend. The First Lieutenant had left for home too which had enabled the Second to be promoted into his position.

The days passed slowly with the normal routine of a blockade. A ship arrived from the north and everyone anticipated news from home and the possibility of a letter which might alleviate the boredom for an hour or two. From time to time they put in to Gibraltar for water and fresh food. The carpenters carried out a detailed survey of the ship's bows and concluded that some major repairs were required which could not be done at sea; surely this would mean returning home before long. News arrived of the death of the Prime Minister William Pitt and a new government under Lord Grenville. The Captain at once entertained hope of some intervention by the Marquess of Buckingham, Grenville's nephew, on his behalf, which might entail his recall and a move to some activity more interesting than commanding a ship on blockade duty. But the political wheels turned at no great speed and being so far away Captain Fremantle was quite unable to influence the situation. However he was clearly delighted to hear that he had been presented, in his absence, to the electors of Sandwich and had duly become a member of Parliament. The seat was under the control of the Admiralty. Tom Grenville, the Marquess's younger brother, had been appointed First Lord of the Admiralty and had agreed that Fremantle would be a useful member of the Admiralty Board and Parliament. Apart from anything else this might mean that orders would soon be sent to Admiral Collingwood to send him home. His friends had done everything he could have asked of them.

At the beginning of October Admiral Collingwood invited the Captain to dine, and during the course of dinner he said that he had received an order to send Captain Fremantle home by the first possible opportunity. Given the need for dockyard repairs to Neptune's bow the Admiral declared that he should sail north in Neptune at once.

'I know this is what you have been hoping for', said the Admiral, 'You have made it quite clear that you are bored by being here, and I confess I share your view entirely. A new challenge evidently awaits you. Before you take your leave I must tell you that I have been pleased to have you here and have always felt that I could rely upon you and Neptune to be ready for any service which might be required'.

'Thank you for your kind words', Fremantle replied, 'And I can only hope that I may continue to serve my King and country equally well in this new role. But it makes me very happy to be heading back towards my wife and family who mean so much to me. And may I wish you the best of good fortune in your command here and that in due time you too may be relieved and travel home to your family'.

Neptune headed at once to the north and everyone onboard knew that they were on the way home. On 26th October Neptune anchored at Spithead and the Captain received a bag of despatches. Shortly afterwards he sent for the First Lieutenant.

'I must leave the ship at once and go first to Westminster and then to Sandwich. You will have acting command of the ship until a new Captain is appointed. I should be grateful if you would have my things packed up and sent to Swanbourne; young Luckett can accompany them. I will take Mr Luckett senior with me; please send him to me now. Oh, and, I have an unpleasant feeling that Mrs Fremantle may well arrive here after I have left because I asked her to meet me here when I wrote earlier. Would you please tell her that I have gone to London and to my constituency at Sandwich. I will leave word with my brother William about my movements. And please tell her I am anxious to see her just as soon as my duties will allow'.

Ben quickly got the message and reported to the Captain.

'Thank you Luckett. I have just received papers which make it imperative that I visit my constituency in Sandwich and meet the electors who will vote me back in as MP on 3rd November. Then I shall need to go up to London and take up my position as a Lord of the Admiralty. I should welcome your company for this although it will entail you being paid off from Neptune. I have arranged for Thomas to accompany all my belongings directly back to Swanbourne so he should arrive there before us'.

'Very good, Sir. How soon do we leave?'

'How long do you need? Can you be ready within two hours?'

'Of course, Sir. I will send a few things with Thomas and keep as little with me as will serve for a few days'.

'Thank you. On the gangway in two hours'.

Ben knew that he should be ready well before the two hours was up and went swiftly to inform the purser and First Lieutenant that he would be leaving at once. His pay could be sent on to his agent, John Sykes, who he might well call upon in London if there was time.

It only took him minutes to sort out the few items of kit he would need with him and the rest of his belongings he packed in his small chest, which he marked up clearly and left in the care of Thomas.

'It looks like we've finished with Neptune now', Ben said to his son, 'and you will be home before me in all likelihood. I am going with the captain to Sandwich where he has been elected member of Parliament, and he is to be a Lord of the Admiralty too it seems. That should stop him complaining about having too little to do whilst at sea on blockade'.

Father and son parted company with a wave and Ben went to wait at the gangway until the Captain should be ready. He looked about the great ship and paused to think about the experiences not just on blockade, but in battle and during the aftermath. He thought of the few men of Neptune who had been killed and wounded and thanked God for the fact that both he and Thomas had survived. He thought of that terrible storm after the battle and struggling in the boats across to Santisima Trinidad to take as many off as they could, and for those who had to be left behind to drown. It was a cruel world, but he had survived to meet the next challenge.

Chapter 31

After the Captain and Ben landed in Portsmouth they caught the next mail service to London and within the hour they were on the road and heading north.

'This is a completely new venture for me,' mused the Captain, 'although it's one for which I have been hoping for some time. Time spent cultivating the Marquess of Buckingham has finally paid off, now that his uncle has the government, and his brother has just been appointed First Lord of the Admiralty. I suppose that being a member of Parliament will give me the chance to influence policy on all sorts of matters although I shall have to be careful not to offend the ministers'.

'That's why I'd be no good at such a job', said Ben, 'I'd only be able to tell it as I saw it – whatever that might be – and I don't think I could ever adjust my message just to fit in with what the government wants to hear'.

'It might be better to stick with what we know, about ships and the sea and what can be done with ships if they are properly manned and equipped'.

Their journey was uneventful as they sped through the beautiful English countryside in early autumn. It was warm and sunny and a joy to be out on the road.

'We'll call on my brother William once we are in London. We can probably stay a night with him and it would be useful for me to hear his view of the current politics. We can also leave word there for Mrs Fremantle as I suspect she will have received my last letter from sea and will have gone down to Portsmouth'.

On the Monday morning they travelled down to Sandwich and the Captain began meeting his electors and getting a measure for the issues which were of greatest importance to them. It was clear that they would need to remain there at least until the day of the election which had been set for 3rd November. The Captain would dine with the Electors on the following day to thank them for their confidence and they would go to London immediately afterwards so that they could be there on the morning of 5th.

They made a very early start and were at Russell Place where they knew Betsey would be by 7am. The reunion was no less warm for being so long delayed, and of short duration. The Captain left an hour later and then spent the rest of the day at the Admiralty while Ben collected the two boys, Thomas and Charles, from their school in Hampton. He returned for dinner, and the boys were duly excited to see their hero father returned safe from the Battle of Trafalgar about which they had heard many reports. They had much to chatter about as Ben returned them later in the day to the school.

On the following day the Fremantles rented a house on Sackville Street until an Admiralty house would be available for them, and the real work of a Lord of the Admiralty began, occupying the captain from 10am until 6pm every day and considerably constraining the possibility of social activity. There was nothing more Ben could do for them and it was time for him to return home.

But before setting off he went to call on John Sykes to hear news of Governor King.

'Have you not heard?' said John Sykes, 'the Governor asked to be relieved some time ago. But the Admiralty and the Government were completely pre-occupied with the war and the need to defend the country from invasion. Resolving affairs on the other side of the world was not a high priority. So it was not until earlier this year that they decided to appoint Captain Bligh, who set off at once'. He paused just long enough to allow Ben to interject.

'You mean the same Captain Bligh of the Bounty whose crew mutinied. He was a great navigator and a brave man but I wonder if his style of leadership and supposed addiction to the cat will serve him well in Port Jackson'.

'Yes, it's the same man. And you may well be right. But you can understand the government being reluctant to send one of their best commanders out there during a war. Captain Bligh should have arrived in Port Jackson in August so I'd expect Governor King to return next spring'.

'And have you heard from Mr Enderby, or had news of young Phillip?' asked Ben.

'The Enderby's whalers seem to be doing quite well and when I last heard Anna Maria is well. As for Phillip he is at the naval school'.

'May I leave a letter for you to give to the Governor when he eventually returns. I should like to see him again and hear about all his projects'.

'Of course. But I fear you may be disappointed. His health has evidently declined significantly and the difficulties of his position have made that far worse. There's been a continuing burble of criticism in the press here about the high-handed behaviour of the Governor and with the war on no politician has felt able to defend him openly'.

On that gloomy note Ben sat down and wrote a brief note to be left with Sykes and given to the Governor when eventually he returned.

Ben's arrival Swanbourne was greeted with joy and delight not only by his own family but by the whole village. Thomas had been back for a few days and basked in the admiration of the neighbours at his part in the victory at Trafalgar. Ben's reunion with Sally was warm and affectionate and he was pleased to see that Sally would be bringing another child into the world with a few weeks. During their fifteen years together they had known joys and sorrows, excitement and boredom, delight and horror. Whilst he had been away Sally had buried both her parents, but she had made good friends in the village. She had got to know more of Mrs Fremantle who had evidently been buying land and houses in and around Swanbourne whenever the opportunity arose. Their oldest daughter Sarah, now 12, was employed at Swanbourne House and it would not be long before James would be ready to decide the direction of his life. He was a bright lad and with good luck combined with hard work and a helping hand he might well rise above his agricultural roots; keeping on the right side of the Fremantles and impressing the Captain would undoubtedly give him a better chance in life.

Ben declared that his days at sea and adventuring around the world were at an end, and he set himself to working out a future which would see the family secure and which would enable him to give all his children the best possible life chances.

Life is not only about hard work, he decided, it is also about making the right friends and ensuring that at least one relationship matures and stands the test of time. He had seen how the virtues of the Christian faith had supported those he had grown to respect most, Lord Nelson, Governor King and Captain Fremantle. He recognised that many of the details of the faith were beyond his understanding and would probably always be so. He had certainly been given ample evidence that a good life depended more upon love in its broadest sense than anything else. He would do his best to lead the rest of his life accordingly.

Epilogue

Governor and Mrs King arrived home with their younger daughters Elizabeth and Mary in September 1807. The Governor was in a poor state of health and there had been moments when he feared that he would not survive long enough to get home. But on the voyage he had begun to feel slightly better and began thinking and planning how to secure the attention of the Secretary of State, his reputation and his financial future. He was met with a high degree of disinterest by all those in government who were wholly pre-occupied with the war against Napoleon. A little sympathy was expressed for his predicament, but no-one was prepared to fight his corner with him and secure the pension he so richly deserved, or to defend him from all the allegations of abuse presented by the Irish and other malcontents whose nefarious schemes he had undermined.

Over the following twelve months his health declined and eventually he succumbed in a small house he had taken in Tooting. He was laid to rest with the minimum of ceremony in the churchyard of St Nicholas, Tooting. Anna Josepha remained in the London area for some months, trying to secure for herself a reasonable pension in recognition of her husband's sacrifice. Living on the pension of a Captain's widow at £80 a year was challenging but eventually she persuaded the government to grant an annuity of £200, although this cancelled the widow's pension. Twenty five years after her husband died, she was persuaded in 1832 by her son Phillip, by then a respected naval lieutenant and hydrographer, to move back to New South Wales where she was soon joined by several others of her family. She saw out her days on the grant of land near Parramatta to which the family was gradually able to add. Their son Phillip became the first Australian-born Admiral, celebrated for his surveys, in particular of the Magellan Strait. He and his sisters, who also lived in Australia, married and brought up large families, and his descendants are well spread in Australia and elsewhere in the world.

Captain and Mrs Fremantle became more rooted in Swanbourne as their family grew. The Captain's stay at the Admiralty was cut short by a change in government and he was appointed in command of a Royal

Yacht, a duty which appears to have allowed him ample time for other pursuits. Whilst still in Neptune, he had been selected by his colleagues to lead the committee to create a memorial to Lord Nelson outside Portsmouth. The obelisk remains close to Fort Nelson on the ridge overlooking Portsmouth and is an important leading mark for vessels approaching the harbour. In 1810 he reached the rank of Rear Admiral and was appointed to the Mediterranean fleet under Sir Charles Cotton and, later, Sir Edward Pellew, who detached him to support activities in Sicily. His last naval service was as Commander in Chief in the Mediterranean in 1818. He had been in his flagship Rochfort on a mission to North Africa when he became ill and returned to Naples where Betsey and his daughters were living. There he died, much to their distress, and was buried. His place of burial appears to be under what is now a car park, and no memorial has been found there. However the Captain and officers of Rochfort subscribed to and built an impressive memorial which is placed overlooking Grand Harbour in Malta.

Thomas and Betsey had become very well established at Swanbourne where descendants still live, and which is regarded as the heart of a much wider family now spread all over the country with branches in the USA and on the continent. Each of the next four generations boasted an Admiral. Their son became Admiral Sir Charles who was celebrated for escorting the first settlers to Western Australia, who named the port where they landed after him. Less known is the fact that in 1824 he was awarded the first gold medal for saving life at sea for his part in a rescue off the South coast of England. One of their grandsons became Admiral Sir Edmund Fremantle, another winner of the Royal Humane Society gold medal, who served in the Mediterranean and Indian Oceans before being appointed to command on the China Station at the end of the nineteenth Century. His son became Admiral Sir Sydney Fremantle who after acting as Deputy Chief of Naval Staff in the closing days of the First World War was appointed to command the First Battle Squadron, which was on duty at Scapa Flow when the German fleet was scuttled in 1919. The Admiral of the following generation was Admiral Sir Edward(Ted) Parry, whose mother was born Fremantle, who captained Achilles at the battle of the River Plate, and went on to become the first Commander in Chief of the Indian navy after independence.

Bibliography

I have read many books about the subject matter of this book and I considered listing references in the text. However, as this is a novel, and is not intended as a scholarly work I decided they would tend only to interrupt the story and divert the reader. Listed below are the principle sources I have used.

Nelson and his navy
I have a large number of biographies of Nelson and accounts of various aspects of ships and the navy of the time. I have not listed them all. John Sugden's masterly work has provided the majority of the detail in Part One.

Adkins R; Trafalgar; The Biography of a battle; Little, Brown 2004
Adkins R & L; Jack Tar; Abacus 2009
Corbett J; The Campaign of Trafalgar; Longmans Green & Co
Colville Q & Davey J (Ed); Nelson, Navy and Nation; Conway 2013
Fothergill B; Sir William Hamilton; Nonsuch Publishing 2005
Howarth D; Trafalgar, the Nelson Touch; Collins 1969
Masefield J; Sea Life in Nelson's Time; Sphere Books 1972
Oman C; Nelson; Hodder and Stoughton 1948
Pocock T; Horatio Nelson; The Bodley Head 1994
Sugden J; Nelson; A dream of Glory; Jonathan Cape 2004
Sugden J; Nelson; The Sword of Albion; The Bodley Head 2012

Australia
The National Archives of Australia holds the King family archive. Of particular note are King's journals the first of which was published without his authorisation at the end of Captain John Hunter's Journal. The second has not been published but the archives contain a fair copy written in several hands and with margin notes in King's handwriting. I transcribed this journal and provided the Mitchell Library with a digitised version to be put on line and made generally available. I have read through a mass of other relevant correspondence which is in the Mitchell Library on microfilm.

The British National Archive at Kew contains all the Colonial Office records, where one can find correspondence to and from New South Wales. Much of this documentation is also reproduced in The Historical Records of New South Wales, Volume 3 of which is relevant to King's time as Governor, was published in 1896. The Historical Records of Australia contains almost the same material for the period and the relevant volume was published in 1922. The editors of these volumes have very different views about Governor King. Both volumes are available online and can be downloaded.

I have also used the following books amongst others. Two are novels but provide some very graphic descriptions of early Australia and Norfolk Island.

Bassett M; The Governor's Lady; OUP 1956
Body M; The Fever of Discovery, the story of Matthew Flinders; New European   Publications 2006
Duffy M; Man of Honour, John Macarthur; Macmillan Australia 2003
Ellmers C & Payton C (Ed); London and the Whaling Trade; Docklands History Group, 2013
Grenville K; The Secret River; Text Publishing Australia 2005
Keneally T; The Commonwealth of Thieves; Chatto & Windus 2006
Keneally T; Australians; Allen & Unwin 2011
King J and King J; Philip Gidley King; Methuen Australia 1981
Lagstrom T; Prisoners in Paradise; T&J Lagstrom 2008
McCullogh C; Morgan's Run; Arrow Books 2001
Moorehead A; The Fatal Impact; Mead and Beckett 1987
Stackpole E; Whales and Destiny; University of Massachusetts Press 1972

Fremantle
The family archive is held in the Buckinghamshire County Archive Office in Aylesbury where I have found relevant material and correspondence. However, the majority of the material I have used is taken directly from the Wynne Diaries, edited by Anne Fremantle and published in three volumes by OUP in 1935. A single volume edition in paperback was published in 1982. These books are out of print and any secondhand copies which come onto the market seem to be sold very quickly.

Hounslow E; Nelson's Right Hand Man; History Press 2016.

Glossary

Altitude at midday. Before the days of accurate chronometers astronomical navigation depended greatly on the midday sight. The altitude of the sun above the horizon when it reached its highest point in any day would enable you relatively easily to calculate your latitude. Whilst this would be the particular responsibility of the Master, the Captain and many other officers would make a habit of using their sextants regularly to take this measurement. Many captains insisted that Midshipmen and other 'young gentlemen' onboard always took the altitude at midday as part of their training.

Anchor. When in harbour ships would generally be anchored rather than being secured alongside a quay. The anchor would be **'Let go'** as the ship reduced speed and when stopped the ship would **'Ride to the anchor'**. When ready to sail the order would be given to **'Weigh anchor'**. At this order the sailors would start to push on the **capstan bars** and begin to wind the anchor cable into the ship.

Bells. The ship's bell was used to mark the passage of time. In the days before reliable clocks time was kept by an hourglass which must be turned each hour. Each half hour was marked by a ring of the bell. So four bells of the forenoon watch was 10am. Eight bells signified the change of the **watch** (q.v.).

Binnacle. The structure on the quarterdeck, close to the wheel, in which the ship's compass is housed and displayed.

Bosun's call, or pipe. This is a specially designed whistle which can produce two notes and a trill. It is shrill and can be heard above considerable background noise. They were used by the Bosun and his mates to give orders.

Bowrope. A rope used to secure the front of a ship or boat to a jetty, quayside or another boat.

Braces – nothing to do with trousers. These are the ropes which control the angle of the yardarm. The **mainbrace**, controlling the yardarm on the mainmast was a very large rope. If it was broken – perhaps by enemy shot – it would have to be spliced, or rejoined. This was a very difficult task which would take several hours of hard and skilled work. Once it had been done it was customary to **'Splice the mainbrace'** which entailed issuing everyone an extra tot of rum.

Broach. This is a verb used to describe what tends to happen to a boat approaching a beach in surf. The waves, travelling faster than the boat, force the stern to one side and the boat is then in danger of being rolled over.

Broad Pennant. Senior officers above the rank of Captain have a distinguishing flag, and are known as Flag Officers. A Commodore, the senior amongst a group of captains, flies a Broad Pennant.

Broadside. A broadside would be fired when a ship was running about parallel to an enemy's course. All the guns on one side of the ship would be fired at the same time. In a frigate like Inconstant this would mean that about 250 pounds weight of cast iron would be shot at the enemy. In a 96 gun ship like Neptune a broadside would weigh over 1000 pounds weight. After the first broadside, gun captains were usually ordered to fire as soon as they had a target. British ships were well-trained and practised and could fire much faster and more accurately than French or Spanish whose ships were frequently blockaded in port.

Calavances. Chick peas.

Cat or cat-o'-nine-tails. A length of rope providing a hand grip at one end, split into nine strands at the other, usually knotted at intervals. It was used for flogging sailors. Captains varied enormously in their use of the cat from those who would make every excuse to reduce the number of strokes, to those who would require it to be used fiercely at the slightest misdemeanour.

Cathead. A substantial piece of timber which projected from each side of the bow. This was normally where the anchors would be secured whilst the ship was at sea. It also provided a suitable projection upon which a man might stand when he was about to be hung. The rope would be led to the fore yardarm above his head and back to the deck where a group of sailors would be ready to run away with the rope and haul the man to the yardarm.

Coxswain. The sailor or warrant officer steering a boat or ship. A senior officer would appoint a Coxswain who would steer his boat, but would also act as a personal assistant in whatever way the officer required.

Crow's nest. A platform at the top of the mainmast from which a lookout could watch the horizon for other ships or land.

Fathom. The basic unit of measurement, equal to six feet (1.829m). 100 fathoms made a **cable**, and 10 cables a **nautical mile**. Three miles made a **league**.

Foc's'le, or forecastle. This is the forward end of a ship and was generally where the sailors were able to relax in such spare time as they had.

Fore and aft rig. This is the alternative to square rig. Sails were mostly triangular in shape. For'ard of the mast the leading edge of the sail would be attached to a stay (a rope which supported the mast) and the third corner would be controlled with a 'sheet'; these were known as **staysails** or jibs. Aft of the mast the leading edge was attached to the mast. Sometimes the mast would effectively be extended by a **gaff**, a spar attached to the mast at one end, along which the top of a sail could be tied. In frigates and smaller ships the mizzen often carried such a sail which was known as a **spanker.**

Gash. The sailor's word for rubbish. A piece of gash rope would be a short length for which there was no use, or which had been used so much it had been weakened and made unsafe. Gash rope was unpicked and turned into **oakum** which was then forced between the deck planks and sealed with pitch to make them watertight (**caulking**).

Gig. Frigates and larger ships would carry a small boat for ferrying the captain. It would have five or six oars and being of light construction would be relatively fast.

Give way together. The order given by the coxswain of a boat for the oarsmen to begin to pull their oars, thereby getting the boat under way.

Gundeck. A frigate would normally have only one gundeck with about 14 guns on each side. The largest ships of the line had three decks and the French and Spanish had a few four deckers (eg Santisima Trinidad).

Gunwhale. Pronounced gun'l. The top edge of a boat's side.

Hammock – everyone knows about a hammock. The ones used in the navy were made of a piece of canvas with a number of eyes along each end. Short lengths of rope (**clews**) were attached to each eye and joined together in a steel ring. When the hammock was '**slung**' the ring at either end was hooked onto a hook in a deckhead beam. The hooks were screwed into the beams at 14 to 18 inch intervals. When slung the hammock would normally be fitted with a **stretcher** across the head end so that this would lay fairly flat and thus be much more comfortable.

Harden up. The order given to steer closer to the wind and tighten the set of the sails accordingly.

Heave to; hove to. This describes a particular set of the sails of a ship which keeps the vessel stationary, so that a boat can be lowered or hoisted.

Helm. A general word used to signify the steering of a boat or ship. As a verb it means to steer. As a noun it refers to whatever implement is being used to steer; in a boat this would be a **tiller**, attached directly to the rudder; in a ship it would be the **wheel**. **'Give him the helm'** is an order to hand the tiller or wheel to someone else.

Holystoning. The decks were scrubbed with special blocks of sandstone to ensure that they were clean. They became known as holystones because the sailors had to be on their knees to use them.

Jib. This was the foremost sail in a boat or ship, triangular in shape. It is particularly important for sailing into to the wind. **'Aft the jib'** is the order given to tighten the sail as the boat turns towards the wind. **'Check the jib'** is the opposite.

Kedge anchor. A small anchor which could be carried in a boat away from the ship. Heaving in the anchor cable would move the ship towards the anchor. The kedge is often used to pull a ship off a sandbank or other obstacle.

King's shilling. Every man who volunteered to serve in the navy was awarded a bounty of one shilling (5p in modern money) which was at that time a bonus worth having.

Lash up and stow. Each day the Bosun's mates would use their bosun's calls to waken the sailors who were not on watch. The calls were accompanied by the order 'Wakey, wakey, rise and shine; lash up and stow.' Once out of his hammock each man would lash up his hammock in a carefully prescribed manner so that it would pass through a **hammock ring**, ensuring that all lashed hammocks were the same size. They were then placed in **hammock netting** which ran along the upperdeck of the ship. Once secured there the hammocks would provide some cover from enemy fire to men on deck.

Marlin spike. A tapered and heavy piece of metal with a sharp point at one end and a thicker rounded surface at the other. It was used mostly for opening a gap between the strands of a rope so that it could be spliced. Made of wood it is called a **fid**.

Painter. This is the rope secured to the bow of a boat; it might be used as the bowrope.

Paying off. At the end of a ship's commission the ship would be **'paid off'**. This entailed the whole ship's company being paid all outstanding wages, the ship's accounts being closed and the ship being de-stored and made ready for repairs or, in peace time, to be **'laid up'** pending a decision on future employment or scrap.

Prepare for sea. This order would be given to ensure that movable items were secured before going to sea. Other preparations would have to be made such as removing lashings from the **anchor cable** and putting bars into the **capstan** ready for the sailors to push the capstan round and raise the anchor.

Pulling a boat. This refers to the action of the men at the oars of a boat. Sailors pull a boat; they do not row it.

Purser. The Purser was the officer in charge of stores and supply. He was responsible for ensuring that a ship went to sea with sufficient material to sail and to repair itself, sufficient food and water, and clothing material. Clothes issued by the Purser were known as **'slops'**.

Quarter. Standing on the deck of a ship looking forwards is **ahead**, behind you is **astern**, to the left the **larboard beam** and to the right the **starboard beam**. In the early 19th Century the term **port** was introduced for the left to avoid possible confusion between larboard and starboard. The quarters were half way between astern and the beam – starboard quarter, larboard quarter. A **quarter wind**, when the wind was coming from that direction, was very favourable for sailing in a square-rigged ship.

Quarterdeck. This is the after part of the upper deck from which the captain would control the ship. Larger ships often had a **Poop** which was above the quarterdeck for this purpose. The quarterdeck was reserved for officers and only sailors with a particular duty there, helmsmen, topmen, were normally permitted access.

Sails. The majority of ships in this period would be fitted with three masts – a **foremast**, **mainmast**, and **mizzen**. On each mast there would be a sail at the lowest level – the **foresail**, **mainsail** or **mizzen**. Above these were a number of sails of decreasing size; the **topsail**, the **top-gallant** and, in the largest ship, the **royal**.

Sheerlegs. Two lengths of timber, perhaps 3 metres long, lashed together at one end and standing apart at their foot to form a triangle. A block would be rigged at the head and a rope run through it. The sheerlegs are held in a near vertical position by stays.

Sheets – nothing to do with beds or areas of canvas. Sheets are the ropes which are used to control the set of the sails by varying the amount of wind that is allowed to billow into them.

Signal flags were used as an important communication. Different shapes, markings and colours were intended to be distinguishable at long range. Once seen and understood the recipient would hoist an **answering pennant** or the whole of the signal received. A code book was used to define the meaning each flag or combination of flags. In battle it quickly became impossible to see flags through the smoke.

Slops. Clothes and material issued to sailors by the Purser(q.v.).

Spilling wind. This refers to a technique of using the sheets to adjust a sail to prevent the wind catching in it. The effect would be to slow the ship down.

Square rigger. The line of battle ships and most frigates were square riggers, powered principally by square sails, secured along their top edge to a **yardarm** with their bottom corners controlled by sheets. Smaller ships might well have a combination of square sails and fore and aft sails(q.v.). The smallest ships and boats would have only fore and aft sails.

Starters. Bosun's mates carried short sticks, known as starters, which they used to encourage sailors to get moving and act more quickly. Their use varied from ship to ship sometimes being used to excess.

Stays. The ropes that hold the masts up, fore and aft. A **'staysail'** is fixed to a stay. The ropes to the sides of the mast are known as **shrouds**.

Stern sheets. This is the space towards the stern of a boat where passengers or officers would sit or stand. The coxswain would also stand there to be in a position to steer his boat and command his crew.

Still. One of the calls made on the bosun's call is the still. This is used to salute an officer when coming onboard. The officer will respond with a salute and then the **'Carry on'** will be piped enabling everyone to continue with their work.

Stove in. Originally to break the top of a barrel to gain entry but more widely used in the navy to mean breaking the side of a boat.

Tack. A ship cannot sail directly into the wind. In good conditions a square rigger might be able to point about 45 degrees off the wind. In order to make progress in the direction the wind is coming from the ship must turn about 90 degrees, her bow passing through the wind. This process is called tacking. If the wind is coming over the starboard side, the ship is on the starboard tack. Square riggers were difficult to turn and if they were not moving fast enough they would be unable to turn through the wind – **'make stays'**. With plenty of space it would be possible to turn back – **'pay off'** – allow the speed to pick up and then try again. Sirius was too close to the reef and ran catastrophically aground.

Taffrail. The barrier around the side of the upper deck preventing anyone falling accidentally over the side. Sailors are always discouraged from leaning on it however safe and secure it seems.

Topmen were the ship's elite in terms of fitness, agility and fearlessness. They were responsible for looking after the sails above deck level and would spend much of their time working the sails and repairing worn or chafed rigging.

Toss oars. The order given in a boat when approaching a ship or jetty, at which the oarsmen would lift their oars into a vertical position, enabling the boat to come alongside without the oars fouling the ship or jetty.

Watch. Sailors were allocated to a watch – larboard or starboard – and would take it in turns to be on watch. A watch was four hours, except in late afternoon when two **'dog watches'** were two hours long. The **first watch** was from 8pm until midnight; **middle, morning, forenoon** and **afternoon watches** followed.

Wear the ship. Nothing to do with clothing. This describes a ship turning her head away from the wind so that the wind crosses her stern. When **tack**ing the wind crosses the bow; when **wear**ing the wind crosses the stern. In modern small boats the term **jibe** is used instead of **wear**.

Weather helm. When the wind is ahead of the beam a ship will set the sails to suit the chosen course. If the ship is badly designed or the sails are badly set the head of the ship will tend to turn into the wind and the helmsman will have to apply the rudder to hold his course. In extreme cases the strain on the rudder will prove too great as it did in the Porpoise.

Yardarm or yard. This is a **spar** fixed horizontally onto a mast, from which a square sail could be hung. In harbour the sail would be **furled** – pulled up and tied to the yardarm – and the sail would be **shaken out** when it was required for use. A **block** (pulley) would be fitted to the end of a yardarm from which a convicted man would be hung. Sailors working on the yardarms had **footropes** to stand on but no safety harness; if they fell they were almost certain to be seriously injured or drowned.